AF539161

The Maverick Republic

An alarming paradox emerges from witnessing prevalent national currents over the past three decades. The ominous paradox is that despite the demonstrable political wisdom of the humble voter and the valiant attempts of the common citizen to seek a semblance of material progress and social equity, those with money, power and influence have relentlessly pushed the country into a wildly individualistic quagmire of greed, self-indulgence and cruelty. A country where there are no standards, no rules or principles to carry out even the simplest transaction, where everything is permissible, where anything goes. The largest democracy has become The Maverick Republic.

Jawid Laiq, a noted journalist, writes on current political and economic issues for a number of distinguished newspapers and journals, including *The Times of India, The Indian Express, Outlook* and *Economic and Political Weekly.* He has reported and commented on major news events within the country since 1970. As a Research Officer from 1987 to 1994 with Amnesty International, London, he travelled to remote refugee camps and tribal villages in far corners of the globe to investigate human rights abuses committed by lawless government agencies. He has also been a Research Fellow with the Centre for Policy Research, New Delhi. He is the author of a monograph on *Globalisation and Resistance.* He was educated at Cathedral School and Elphinstone College, Bombay, and at London University.

The Maverick Republic
Thirty Years of Coverage

OTHER LOTUS TITLES

ANIL K. JAGGIA SAURABH SHUKLA	*IC 814: Hijacked! The Inside Story*
ARJAN SINGH	*Arjan Singh's Tiger Book*
CLAUDIA PRECKEL	*Begums of Bhopal*
DHANANJAYA SINGH	*The House of Marwar*
ERIC S. MARGOLIS	*War at the Top of the World*
E. JAIWANT PAUL	*'By My Sword and Shield'*
GERALDINE FORBES (ed.)	*The Memoirs of Dr. Haimabati Sen*
HARINDER BAWEJA (ed.)	*Most Wanted: Profiles of Terror*
INDIRA MENON	*The Madras Quartet*
IRADJ AMINI	*Koh-i-noor*
JOHN LALL	*Begam Samru*
JYOTI JAFA	*Really, Your Highness!*
KHUSHWANT SINGH	*Kipling's India*
KANWALBIR PUSHPENDRA SINGH	*The Ruse*
K.M. GEORGE	*The Best of Thakazhi Sivasankara Pillai*
LAKSHMI SUBRAMANIAN	*Medieval Seafarers*
M.J. AKBAR	*The Shade of Swords*
MANOHAR MALGONKAR	*Dropping Names*
MAURA MOYNIHAN	*Masterji and Other Stories*
MUSHIRUL HASAN	*India Partitioned. 2 vols*
NAMITA GOKHALE	*Mountain Echoes*
NINA EPTON	*Mumtaz Mahal: Beloved Empress*
P. LAL	*The Bhagavad Gita*
RALPH RUSSELL	*The Famous Ghalib*
ROMESH BHANDARI	*Goa*
RUSKIN BOND	*Ruskin Bond's Green Book*
SHOVANA NARAYAN	*Rhythmic Echoes and Reflections: Kathak*
SUDHIR KAKAR (ed.)	*Indian Love Stories*
SUJATA S. SABNIS	*A Twist in Destiny*
SUMATI MUTATKAR	*Shrikrishna Narayan Ratanjankar 'Sujan'*
V.S. NARAVANE (ed.)	*Devdas and Other Stories by Sarat Chandra*

FORTHCOMING TITLES

MAJ. GEN. I. CARDOZO	*The Paramvir Chakra Winners*
MAJ. R.P. SINGH	*Sawai Man Singh II*
SYLVIA FRASER	*The Rope in the Water*

The Maverick Republic

Thirty Years of Coverage

Jawid Laiq

Lotus Collection

© Jawid Laiq 2002
All rights reserved. No part of this publication may be reproduced or transmitted, in any form or by any means, without the prior permission of the publisher.

This edition first published 2002
The Lotus Collection
An imprint of
Roli Books Pvt Ltd
M-75, G.K. II Market
New Delhi 110 048
Phones: 6442271, 6462782, 6460886
Fax: 6467185
E-mail: roli@vsnl.com; Website: rolibooks.com
Also at
Varanasi, Agra, Jaipur and the Netherlands

ISBN: 81-7436-213-4
Rs. 295

Typeset in Minion by Roli Books Pvt Ltd and
printed at Pauls Press, Okhla, New Delhi-110 020

Contents

To
Nazoo, Noonoo
Bhartu, Mumsee, Abba

Preface

THE chapters in this book represent the major themes which have emerged from over 30 years of reports, comments and analyses written by me. They have been put together, hopefully, as an indicator of issues which are of crucial significance to the human condition within this nation. These chapters are not meant to be read as a chronicle or comprehensive record of national events.

For the major part of the past three decades I have been a journalist with a broad range of print media organisations. I have occasionally moved away from journalism for intervening periods of several years to look at events from the wider perspectives of academic research at the Centre for Policy Research, New Delhi, and of human rights research at the London-based secretariat of Amnesty International. I have always returned to my first calling – journalism – where I have had the opportunity to interact with many fine professional colleagues and friends including (the late) S. Mulgaokar, Kuldip Nayar, Ajit Bhattacharjea, M.J. Akbar and Vinod Mehta.

My closest colleague, friend and critic has been my wife, Bharati Bhargava, whom I met during the dramatic years of the Emergency when we were both working at the *Indian Express*, New Delhi. Since then, my sharpest critics have turned out to be my daughter, Nur, and my son, Niyaz, without whose charming modes of constant harassment I might not have pulled myself together to compile this volume.

To Qamar Ahmad, my mother, and to Nayer Laiq Ahmad, my late father, I owe the deepest feelings of gratitude for their generosity of spirit and their clear sense of right and wrong. To my sisters,

Naheed and Subur, I owe many happy moments as I also do to my particular friends, Nasser Munjee and Arati Bhargava.

I specially wish to thank Mushirul Hasan, Pramod Kapoor, Harinder Baweja and Veena Baswani whose unstinting encouragement helped me to complete this project.

New Delhi
June 2002

Introduction

A Reporter's Buzz

THE benefits of automation and instant communication have ruined the excitement of walking through the freezing cold at the dead of night into a wooden shack serving as the telegraph office in Kotdwara, the town which is the gateway to Pauri Garhwal, waking up the telegraphist who lives next door, and seeing him tap out in Morse Code with his thumb and forefinger each letter of every word of my report which I have banged out on a white sheet of paper on my trusty Olivetti portable. The obliging telegraphist transmits the urgent press telegram so accurately that the report on the maneater of Pauri is reproduced flawlessly on the front page of the *Indian Express* next morning in Delhi, after being personally delivered past midnight by a bicycle messenger from the Central Telegraph Office. Now the phones work, the fax replicates a page a minute and the e-mail flashes the entire report in a second or two. The skilful old telegraphist at his ancient, polished mahogany table has disappeared.

To be alone and on the road in glorious anticipation of freedom and adventure is the essence of being a reporter. I get that wonderful thrill down my spine whenever I drive out of Delhi in my rundown old Fiat to seek a 'story', the reporter's pseudonym for a news item. Whether it is north towards Amritsar on the Grand Trunk Road, south on the Mathura Road, south-west to Alwar or to Jaipur, east towards Rampur or Dehradun and onwards to the pine-carpeted hills and gurgling streams of Kumaon and Garhwal. Taking the train is almost as exhilarating, though it was more so when I could lie with my head by the open window of the spacious old First Class compartments – hearing the haunting night sounds and smelling the rain-soaked earth of the monsoons or the smog of winter. Travel in a cramped 2-tier AC carriage has diminished some of the delight of rail travel. The dullest passage out of Delhi is through the plastic departure lounge at Palam, aboard an airborne, metal capsule.

The best way to travel if you wish to gauge the popular mood is by a local, ramshackle, state roadways bus. If you are covering an election, there can be no better way for a reporter to transport himself towards an accurate election forecast. The bus keeps stopping, dropping and picking up passengers at every village and small town. You can quickly pick up what is of concern to the people inhabiting the constituencies along the way. My favourite state for road travel in northern India is Madhya Pradesh. The bus conductors are relatively courteous, the bus drivers are not like the maniacs who steer Punjab and Haryana Roadways buses, the co-passengers are polite without being nosey, the roads are not invaded by an enraged mob of trucks and traffic is blissfully scarce.

I have done a reporter's journey out of Khajuraho and through the roads of central India thrice – January 1978, December 1984, April 1996 – and countless other private journeys. Each time the enchantment increases. Out from the shimmering ponds, fields and temples of Khajuraho, up the narrow winding path which climbs up the sal-covered hills which look down on the valley of the diamond town of Panna, to the bustling market town of Satna, and on to the lush, wooded hills which surround Amarkantak, the source of the Narmada, where the sight of thousands of blind people is being restored in a cataract surgery camp. I also get my rotting molar removed painlessly without any anaesthetic by a magical ayurvedic dentist who is providing the same free service for hundreds of other sufferers at the Amarkantak medical camp.

On two other occasions, from Khajuraho to Satna, to the princely town of Rewa whose Maharajas had once bred white tigers, and then onwards to Allahabad which is both a spiritual and political Sangam where the reporter can garner political opinions from the entire Gangetic belt. From the tidy and neat tribal villages of sparsely populated Madhya Pradesh to the messy disorder of crowded Uttar Pradesh is unnerving, though the sophisticated political articulation of the humblest UP individual makes up for the muck and grime of his physical surroundings.

On the road to Pauri Garhwal in the Himalayan foothills via a bridge of boats over the Ganga near Bijnor, I repeatedly see and hear that the UP villager is long suffering, whether in the plains or the hills (now in Uttaranchal). Maneating leopards lurk around some of the remoter villages of these hills, preying on the angelic, rosy-cheeked, *pahadhi* children and their frail, pretty mothers. The well-fed, flatulent, wildlife and forest officials mouth excuses for the leopards. It is not their children who are being eaten for supper by protected wildlife.

A year later, I am reporting from a broken down hired Ambassador on an Arabian nights camp in the Rajasthan desert, 70 kilometres from the fortress town of Jaisalmer, where Saudi princelings are hunting rare birds by sending their trained falcons soaring into the sky from wireless equipped Toyota pick-ups. But to beat all road journeys, is a moonlit night trip through the glistening white Little Rann of Kutch to arrive at dawn at the gloriously medieval, walled town of Bhuj before it became a sad ruin after the January 2001 earthquake. The snow-white effect is the reflection from the miles of salt-pans and sand-dunes on either side of the causeway across the Little Rann which becomes a shallow inland sea during the short rainy season. I am travelling on a bus with 'sleeper berths'. I do not get a wink of sleep as I have to stop myself from falling off the upper 'berth' which is a hard wooden plank, 10 inches wide and five feet long. The white magic is adequate compensation even when seen through the wire mesh of the tiny tin cage which passes for a compartment in the 'luxury' night bus from Ahmedabad to Bhuj. All part of the pleasure of covering the March 1998 election.

Spontaneous and open expression of views on forthcoming elections and generally on society and politics in direct and pithy words is the norm in the countryside. The practical wisdom of the village peasant, labourer and artisan is in stark contrast to the convoluted, deceitful and self-serving ramblings of the metropolitan sophisticate. I can never forget the rickshaw-puller whom I met minutes after I stepped off the train at Sultanpur station, near Sanjay Gandhi's prospective Amethi constituency, on a February 1977 morning. He angrily told me that nobody would vote for the Indira-Sanjay duo and the Congress party which had inflicted so many brutalities on the common folk during the Emergency. His words proved to be a more accurate forecast of the electoral debacle suffered by the Congress in northern India in March 1977 than all the complex opinion polls engineered by various organisations.

In every election in the past three decades – except in the December 1984 election held soon after Indira Gandhi's assassination in October when national integrity and security had become the prime issue – the major concerns of the vast majority of voters have been economic and material. Even after the Kargil conflict, the BJP was not able to shift the electorate's focus substantially towards defence and security issues in the 1999 election. Unemployment, inflation, lack of medical, educational and transport facilities are the basic concerns of the rural voter despite repeated attempts by politicians to distract him into the dark alleyways of caste and community. At every election, candidates make promises which are rarely fulfilled. Yet, the so-called uneducated rural working man and woman continues to retain a sense of balance and fine political judgement tempered by a cynical and humorous disdain for the political charlatan. I have never felt the need for hero-worship but if I revere anyone it is that ordinary rural labouring person who has repeatedly tried to save this country from national disaster by exercising his/her electoral sagacity.

The best vantage point to observe the behaviour of the elected representatives of the people is from the press gallery above the Lok Sabha. The best time is 'Zero Hour' when MPs are expected to raise special and urgent matters of national importance without having given prior notice. Invariably, that crucial morning hour is reduced to bedlam as scores of voluble MPs simultaneously demand the attention of the Speaker to raise issues which are usually of a personal and petty nature. Media reporting of Parliament is a sanitised version of events. The reality is far more colourful but cannot be reported as it would invite contempt of Parliament. The language and behaviour of MPs is often beyond compare.

Interspersed between reporting on societal and political events, I have for long periods sought to reflect and to comment on those events and have noticed the emergence of an alarming paradox. The ominous paradox is that despite all the valiant attempts of the humble voter to seek a semblance of national progress, those with money, power and influence have relentlessly pushed this country into a wildly individualistic quagmire of greed, self-indulgence and cruelty where there are no standards, rules and principles to carry out even the simplest social transaction, where anything is permissible, where anything goes. The largest democracy has become The Maverick Republic.

Chapter-1

Delhi and Punjab 1983-84

THE Congress Party has yet to recover fully from the trauma it set in motion in the early 1980s by propping up an obscure preacher to counter the Akalis in Punjab. Indira Gandhi, then Union Home Minister Zail Singh and various intelligence outfits thought they were executing a brilliant master stroke by promoting the shrill religious cries of Jarnail Singh Bhindranwale. Indira Gandhi and Bhindranwale and thousands of innocents met violent deaths as a consequence of that master stroke which turned out to be a political and human catastrophe that continued throughout the 1980s. It also provided a convenient handle for Pakistani agencies to step up their cross-border activities.

The Frankenstein Congress had created a monster it could not control. The extent of Bhindranwale's charismatic powers and hypnotic appeal among groups of Sikh youth became evident when the army launched its operation on June 5, 1984, to free the Golden Temple at Amritsar of his armed followers. The retinue of smooth-cheeked, 16 and 17-year olds with old rifles I had seen hovering around Bhindranwale a year earlier at the Golden Temple put up a fierce resistance which kept the army at bay for 48 hours. I had thought that these innocent-eyed children would surrender at the first shot. Their grim determination during the battle, assisted by the tactical skills of Shahbeg Singh, the renegade major-general, surprised the army and proved me wrong.

The army action angered even the moderate Sikhs. They considered it to be a violation of the sanctity of their most holy sanctuary. The climate of anger culminated in the assassination of Indira Gandhi and the subsequent mass killing of Sikhs in Delhi and many other places all over northern India. Mob fury at the assassination was evident as soon as news leaked out from the All-India Institute of Medical Sciences in Delhi that Indira Gandhi had died. A menacing mob surrounded President Zail Singh's limousine when he appeared some hours later at the Institute to pay his respects to Indira Gandhi's remains. I could see and hear this escalating vengeance against innocent Sikhs gathering momentum as I moved around the city's streets. It was a spontaneous anger which was later commandeered by some Congress leaders. The signal failure was by the administration, particularly Home Minister P. V. Narasimha Rao, to summon the army to assist the civil power with explicit orders to quell forcefully the mobs which had taken over the country's capital. Mob rule continued in Delhi for three days till Indira Gandhi's funeral and subsided on its own while Rao prevaricated. As Prime Minister, Rao was to repeat his dilatory tactics during the Ayodhya episode in December 1992 and again allow the mass killing of Muslims by Shiv Sena mobs in Bombay in January 1993.

Indira Gandhi's assassination also led to two major, related political mishaps. It catapulted Rajiv Gandhi, a total political novice, to prime ministership, surrounded by his coterie of juvenile operators. It aroused mass political emotions which presented Indira Gandhi's son and the Congress with an undeserved and unprecedented majority in the December 1984 Lok Sabha election. The huge majority evoked a false sense of unrestrained power among Rajiv Gandhi and his band of boys. They proceeded to take crucial decisions without any planning or forethought. Their mindless decisions ended in a number of fiascos. Hopelessly unbalanced budgets and unrestricted imports initiated by the Rajiv regime inevitably pushed the economy towards the fiscal and foreign exchange crisis of 1991. The reversal of the Supreme

Court judgement on the payment of alimony to Shah Bano, a divorced Muslim woman, and the unlocking of the Babri Masjid gates, both in 1986, revived the BJP and Hindu communal forces. The notorious Bofors gun deal of 1986 sealed Rajiv's political fate with his defeat in the November 1989 Lok Sabha election. India's military intervention in Sri Lanka in 1987 sealed his personal fate with his assassination at the hands of the vengeful Tamil Tigers in May 1991.

In Punjab, the Akalis, backed by the BJP, returned to power with a vengeance in 1985 after the ending of Presidential Rule. Finally, the corruption and ineptitude of the Akali ministry led by Chief Minister Prakash Singh Badal saw the Congress return to power in the state in 2002.

Assassination

MOST URGENT FLASH

INDIRA SHOT BY SIKH GUARDS AND CRITICALLY INJURED

FROM JAWID LAIQ

NEW DELHI, OCT 31 (KUNA) - INDIA'S PRIME MINISTER INDIRA GANDHI WAS SHOT IN HER HOUSE WEDNESDAY MORNING BY TWO SIKHS OF HER PERSONAL SECURITY STAFF.

SHE IS LYING CRITICALLY ILL IN HOSPITAL WITH 16 BULLET INJURIES.

THE TWO SIKH BODYGUARDS SPRAYED HER WITH BURSTS FROM THEIR SUB-MACHINE GUNS.

(END) JL

HOW RECEIVED IT PL? +

MMMM JAWID, HERE IS AJEERY

WE RECEIVE WELL BUT APPRECIATE A DETAILED ROUNDUP WITH SPECULATION ON SUCCESSOR WITH A FEW GOOD QUOTES FROM OFFICIALS ON INCIDENT AND THE SURROUNDING CIRCUMSTANCES

OK A BIT LATER?+

YES BUT PLS MAKE IT AS FAST AS POSSIBLE. ITS VERY URGENT STORY AND WE ALREADY LATE AND HOPE TO RECOUP WITH A WELL BALANCED AND ELABORATE STORY AND I AM SURE YOU CAN HELP PERFECTLY. MEANTIME AGENCIES REPORT SHE WAS HIT BY EIGHT BULLETS

LATEST IS SHE HAS 16 RPT 16 BULLET INJURIES+

OK THANKS THAT AT LEAST GIVES US A NEW PEG. TKS JAWID

(Above and below are copies of the original telex transmissions sent by the author to the news desk of KUNA (Kuwait News Agency) between October 31 and November 2, 1984. At the time, the author was KUNA's India correspondent. The telex conversations between the editors of the news desk and the correspondent have been changed into italics to distinguish them from the news messages which are in normal type. The abbreviations and symbols used on the telex have been retained. For instance, the + symbol signifies end of transmission/ automated acknowledgement in telex code language. MMMM means 'wait a moment', U means 'you', PLS is 'please', TKS is 'thanks' and so on.)

ZAIL AND RAJIV RUSHING BACK TO DELHI

NEW DELHI, OCT 31 (KUNA) - THE TWO MOST IMPORTANT FIGURES AFTER PRIME MINISTER INDIRA GANDHI, PRESIDENT ZAIL SINGH AND INDIRA'S SON, RAJIV, WERE NOT HERE IN NEW DELHI WHEN SHE WAS SHOT AND CRITICALLY INJURED THIS MORNING AT 9-40 INDIAN TIME BY TWO SIKH BODYGUARDS OUTSIDE HER RESIDENCE.

RAJIV, WHO WAS ON A POLITICAL TOUR OF WEST BENGAL STATE, IS RUSHING BACK TO DELHI. WITH GREAT CONFUSION REIGNING HERE AND NO OBVIOUS CABINET MINISTER DESIGNATED TO TAKE OVER, RAJIV MAY BE APPOINTED ACTING PRIME MINISTER BY PRESIDENT ZAIL SINGH WHEN HE RETURNS TODAY FROM A STATE VISIT TO THE YEMEN ARAB REPUBLIC.

IF RAJIV IS UNWILLING, FINANCE MINISTER PRANAB MUKHERJEE MAY BE MADE ACTING PRIME MINISTER, ACCORDING TO INFORMED CIRCLES IN THE INDIRA CONGRESS PARTY.

POLICE OFFICIALS HERE HAVE TIGHTENED SECURITY AS PUBLIC ANGER IN THIS CITY IS BUILDING UP AGAINST THE SIKH COMMUNITY BECAUSE THE ASSAILANTS WERE SIKHS.

THERE ARE FEARS THAT CLASHES BETWEEN HINDUS AND SIKHS COULD BREAK OUT ALL OVER INDIA.

A MILLING CROWD OF THOUSANDS IS WAITING ANXIOUSLY OUTSIDE THE ALL-INDIA INSTITUTE OF MEDICAL SCIENCES IN NEW DELHI TO KNOW THE LATEST ABOUT INDIRA GANDHI'S CONDITION.

SURGEONS HAVE REMOVED FOUR BULLETS IN AN EMERGENCY OPERATION ON INDIRA GANDHI. HER CONDITION IS PRECARIOUS.

MANEKA GANDHI, THE PRIME MINISTER'S ESTRANGED DAUGHTER-IN-LAW, HAS RUSHED TO THE HOSPITAL ALONG WITH OTHER RELATIVES OF INDIRA. MANY GOVERNMENT MINISTERS ARE ALSO AT THE HOSPITAL.

UNCONFIRMED REPORTS SAID THAT THE TWO SIKH BODYGUARDS WHO SHOT AT INDIRA GANDHI WERE SHOT DEAD BY OTHER SECURITY GUARDS.

(END) JL

(MORE TO FOLLOW LATER)+

ARE YOU ON?? YES

PLS KEEP FOLLOWING STORY URGENTLY AS WE NEED FULL DETAILS

YES

IS THAT JAWID? YES

OK FINE. TELL US HOW TO REACH YOU WHEN WE NEED BECAUSE ITS DIFFICULT TO GET U ON TELEX

WILL BE RUSHING AROUND. THE ONLY WAY TO GET ME IS THROUGH THE TELEX. YOU CAN ALSO TRY MY PHONE NUMBER

OK TKS AND GD WORK. TELL US SOMETHING ABOUT HER CONDITION. WHAT ARE CHANCES OF HER SURVIVAL?

DOCTORS SAY THAT CONDITION EXTREMELY CRITICAL. THEY WILL NOT SAY MORE.

TKS JAWID AND MR AJEERY GIVES U REGARDS +

INDIRA DEAD, REPORTS PTI

NEW DELHI, OCT 31 (KUNA) - INDIA'S PRIME MINISTER INDIRA GANDHI IS DEAD, PTI, THE NATIONAL INDIAN NEWS AGENCY, HAS JUST REPORTED. IT GIVES NO SOURCES FOR ITS REPORT.

EARLIER, A SENIOR DOCTOR AT THE HOSPITAL SAID THAT "SHE WAS BROUGHT TO THE HOSPITAL IN A COMPLETELY COLLAPSED CONDITION AND A DEEP COMA".

SHE WAS KEPT ALIVE BY A HEART-LUNG MACHINE WHILE BEING OPERATED ON.

THE CROWDS OUTSIDE THE HOSPITAL ARE STUNNED.

(MORE TO FOLLOW LATER)

PLEASE BE SURE TO SEND US REACTIONS AND SOME BACKGROUND ETC ON THE ASSASSINATION AND EFFECTS ON THE POLITICAL SCENE, NOTABLY THE ELECTIONS AS SOON AS POSSIBLE PLS+

LET ME FIRST CONFIRM HER DEATH

INDIRA BACKGOUND AND REACTION TO DEATH

NEW DELHI, OCT 31 (KUNA) - INDIA'S PRIME MINISTER INDIRA GANDHI, BORN ON NOVEMBER 19, 1917, DIED SHORTLY AFTER MID-DAY LOCAL TIME WEDNESDAY, HOSPITAL SOURCES CONFIRMED, OF BULLET WOUNDS

INFLICTED EARLIER THIS MORNING BY TWO SIKH BODYGUARDS OF HER OFFICIAL SECURITY STAFF. THEY FIRED 16 ROUNDS INTO HER AT CLOSE RANGE WITH THEIR SUB-MACHINE GUNS AS SHE STEPPED OUT OF HER RESIDENCE. THE TWO BODYGUARDS WERE IMMEDIATELY SHOT DEAD BY OTHER MEMBERS OF HER SECURITY STAFF.

(It was later learned that one of the bodyguards had survived after being shot – author.)

THOUSANDS OF PERSONS, MANY OF THEM TEARFUL, BUT MOST OF THEM SHOCKED AND SILENT, ARE GATHERING OUTSIDE HER RESIDENCE AS NEWS OF HER DEATH IS SPREADING THROUGH THIS CITY.

INDIRA GANDHI BECAME INDEPENDENT INDIA'S THIRD PRIME MINISTER ON JANUARY 24, 1966, FOLLOWING THE DEATH BY HEART ATTACK OF PRIME MINISTER LAL BAHADUR SHASTRI. INDIRA'S FATHER, JAWAHARLAL NEHRU, WAS THE COUNTRY'S FIRST PRIME MINISTER AND INDIRA GANDHI HAD A LONG POLITICAL EDUCATION UNDER HER FATHER'S GUIDANCE.

INDIRA GANDHI USED HER SHARP POLITICAL ACUMEN WITH DEVASTATING EFFECT, COMPLETELY OUT-MANOEUVRING HER POLITICAL OPPONENTS WITHIN HER CONGRESS PARTY AND OUTSIDE IT.

SHE USED POLITICAL SLOGANS LIKE "REMOVE POVERTY" AND "ELECT A GOVERNMENT THAT WORKS" TO WIN THE 1971 AND 1980 PARLIAMENTARY ELECTIONS, RESPECTIVELY, WITH OVERWHELMING MAJORITIES.

THE ONLY TIME SHE MISCALCULATED THE NATIONAL POLITICAL MOOD WAS WHEN SHE ESTABLISHED SEMI-DICTATORIAL RULE IN INDIA FOR 19 MONTHS FROM JUNE 1975 TO EARLY 1977.

SHE SUFFERED A MASSIVE DEFEAT IN THE 1977 ELECTIONS BUT DUE TO THE FACTION FIGHTS WITHIN THE JANATA GOVERNMENT SHE WAS RETURNED TO POWER IN THE 1980 ELECTIONS.

HER PARTICULAR ABILITY AND INTEREST WAS IN FOREIGN POLICY. SHE WAS UNANIMOUSLY CHOSEN AS CHAIRMAN OF THE NON-ALIGNED MOVEMENT IN MARCH 1983.

HER GREATEST TRIUMPH WAS IN THE DECEMBER 1971 WAR WITH PAKISTAN WHICH LED TO THE BIRTH OF THE NEW NATION OF BANGLADESH. SHE CAME TO BE KNOWN AS "THE EMPRESS OF INDIA".

HER SEVEREST TEST CAME THIS YEAR IN HOW TO HANDLE EXTREMISTS IN THE WARRIOR-LIKE SIKH COMMUNITY. AFTER MUCH HESITATION, SHE ORDERED THE INDIAN ARMY TO STORM THE HOLY SIKH GOLDEN TEMPLE AT AMRITSAR ON JUNE 5 AND 6, 1984. THIS LED TO AN ANGRY REACTION AMONG MANY SIKHS, TWO OF WHOM TODAY TOOK HER LIFE.

(END) JL

POLITICAL CONSEQUENCES OF INDIRA DEATH

NEW DELHI, OCT 31 (KUNA) - PRIME MINISTER INDIRA GANDHI'S ASSASSINATION TODAY HAS LEFT AN IMMENSE GAP ON THE INDIAN POLITICAL SCENE WITH NOT A SINGLE POLITICAL FIGURE WHO COMMANDS ANYTHING LIKE THE NATIONAL SUPPORT ENJOYED BY HER.

INDIRA GANDHI'S PERSONAL STYLE OF LEADERSHIP HAS ALSO LEFT A NUMBER OF "POLITICAL PYGMIES" WITHOUT ANY POLITICAL BASE IN HER CONGRESS PARTY. THE OPPOSITION PARTIES ALSO HAVE NO OUTSTANDING LEADER.

INDIRA GANDHI'S SON, RAJIV GANDHI, HAS VERY LITTLE POLITICAL EXPERIENCE OR UNDERSTANDING.

THE SENIOR-MOST MINISTER IN HER CABINET IS FINANCE MINISTER PRANAB MUKHERJEE WHO HAS NO POLITICAL BASE IN ANY OF INDIA'S CONSTITUENT STATES.

ACCORDING TO POLITICAL OBSERVERS HERE, INDIA IS LIKELY TO FACE A PERIOD OF POLITICAL AND SECTARIAN INSTABILITY AND AN IMMEDIATE ELECTION IS RULED OUT.

HOWEVER, IF AFTER A COUPLE OF MONTHS, RAJIV GANDHI MANAGES TO ESTABLISH HIS SUPREMACY WITHIN THE CONGRESS PARTY, HE MAY CALL AN ELECTION IN ORDER TO GAIN A SYMPATHY VOTE.

ANOTHER SCENARIO BEING DISCUSSED HERE IS GREATER CHAOS AND COMMUNAL STRIFE WHICH COULD LEAD TO THE EMERGENCE OF THE INDIAN ARMY ON THE POLITICAL ARENA. THE ARMY'S ROLE WOULD BE TO RESTORE ORDER IN THE COUNTRY AS HAS HAPPENED IN SO MANY NEIGHBOURING COUNTRIES.

(END) JL

Succession

URGENT

RAJIV GANDHI SWORN IN AS PRIME MINISTER

NEW DELHI, OCT 31 (KUNA) - RAJIV GANDHI, 39, WAS SWORN IN AS THE NEW PRIME MINISTER OF INDIA WEDNESDAY EVENING, SUCCEEDING HIS MOTHER,

INDIRA GANDHI, WHO WAS ASSASSINATED HERE THIS MORNING.

PRESIDENT ZAIL SINGH CONDUCTED THE SWEARING-IN CEREMONY IN THE PRESENCE OF SENIOR MINISTERS AND OFFICIALS.

RAJIV GANDHI HAS BEEN GENERAL SECRETARY OF THE RULING INDIRA CONGRESS PARTY FOR OVER A YEAR. HE WAS BEING GROOMED BY HIS MOTHER TO SUCCEED HER ONE DAY BUT HE HAS BEEN CATAPULTED INTO POWER BY THE SUDDEN AND TRAGIC DEATH OF HIS MOTHER.

RAJIV WAS DRAFTED INTO THE CONGRESS PARTY BY INDIRA GANDHI SOON AFTER HIS YOUNGER BROTHER, SANJAY, WAS KILLED IN AN AIR CRASH IN JUNE 1980.

RAJIV WAS INITIALLY RELUCTANT TO JOIN POLITICS AND TO GIVE UP HIS CAREER AS AN INDIAN AIRLINES PILOT, BUT HIS MOTHER PERSUADED HIM TO ENTER POLITICS.

RAJIV IS KNOWN TO BELIEVE IN RUNNING GOVERNMENT LIKE A MODERN BUSINESS EXECUTIVE. HE HAS VERY LITTLE EXPERIENCE AND UNDERSTANDING OF POLITICAL TACTICS.

HE IS BY FAR THE YOUNGEST PRIME MINISTER INDIA HAS EVER HAD. INDIRA GANDHI WAS 49 WHEN SHE FIRST BECAME PRIME MINISTER IN 1966.

(END) JL

FUNERAL ON SATURDAY

NEW DELHI, OCT 31 (KUNA) - INDIRA GANDHI'S FUNERAL IS TO BE ON SATURDAY, IT WAS OFFICIALLY ANNOUNCED

HERE WEDNESDAY NIGHT BY H.Y. SHARADA PRASAD, INFORMATION ADVISER IN THE PRIME MINISTER'S OFFICE.

PRASAD SAID THAT INDIRA GANDHI WAS WALKING TOWARDS AN IRISH TELEVISION TEAM FOR AN INTERVIEW BY FAMOUS BRITISH ACTOR PETER USTINOV WHEN SHE WA SHOT BY TWO SECURITY GUARDS, BEANT SINGH AND SATWANT SINGH. ONE OF THESE GUARDS HAD WORKED AS A SECURITY MAN FOR EIGHT YEARS AT THE PRIME MINISTER'S OFFICIAL RESIDENCE.

PRASAD WAS AT THE PRIME MINISTER'S HOUSE THIS MORNING, ACCOMPANYING THE TV TEAM, WHEN HE HEARD A VOLLEY OF SHOTS AT 9-15 A.M. LOCAL TIME. HE SAID THAT HE RUSHED TOWARDS THE SOUND OF THE FIRING AND SAW INDIRA GANDHI BEING LIFTED OFF THE GROUND AND RUSHED TO HOSPITAL IN A CAR.

PRASAD SAID THAT HE SAW RAJIV GANDHI'S WIFE, SONIA GANDHI, RUSHING OUT ONTO THE LAWN IN A NIGHT-GOWN ON HEARING THE SHOTS.

PRASAD SAID THAT THE HOSPITAL DOCTORS OFFICIALLY PRONOUNCED INDIRA GANDHI DEAD AT 2-30 P.M. LOCAL TIME.

HE SAID THAT RAJIV GANDHI WAS CHOSEN AS THE NEW PRIME MINISTER TODAY AT A MEETING OF THE PARLIAMENTARY BOARD OF THE RULING CONGRESS PARTY. THIS CHOICE WAS CONVEYED TO PRESIDENT ZAIL SINGH WHO SHORTLY AFTERWARDS SWORE RAJIV IN AS HEAD OF THE INDIAN GOVERNMENT.

PRASAD SAID THAT ACCORDING TO THE INDIAN CONSTITUTION THERE IS NO SUCH POSITION AS AN ACTING OR INTERIM PRIME MINISTER. THIS IMPLIES THAT RAJIV

GANDHI IS FULLY CONFIRMED AS THE NEW PRIME MINISTER OF INDIA.

P.V. NARASIMHA RAO, PRANAB MUKHERJEE, P. SHIV SHANKER AND BUTA SINGH WERE ALSO SWORN IN TODAY AS THE FIRST FOUR MINSTERS OF RAJIV'S NEW CABINET, PRASAD ANNOUNCED. ALL FOUR WERE ALSO MEMBERS OF INDIRA GANDHI'S CABINET.

RAJIV GANDHI WILL BROADCAST TO THE NATION LATER TONIGHT.

(END) JL

Persecution

MANY AREAS OF DELHI ARE BURNING

FROM JAWID LAIQ

NEW DELHI, NOV 1 (KUNA) - EVEN AS THIS CORRESPONDENT IS TYPING HIS REPORT, HE CAN SEE THICK BLACK SMOKE BILLOWING SOME HUNDREDS OF METRES AWAY IN ALL FOUR DIRECTIONS THURSDAY AFTERNOON.

ANGRY HINDU MOBS ARE SETTING FIRE TO SIKH HOMES, SHOPS AND TEMPLES ALL OVER DELHI. THE POLICE IS UNABLE TO CONTROL THE MOB FEROCITY WHICH HAS GROWN SINCE LAST NIGHT ON HEARING THAT THE KILLERS OF INDIRA GANDHI WERE TWO SIKH BODYGUARDS.

THE ARMY HAS BEEN CALLED TO TRY AND CONTROL THE VIOLENCE IN DELHI. CURFEW IS BEING IMPOSED ALL OVER THIS CITY.

SEVERAL MAIN ROADS ARE LITTERED WITH THE BURNED OUT WRECKS OF CARS AND BUSES WHICH WERE BEING DRIVEN BY SIKHS.

ABOUT ONE KILOMETRE AWAY FROM THE PRESS TELEX OFFICE WHERE THIS CORRESPONDENT IS SITTING, A MOB HAS ATTACKED THE MAIN BANGLA SAHIB SIKH TEMPLE AND THE SIKHS INSIDE HAVE RETALIATED BY OPENING FIRE. THE SHOTS OF RIFLE-FIRE CAN BE HEARD.

SEVERAL PERSONS HAVE DIED. BUT WITH NO OFFICIAL INFORMATION AVAILABLE, IT IS IMPOSSIBLE TO ESTIMATE THE NUMBER OF KILLED AND INJURED. MOBS HAVE ALSO TAKEN TO THE STREETS IN CITIES AND SMALLER TOWNS ALL OVER NORTHERN INDIA. AT LEAST FIVE CITIES ARE UNDER CURFEW. THESE CITIES ARE JAMMU, KANPUR, PATNA, SAGAR AND VARANASI.

INDIRA GANDHI'S DEATH IS LEADING TO A NATIONAL DISASTER.

(END) JL

ATTENTION EDITORS. IT MAY PROVE DIFFICULT TO SEND MORE REGULAR REPORTS AS MOB RULE IS SPREADING AROUND THIS PLACE. HOW RECEIVED PLS?

MMMM PLS TRY YOUR BEST TO PROVIDE US WITH MORE DETAILS

OKOKOK+

BURNING BODIES BY MOB RULE

NEW DELHI, NOV 2 (KUNA) - MOB RULE IN THIS CAPITAL CITY OF INDIA FRIDAY SPREAD TO POORER EASTERN AREAS FROM THE UPPER CLASS, GARDEN SUBURBS OF SOUTH DELHI

WHERE COUNTLESS SIKH HOMES, SHOPS AND VEHICLES WERE GUTTED AND LOOTED THURSDAY BY EXCITED MOBS AND AT LEAST 50 PERSONS, MOSTLY SIKHS, WERE KILLED. MORE THAN 30 OTHER TOWNS IN NORTHERN AND EASTERN INDIA ARE ALSO AFFECTED BY VIOLENCE DIRECTED AGAINST SIKHS FOLLOWING THE ASSASSINATION ON WEDNESDAY OF INDIRA GANDHI BY TWO OF HER SIKH BODYGUARDS.

WHILE VISITING VIOLENCE-TORN EAST DELHI FRIDAY AFTERNOON, THIS CORRESPONDENT SAW ONE FIERCELY BLAZING BODY AND TWO BURNED BODIES LYING WITHIN A 50-METRE STRETCH OF THE NATIONAL HIGHWAY WHICH LEADS TO UTTAR PRADESH STATE.

THE BLAZING BODY'S FACE WAS COVERED WITH FRESH BLOOD AND HE HAD OBVIOUSLY BEEN JUST BEATEN TO DEATH AND SET ABLAZE BY A MENACING MOB WHICH WAS STANDING AROUND. THERE WAS SOME JUTE SACKING PLACED ON THE LEGS OF THE BODY TO HELP COMBUSTION. AS THE MOB WAS COMPOSED OF HINDUS, THE VICTIM WAS PROBABLY A SIKH.

THE TWO OTHER BODIES HAD BEEN BURNED SOME TIME BACK AND WERE JUST CHARRED REMAINS.

ABOUT 100 METRES DOWN THE HIGHWAY FROM THE BLAZING BODY, THIS CORRESPONDENT TALKED TO DELHI POLICE SUB-INSPECTOR AMAR SINGH (NOT A SIKH, DESPITE THE NAME SINGH). HE SAID, "EVERYTHING IS UNDER CONTROL". I POINTED TOWARDS THE BURNING BODY, 100 METRES AWAY. "THAT IS A BURNING LOG OF WOOD", THE SUB-INSPECTOR SAID WITH A COMPLETELY HONEST EXPRESSION ON HIS FACE.

THE MOBS IN THE LANES GOING OFF THE HIGHWAY WERE LOOKING GRIM AND MENACING. AN AXE-WIELDING RUFFIAN

CAME CLOSE. THIS CORRESPONDENT TURNED BACK TO PASS THE BLAZING BODY AGAIN.

AN ARMY CONVOY OF FIVE INDIAN-BUILT JONG-JEEPS DROVE UP AND ONE OF THE VEHICLES, CARRYING A MIXED HINDU AND SIKH GROUP OF SOLDIERS, STOPPED NEAR THE BLAZING BODY.

ONE OF THE SIKH SODIERS JUMPED OUT ON SEEING THE BODY AND JABBED HIS QUIVERING RIFLE TOWARDS THE MOB. THE OTHER SOLDIERS TOLD HIM TO GET BACK INTO THE JONGA-JEEP. AFTER A MOMENT'S HESITATION, THE SOLDIER GOT IN AND THE CONVOY DROVE OFF TOWARDS A BILLOWING CLOWD OF SMOKE ABOUT TWO KILOMETRES AWAY WHERE OTHER MOBS WERE REPORTED TO BE BURNING, KILLING AND LOOTING.

(END) JL

HOW RECD PLS?

WELL RECD.... TKS....

TKS

Insurrection

Bhindranwale – Preacher with a Pistol

Amritsar

JARNAIL Singh Bhindranwale, the man who is regarded by millions of Sikhs as their spiritual and political leader, here in this holy Sikh city accused the Indian Government of fraud in its dealings with the Sikhs.

Reclining on a string-cot, a revolver strapped to his waist and a sword by his side, the Sikh fundamentalist leader told this correspondent in an interview that the recent religious concessions allowed by the Indian Government "are a fraud".

Bhindranwale said that these concessions had not been given in writing and were therefore meaningless.

He said that the personnel of the Central Reserve Police Force were still smoking cigarettes near the holy Sikh Golden Temple and the Sikhs had not been allowed to have a radio station of their own to broadcast their religious scriptures.

(Among the concessions announced by the Government are a ban on smoking near the Golden Temple and the broadcasting of Sikh scriptures by a Government radio station. The Sikh faith forbids smoking.)

Answering questions in his bare room in a hostel attached to the sparkling Golden Temple, the most sacred shrine of the Sikh religion, Bhindranwale said that "the Government is creating" the riots between Sikhs and Hindus over the past few days in the town of Patiala (about 100 kilometres south of Amritsar).

Asked why the Government would instigate riots, he said that it was doing so "to defame" the Sikhs and the Sikh Akali Party in particular.

Regarding the concept of an independent Sikh homeland called Khalistan, he said he was not for it or against it.

While a regular stream of pious Sikhs flowed in and out of his room to touch his feet as a mark of devotion, Bhindranwale declared that the Sikhs "want to live in India but it is for the Central Government of India to decide whether it wants to live with the Sikhs".

Regarding further negotiations between the Indian Government and the Akali Party about Sikh demands, he said that talks could be held again if responsible leaders of the government came to the Golden Temple Complex in Amrtisar to hold them. But the final decision for resuming talks rested with the Akali Party and the Government.

He said that he was ready to participate in these talks if asked to do so by the Akali Party.

Asked whether the outlawed Secretary-General of the National Council of Khalistan, Balbir Singh Sandhu, was staying in the same hostel as him, Bhindranwale said that it was not his business to know about such matters.

A few minutes later, this correspondent met Sandhu who stays on a lower floor of the same hostel. Unlike Bhindranwale, Sandhu is not surrounded by a crowd of devout visitors and armed attendants.

Sandhu openly declares that Khalistan is bound to become a reality some day, but he cannot say when.

Sandhu says that the creation of Khalistan is inevitable now that Sikh consciousness has reached its present stage.

The Sikhs have realised through their 36 years of experience of living in independent India that they will not be able to get a nation of their own except through war, he says.

Sandhu, who looks like an old grey-bearded university professor, says that both Bhindranwale and the Akali Party have raised the political and religious consciousness of the Sikhs and thereby helped the movement for Khalistan.

While brewing some tea for himself and his visitor on a tiny electric stove, Sandhu says that religion and politics are inseparable in the Sikh creed. On the floor above, Bhindranwale had uttered exactly the same phrase.

From Sandhu's window, the dome of the Golden Temple can be seen all aglow and the devout crowds can be heard chanting the holy Sikh verses.

KUNA (Kuwait News Agency), **May 8, 1983.**

Hide-and-Seek in the Golden Temple

Amritsar

OVERLOOKING the cool green waters which enclose Sikhism's holiest shrine, the Golden Temple, are two white-washed buildings where the current Indian political thriller is being played.

Reclining or sitting cross-legged on rough beds in the two buildings are two white-bearded men and a younger black-bearded man who hold the keys to the future of the troubled state of Punjab which has been both India's sword-arm and its granary.

In the formal hierarchy of Sikh politics, Harchand Singh Longowal is the top man. He is the President of the Akali Party and the "dictator" of the mass Akali agitation which has been going on for exactly a year. The Akali Party, whose membership is confined to Sikhs, has been demanding more religious concessions for the Sikhs and greater political autonomy for Punjab state whose population is 52 per cent Sikh and 48 per cent Hindu. (In India as a whole, Sikhs make up less than 2 per cent of the total population while Hindus make up the vast majority at 85 per cent. Muslims form about 10 per cent of India's population.)

But Sikh power is shifting inevitably into the hands of the black-bearded messiah, Jarnail Singh Bhindranwale, a 37-year-old preacher whose clever mixture of religion and politics is firing the emotions of the Sikh peasantry, India's toughest and most technically skilled farmers who provide a disproportionately high share of India's grain production and soldiers.

In the background is Balbir Singh Sandhu, a quiet unassuming man who talks of blood, war and an independent Sikh state called Khalistan which would be carved out of India.

According to Indian laws, Sandhu's statements are seditious and treasonable and he faces several criminal charges. Yet, he is living in room 32 in one of the two white-washed buildings. Two floors above, in the same building, Bhindranwale feigns ignorance about Sandhu's whereabouts. In the other white-washed building, 20 metres away, Longowal also pretends he does not know about Sandhu's presence.

Sandhu's open demand for Khalistan is not yet echoed by Bhindranwale who is ambivalent about it. Bhindranwale tells me that he is neither a supporter nor an opponent of Khalistan. Longowal tells me that the Akali Party is not for Khalistan.

However, the Akali agitation for Sikh rights led by the sad-eyed Longowal and the angry allegations of Hindu discrimination against Sikhs made by the hawk-nosed Bhindranwale are subtly helping Sandhu's cause. But Sandhu has no mass support. The man who is gathering increasing support by the day is Bhindranwale.

In his dingy room, Bhindranwale the young preacher, receives a constant stream of devotees and admirers, high and humble. Most of them touch his feet and drop currency notes on his bed. He blesses them.

He leads an ascetic life in his bare room. His only possessions seem to be the Sikh holy book and an alarm clock of the cheapest make.

For the Sikhs, he appears to be fast becoming a politician-saint, a phenomenon peculiar to India. This saint could be a Sikh warrior version of Mahatma Gandhi. He has a revolver strapped to his waist.

KUNA (Kuwait News Agency), **May 9, 1983.**

Provocation

Simmering Tensions

Jullundur

ON the surface of the politically volatile northern Indian state of Punjab there is no tension except in the riot-hit town of Patiala. A drive of several hundred kilometres through

Punjab over the past few days by this correspondent reveals a placid countryside with tractor-trailers brimming with a record wheat harvest and bustling towns with business carrying on as usual.

But beneath the placid surface there are simmering tensions which emerge in many conversations.

A number of violent incidents over the past two years have made Punjab's Hindu community feel increasingly insecure, Romesh Chander tells me. He is the owner-editor of the Jullundur-based *Hind Samachar* newspaper group which has the highest circulation in Punjab.

Chander knows the feelings of the Hindu community which forms 48 per cent of the population of Punjab while the Sikh community forms the other 52 per cent. Chander's father, Lala Jagat Narain, who was a vocal spokesman for Punjab's Hindus and a critic of Sikh separatist demands, was murdered in September 1981.

The police arrested Sikh fundamentalist leader Jarnail Singh Bhindranwale for possible involvement in Narain's murder but let him off for lack of evidence. Chander says that Bhindranwale was released for political reasons by the Government due to his strong support base among Sikhs.

Bhindranwale, on the other hand, told me in Amritsar, 100 kilometres north of Jullundur, that the Government was continuously repressing the Sikhs and favouring the Hindus.

Striking evidence of the growing gap between Hindus and Sikhs is provided by Chander who says that very few Sikhs now read his newspapers. The large circulation of his newspapers is almost entirely among Hindus. The Sikhs mostly read Sikh-owned newspapers.

The simmering tension has also affected business relations. In Kartarpur, a small furniture-making town near Jullundur, Bhushan Kohli, a shop-owner, says his sales are down by 70 per cent. Buyers from other towns now rarely come to Kartarpur. There is so much mental insecurity that people no longer wish to invest in household luxuries like furniture.

Kohli no longer offers credit to prospective buyers. In this atmosphere of lawlessness, he says, who knows whether loans will be returned? Kohli's doubts are echoed by several other businessmen.

In Chandigarh, 120 kilometres south-east of Jullundur, V.N. Narayanan, deputy editor of *The Tribune*, Punjab's leading English language daily, takes a more detached view of the situation. He has worked in Chandigarh for some years but is an outsider as he is from the southern Indian state of Tamil Nadu.

Narayanan points out that among the Sikhs, it is only the Jats (the landowning-soldier caste) who support the Akali Party and its agitation for greater political autonomy for Punjab state. The Jats form only about 30 per cent of the Sikh population in Punjab.

He reasons that the Hindus in Punjab are needlessly suspicious about the Sikhs.

About the political prospects of Punjab, he is unsure. He cannot forecast what shape the political emotions now being stirred up in Punjab will take.

KUNA (Kuwait News Agency), **May 11, 1983.**

Confrontation

Battle of the Golden Temple

Amritsar

GUN-SLITS carved out of marble walls, machine-gun nests on minarets, sand-bagged sniper points on ancient balconies, drainage-holes turned into firing positions, a holy building converted into the command bunker of Sikh militant leader Jarnail Singh Bhindranwale who died with a bullet in his head in his last redoubt.

These are the fortifications built by Sikh militants that I saw today during a hurried, army-conducted tour of the Golden Temple complex in Amritsar, 400 kilometres north of New Delhi. The militants had, with great martial skill, converted the area around the Sikh faith's most holy shrine into a fortress which the Indian Army penetrated and occupied at great cost on June 5 and 6.

At a press briefing by three army generals in the Sikh holy city, Monday, Lieutenant-General Krishnaswamy Sundarji, the overall commander of the Golden Temple operation, said that the resistance by Sikh militants had been even stiffer than he had foreseen. Answering a question, he agreed that the Government's intelligence agencies had been unable to provide adequate information about the battle preparations of the militants.

Sundarji pointed out that the army was also severely handicapped by an order not to fire back at the central Golden Temple building which houses the Sikh Holy Book. Despite continuous machine-gun fire from the central temple, troops obeyed the order and suffered 83 dead and 248 wounded while storming the other buildings around the central temple.

Sundarji said that the machine-gunners within the central temple surrendered only after most of the surrounding buildings had been taken by the army.

Bhindranwale, in his bunker in the second holiest building, held out till the last and died in the fighting along with 491 other Sikh militants, according to the latest figures given out today by the army.

Lieutenant-General Ranjit Singh Dayal, military adviser to the Punjab Governor, said at the press briefing today that the army would now proceed to flush out terrorists from the rural countryside of Punjab state. After that task was accomplished, the army would withdraw in stages and hand back the business of keeping order to the civilian authorities. Dayal said that he could not provide any time frame for completing the army's programme.

KUNA (Kuwait News Agency), **June 18, 1984.**

Chapter-2

Miracle Dentist in Amarkantak, Maneater in Pauri

I HAVE spent the night in some strange places while following an interesting trail. The creeping tingle of excitement sharpens as darkness descends on eerie surroundings. A lurking presence adds to that tingle. Lying wrapped in my father's 55-year-old overcoat on the planked floor of the headman's hut-on-stilts on a cold February night in the Pauri Garhwal mountain village of Birmoli, with a maneater possibly prowling under the floor, gives me a better high than any drink or drug. On an another cold night wrapped in the same ancient overcoat, lying on the sand under the chassis of a machine-gun mounted Land Rover of the Western Sahara's Polisario guerrilla fighters, with the looming threat of a night attack by the Moroccan army, provides a greater high than Birmoli. By far the coldest night, when the chill seeps into every knuckle and bone, is in a roadside hutment on the Zoji-la pass which connects Ladakh with the vale of Kashmir. The Border Security Force is transporting a load of reporters to its outpost in Drass which is reputed to be the coldest inhabited place after Siberia.

That hutment on Zoji-la is not as uncomfortable as the stringy *charpai* I occupy for the night in the pitch-dark pump-house of an irrigation channel while chasing Sanjay Gandhi's election manoeuvres in Amethi constituency. Chasing the Gandhi entourage can get extremely claustrophobic. Staying the night in a cupboard-sized cubicle in the cheapest doss-house in the industrial Italian town of Turin, while expecting to interview Sonia

Gandhi's father the following morning, has to be endured as my precious foreign exchange is running out.

A reporter's bed is not always uncomfortable. In Jullundur, the recently ousted Chief Minister of Punjab is more than happy to be interviewed on a blistering hot afternoon in my room at Skylark, the only air-conditioned hotel in town. Zail Singh walks in, takes off his white turban to reveal an entirely bald pate, lies down on the soft bed, asks for refreshments and politely indicates that I may proceed with the interview. After a cool rest, a soothing cup of tea and some pointless answers to my desultory questions, the future President of India thanks me most graciously and departs while I remain transfixed to my bedside chair in idiotic bemusement

I do not drink tea with Zail Singh as I am not particularly fond of that beverage, unlike most reporters who swallow gallons of tea through the working day. My special problem while reporting from strange places is not food or accommodation but the endless hunt for clean drinking water. I usually carry a large plastic jerry-can of boiled water when I set out. This runs out in a couple of days. Bottled mineral water is unsafe and the sugar content of Cokes, Limcas and Fantas increases my thirst. I keep scrounging for tightly capped bottles of fizzy soda at every roadside *dhaba*. At times, I walk into strange kitchens and request the amused cook to boil a *degchee* of water in my presence so that I can refill my jerry-can.

Wonder Dentist

Amarkantak (Madhya Pradesh)

A WONDER dentist who can remove deeply embedded problem teeth with a little finger pressure on the head and chin, a quick Vedic chant, the flick of a wrist and hardly any pain. Not a myth but a living ayurved who has removed the teeth of about two lakh suffering men and women in 340 medical camps since the year of the country's independence.

His name is Labhshanker Fulshanker Shukla and he hails

from Rajkot in Gujarat but travels all over the country, removing teeth without payment but charging something for his ayurvedic dental powder. In a medical camp in this remote area, I saw him repeatedly removing teeth in seconds from patients who winced not a bit.

Just to make absolutely sure, I lined up to have a firmly embedded molar tooth at the back of my mouth removed. Within seconds it was all over with just a slight stab of pain and no anaesthetic. A quick gargle with some blood red concoction and the bleeding stopped immediately. No pain at night or the following day.

The secret appears to be slight finger pressure on the middle of the head and under the chin just before Dant Vaidya (Dentist) Shukla flicks out your tooth with a tweezer. If the tooth is already loose, he opens your mouth and pumps your cheeks and hey presto, the troublesome tooth flies out and drops to the ground at your feet.

Dentist Vaidya says he leant the science from an ayurved called Dr K.B. Gupta who had in turn been taught by Swami Nananand Bharati, a guru who lived many decades ago in the Himalayas. Dentist Vaidya has taught his daughter, Saroj, the refinements of his science. He has also taught 15 other young people. He says that it takes two years to complete the training after the students have graduated from an ayurvedic college. May his science prosper!

Indian Express, **January 16, 1978.**

A Thousand Eyes Can See Again

Amarkantak (Madhya Pradesh)

DEEP in the wooded hills overlooking the bowl where the river Narmada begins its thousand-mile sojourn to the sea, a thousand and one eyes can see the sun again.

After months or years of darkness, the sun peers into the

retinas and the souls of Sarpraj, the six-year-old son of a coal-trolley pusher, and of Gyarsibai, the 43-year-old wife of a labourer, and of many other persons, all because of a simple operation in a bamboo and jute-sacking medical camp.

The camp is a temporary, three-week hospital to bring some relief in this tribal area of Madhya Pradesh, notoriously neglected by government and other agencies. The relief can only be for those ailments which are immediately curable or require relatively minor but skilled surgery.

At the camp, the focus is on easily curable eye defects like cataract, latent glaucoma and festering tear-sacks. Eye surgeons from Gujarat and Bombay, during the last week of December and the first week of January, have restored the sight of 2,100 cataract patients and others affected by glaucoma.

Without the camp, many of these patients would have continued to live in darkness and misery as they cannot afford any kind of medical aid. Around Amarkantak in the entire district of Shahdol there are only two hospitals equipped to do even minor surgery and due to the pressure of demand on them, only money or influence can get a sick person into these hospitals. In the circumstances, quack doctors, charging a rupee or two, have a field day.

Apart from eye diseases, the medical camp has discovered a large number of cancer cases in the area. Those at the initial stage, particularly cancers of the cervix, have been operated on and 40 women can now hope to live out their normal spans.

About 200 other gynaecological operations have been done at the camp. The operations are mainly to untie or open tubes to help make sterile women fertile. Due to malnutrition, male sterility is also quite prevalent in the region. Fortifying vitamins and other drugs are supplied by the camp for a limited period but these may not be enough as the medicines must be taken for long periods.

Other ailments which require long-term or preventive medicine are beyond the capacities of this temporary medical camp. But at least the camp has saved the sight and lives of those who required minor surgery and had nowhere else to go. The camp has been a temporary oasis of free and effective welfare organised mainly by the Girivanvasi Pragati Mandal of Bombay and the Gujarat Blind Relief and Health Association.

For many local diseases there is no medical cure. These are the diseases of poverty and prolonged hunger. Thousands of poor tribals and others roam around Shahdol and its neighbouring districts with large goitres because they cannot afford to salt their food properly. They use a rough local rock-salt which has no iodine in it. The lack of iodine leads to steadily developing goitres. A proper diet would cure them but when can they hope for that?

Indian Express, **January 16, 1978.**

Freshly Picked Diamonds

Panna (Madhya Pradesh)

SPARKLING in the palm of my hand is a tiny gem, freshly picked from one of the oldest diamond areas of the country. Weighing just a carat (two grams), the little gem will sell at about Rs 1,200 to diamond cutters and polishers.

Let any lady who finally adorns her ear or finger with it remember that this little diamond is the end result of sifting from around ten tonnes of diamond-bearing rock. Naturally it costs so much.

The final sifting at the government-owned Majhgawan mine near Panna is done by four women with delicate hands and quick eyes who earn just six rupees and fifty paise per day. They wear chunky tribal jewellery while they pick the diamonds for other maidens. They and all visitors are watched closely by the hawk-eyed men of one of the Central security forces. Any thoughts of niftily pocketing a worthwhile piece are soon parted.

The long process of crushing, grinding, washing and sizing the diamond-bearing rock begins at the bottom of a huge 30-metre deep pit where the rock is blasted out of the earth. From then on, sophisticated machines do the job of slowly reducing the size of the rock. Under impact of these machines, any big diamond would pop out of the rock in which it is embedded. There is almost no danger of a diamond being crushed as the jigs used to size the rock operate on the principle of specific gravity rather than brute force.

The General Manager of the Diamond Mining Project at Panna, Mr P.L. Jadeja, is a local man and, as his name suggests, is from a family which used to set diamonds for the princes of Central India. He explains that the mines around Panna were active in Mughal times and did get an honourable mention in the *Ain-e-Akbari*. Then they were left largely untouched for a time till a local maharajah began some diggings at Majhgawan in 1939. The Government of India stepped in at Majhgawan in 1959 and also started operations in a neighbouring mine at Ramkherya.

The diamond pit at Majhgawan is reputed to have a potential of eleven lakh carats of diamonds going down to a depth of 100 metres. In 1976-77, the two government mines around Panna sold diamonds worth two crore rupees.

There was also a private haul of diamonds worth two lakh rupees. If you wish to dig your own diamonds, you can still go to an area in Panna and start shovelling the soil after getting a license for five rupees. The license allows you to dig a 25-metre-foot patch for a month or two and if you manage to pick up a diamond, it goes straight to a government-organised public auction. Eighty per cent of the sale price is yours while 20 per cent is kept by the government as commission. If you wish to retain your diamond, you will have to buy it back it at the auction.

Indian Express, **January 17, 1978.**

Wildlife Officials Protect Child Killer

Dogadda (Pauri Garhwal)

THE maneater which has killed 14 people in Pauri Garhwal is still at large and none of the "experienced" shikaris licensed to kill it is anywhere near its haunt.

Villagers in the 220 square-mile area do not leave their huts at night. A woman who did, had a narrow escape – the animal only managed to get hold of her sari.

Only one adult has been the maneater's victim. The 13 other victims dragged away and partly eaten were children. Those attacked but lucky to survive were mauled lightly. Since the maneater attacks swiftly –in the dark – none of the survivors can tell what animal it is.

From the fang marks on the victims and the stealth of the animal, the Wildlife Warden of Kotdwara, Mr G.N. Chaturvedi, is convinced that the maneater is a panther or a leopard. The two are almost identical species. Some persons who have been attacked think it might be a hyena. There is no mention of it being a tiger. The villagers feel that nothing is being done for their protection. There is no sign of the administration posting a couple of BSF or CRPF personnel in each village to provide some sense of security to the villagers. The usual bureaucratic callousness is pervasive.

Any local application for a permit to kill the maneater has to be personally passed by the Chief Wildlife Warden in Lucknow. The Wildlife Department thinks it must protect wildlife at any cost. A man who shot a tiger which had lifted his cattle was prosecuted under the Wildlife Act. He now says he will not shoot at the maneater since he might be prosecuted again.

The Wildlife Department says that if all and sundry are permitted to try to shoot the maneater, other leopards or tigers will be injured and turn into maneaters. This hypothetical question of course does not worry the maneater.

However, a few token measures have been taken by the authorities. Sixteen guns have been distributed in the area and five wireless sets were bought a few days ago. A district forest official is expected to arrive from Bareilly on February 6 to try to kill the animal.

Indian Express, **February 4, 1978.**

Pauri Maneater Is Human in Cunning

Birmoli (Pauri Garhwal)

IT was a cool moonlit night. Fresh snow covered the ground. The Negi family had just finished dinner. The three daughters and their mother came out onto the terrace to relieve themselves. They lived on the ground floor. A cloud covered the moon. The night became pitch dark. The maneater watched the family from the steps going up to the first floor on the right hand side of the house. They were too close. Only five feet away. He could not spring at them.

He walked round the back of the house to the steps on the left hand side of the house. He waited. The mother was far out on the terrace. The two younger daughters stooped and went in through the low door. The third daughter stooped to go in. The maneater sprang silently at her neck. She died without a sound.

The maneater dragged the 14-year-old girl across the terrace. The mother could only see her daughter's white pyjama moving across the floor. She grabbed her daughter's pyjama leg. The maneater tugged the daughter by her neck. The mother could not hold on. The maneater threw the body 20 feet down from the terrace and dragged it down for another thousand feet though the terraced fields in similar fashion.

Last evening, as the darkness was gathering on that fearsome terrace in Birmoli village, the mother unemotionally recounted all the moves on the night of January 9 when her daughter became the thirteenth victim of the maneater. He was to claim his next kill the next night. January 10 has seen the maneater's last kill so far.

Last night, the villagers and I retreated behind locked doors soon after dusk, for that is when the maneater usually strikes. As it became darker the village Pradhan and I came out for a while. Fear is probably the most sensuous of emotions as it creeps coldly and physically down the spine from the nape of the neck. I felt it creeping down. The Pradhan also did, I think. The Pradhan, who is a retired army piper, blew his Scottish bagpipes to the tune of 'Hundred Pipers' while I probed the darkness with my torch. Lights came on across the valley as former Havildar Tajbir Singh Bisht played his eerie and alien tune. It might also have chased away the lurking animal.

This morning, Tajbir Singh and Gangotri Devi Chopra, the mother of Godambari who was killed by the maneater, repeatedly pleaded that something should be done about this animal which is almost human in its cunning.

The maneater may have been sighted last night in Gaira village, about five miles from here. A panther killed a cow, was chased away by the villagers, came back, sat boldly on the roof of a hut for three hours, then descended and devoured the cow. Was it the maneater? Nobody can tell.

On January 18, at five in the morning, the village headmaster's wife in Saurkhet, across the deep valley from Birmoli, had a narrow escape. The maneater sprang at her but missed by a couple of feet as she moved unexpectedly.

This whole area down to the plains near Kotdwara fears that the creature is bound to claim its fifteenth victim in the next few days.

Indian Express, **February 6, 1978.**

Hunter Becomes the Hunted

Dogadda (Pauri Garhwal)

MOST of the villages which attract the maneater in this Himalayan foothills area of western Uttar Pradesh are accessible to humans only on foot. Even horses or mules cannot negotiate the steep and stony paths leading to the villages which cling to the hillsides. Some of the paths go along fast flowing mountain streams. A wrong step, especially at night, means a nasty fall down hundreds of feet.

In these rugged conditions and with the extremely cunning maneater lurking in the dark, none of the shikaris who have tried to shoot the creature during the past year have attempted to follow the trail leading from a fresh kill in the dark. One local shikari, Mr Umrao Singh, who noticed the droppings of the beast in daylight, followed the trail.

While he was following the trail, the maneater was doing his own stalking and the hunter became the hunted. Both man and beast rolled down the hill together. The maneater had attacked Mr Umrao Singh and caught him by the leg. Hearing his shouts, two fellow shikaris came to his aid but the maneater escaped.

Since the maneater usually attacks in the dark and the villages are almost inaccessible to humans at night, the shikaris have always arrived many hours or days after reports of a kill have reached them. Goats have been tied as bait and the shikaris have waited on machans.

Panthers have been shot at twice from the machans. Both times the animals have escaped. As there are many panthers and other carnivores, like hyenas, in this area, there is no certainty that the shikaris shot at the maneater or some other animal attracted by the easy bait.

In these circumstances, the villagers whose lives have been endangered since January 1977 by the maneater feel that the shikaris will not be able to kill him for a long time. And since there is no Jim Corbett around in the country who will follow the maneater in the dark, there is little alternative but to post armed guards with powerful flashlights in each of the dozens of villages affected over the 220 square mile area. If some innocent animals get shot in the process, it will not be worse than the deaths of 13 innocent children and one woman who have been killed in the area largely because of official apathy, particularly in the Wildlife Department.

Indian Express, **February 8, 1978.**

The Royal Falcon Hunt

Jaisalmer (Rajasthan)

THE twinkling stars seem to fall out of the keen, clear desert night. The white sand is luminous. Strewn around are the dark, ghostly forms of stunted bushes. The only sound in the still night air is the soft hum of a finely tuned generator. In the distance is a dimly lit encampment.

On closer approach, after trudging through the sand by torchlight, a scene straight out of the Arabian Nights confounds the eye. Under two large, low-slung tents are astounding sights. Under one tent are several huddles of Arabs in Bedouin head-dress and flowing robes topped by padded, lamb's wool jackets to keep out the winter cold. They seem to be conferring, sitting cross-legged on the floor. But they are not talking. They are eating from communal, brass thalis, each eight feet in diameter. About ten men eat together from each of the thalis. Prince and retainer share the same vessel in keeping with Saudi tradition.

In the neighbouring tent, sitting perfectly still on small, carved brass stools are at least 20 falcons with sharp talons. Their eyes are hooded so that they do not get distracted. Another dozen hooded falcons are perched on stools outside the tent. It is an eerie fantasy – these bird-like demons of death in a royal Arab camp in the middle of the great Indian desert.

Fantasy is fact. The camp is 70 kilometres from the fortress town of Jaisalmer, that filigreed stonework gem set in the Rajasthan desert. And 40 kilometres from the border post of Longewala, where an epic battle was fought in the 1971 war against Pakistan.

The evening meal is over and Prince Bandar and his sons, Prince Mohammad and Prince Saud, come out of the dining tent accompanied by their retainers. The elder prince sits against a bolster on a white sheet and in a semicircle around him in the sand sit the Bedouins who train and nurse the falcons.

Kahwa (coffee) spiced with cardamom is served in thimblefuls from brass dallas (samovars) which glisten in the red glow of the log fire. Tales are told of the day's hunt. This day, the hunting parties spent hours seeking a falcon which flew away to freedom. They could not coax him back.

As we had imagined a palatial oasis in the desert, complete with dancing girls, the camp proves to be an austere affair. About a dozen canvas tents pitched in the sand. At least outwardly there are no signs of ostentation. Nor are there any women.

To an Indian eye, it is not the camp but the vehicles and electronic gadgets which are luxurious. Instant communication is maintained with the Saudi capital of Riyadh from a General Motors Sierra Classic truck with the latest radio transmitter-receiver. The sense of power is evident. Every member of the richest royal family in the world is expected to keep in touch with the nerve centre of what is becoming the richest nation in the world.

The 'jeeps' are the latest Toyota Land Cruisers and Range Rovers with special low-pressure tyres which glide over the sand. Every vehicle is equipped with a radio intercom system. Pick up the microphone, press a button and you talk instantly to those in another vehicle miles away.

The rear seats in the open Toyotas and Rovers are on raised platforms. The falcons are perched on rods behind the seats. When a hunting ground is reached, a favoured falcon is transferred onto a gloved hand and the hood is removed from his eyes. As a tillor (bustard) is sighted, the falcon is released with a sharp command in Arabic. He soars into the sky and swoops onto his prey, all in one grand symphonic movement.

The hunting falcons are a precious commodity. Baby falcons

are trapped in Syria and the northern reaches of Saudi Arabia. When they are a year old, they are trained for one to three months to swoop down on other birds and hold them down on the ground in their curved talons till the hunting party in its deluxe 'jeeps' catches up. The neck of the hunted bird is cut in halal fashion and is stowed away to be eaten later.

The most delicious of meats is said to be that of the tillor which is the Rajasthani name for the lesser bustard (also known as the McQueen Bustard) which migrates every winter from Siberia to warmer climes. A favourite winter resort of the tillor is the Rajasthan desert. These feathered immigrants apparently stopped going to Arabia and Pakistan when the hunting climate became too hostile.

Both hunter and hunted (falcon and tillor) are about the same size – about a foot high when seated and two to three kilograms in weight. The falcons are specially trained on cloth dummies and live doves to catch tillors in flight or on the ground. As a reward after catching a tillor, the falcons are offered tasty morsels of chicken.

Prince Mohammad, studying Political Science at Seattle University in the United States, gently explains this ancient royal sport while we sip the cardamom coffee by the log fire. He and his family have been coming to this desert area for the past three years and they have never hunted the Great Indian Bustard. In any case, it can never be hunted by such a small warrior as the falcon. (Prince Mohammad apparently does not know that both the Great Bustard and the lesser one are protected species listed under the Protection of Wild Life Act of 1972.)

The Great Indian Bustard (known locally as the godhawan) is six to seven times (upto 20 kilograms) the weight of the falcon and of the tillor. It is a huge bird which struts around the desert in regal style. It is four feet high and looks vaguely like an overgrown goose. It flies only in short hops. For the falcon, it is an impossible prey. No falcon could possibly attack such a huge bird, let alone hold it down in his puny talons.

The day we enter the camp, however, turns out to be the last day of the royal hunt. Unknown to the princes and to us in the desert, the Rajasthan High Court has passed an order against the hunt. The next day, the Minister of State for External Affairs, Mr Samerendra Kundu, flies in from Delhi to convey the news to the princes that the hunt is over. They take this graciously but feel that they should have been openly told from the beginning that they were doing something illegal. We meet Prince Mohammad again the following day. He tells us he will be flying home shortly. He is suave and extremely polite as usual, but there is a hint of irritation. He feels that it is inhospitable to turn out foreign guests once they have been allowed in. He finds it difficult to understand why a huge nation with all its cares should bother about a few hunters seeking a few bustards?

Perhaps he has a point. The only people who are horrified by the hunt are those in Delhi and Bombay and Jaipur who have never seen a bustard but are wildly enthusiastic about trendy issues like wildlife. Contrary to press reports, there is no protesting Vishnoi or Jain community in the hunting area. The locals in Ramgarh, a village three kilometres from camp, are quite happy with the hunters. A few have been employed at fancy rates at the camp and local foods are sold at inflated prices to the royal party. In Jaisalmer, there is some grumbling about the 'foreigners'. But this is clearly mixed with a warm feeling in the pocket. Tourists, especially rich and royal, help the folk of Jaisalmer – who are largely a trading community – to sell everything from silver antiques to varieties of junk.

Will this world of feudal largesse and grandeur last? We ask Prince Mohammad whether the fate of the Shah of Iran will not also overcome the Saudi princes? He says that Saudi royalty, unlike the imperial Shah, are one with the people and tribes of their country. The answer is not entirely convincing.

New Delhi magazine, **April 2, 1979.**

Chapter-3

Who Cares for the Voter?

THE GREAT Indian Voter has cast his vote wisely, patiently and with great sophistication over the past 50 years. Again and again, the voter's main expectation has been that those whom he has elected will bring about some slight improvement in his basic economic condition, some degree of progress in employment, income, water and power supply, health and education. Repeatedly, his hopes have been belied and he has increasingly turned to voting against the party in power. There have been rare exceptions where he has continued to vote sequentially for the same political group as it has provided at least a few minimal, material gains. The Left Front in West Bengal is one such example which has been continually voted back to power.

In frustration, some voters have at times turned towards parties that have whipped up regional, caste or communal emotions. The literate, urban, middle class voter has been shown to be more prone to fall for hysterical, sectarian appeals than the illiterate, rural, labouring class voter. In countless conversations this writer has had with the humble rural voter, her/his political wisdom shines through.

A relatively new trend which has become apparent since the 1996 Lok Sabha election is that the village voter has become as disgusted and disgruntled with politicians and the political system as the opinionated, metropolitan intellectual. The climate of widespread political cynicism points towards a threat to democracy.

The Dumb, the Blind and the Blue-Blooded

Rewa (Madhya Pradesh)

"WE are aiming for the Guinness Book of Records by trying for the biggest election majority in world history", declares K.P. Singh, campaign organiser and family retainer of Congress(I) candidate Martand Singh, the former princely ruler of Rewa, whose main opponent for the Rewa seat is blind social worker Yamuna Prasad Shastri of the Janata Party.

K.P. Singh has put on a Sheikh Abdullah-type cap to accompany the dignified, elderly Maharani of Rewa to the Muslim mud huts of Bichchaiya basti, behind the Rewa city palace. It is the first time the Maharani has visited the basti and an instant crowd gathers to gawk at the Maharani. She walks around the local saint's tomb in ritual obeisance and sits on a charpai under the peepal tree.

She does not say a word and the crowd of women and men continue to gawk. After 15 minutes her chauffeur drives her back to the palace.

Looking on, Mohammad Zahid, 26, a bidi worker who earns five rupees for every thousand bidis he hand-rolls, says, "*Maharaj goonge hai magar vote unko hee dainge*" (The Maharaja is dumb but we will still vote for him).

He elaborates that whenever anyone goes to the "Maharaj" with his problems and grievances, the Maharaja never says a word. Most complaints are passed onto "The Second Maharaj" who is the chauffeur-cum-personal assistant.

Another bright-looking bidi worker, Sarfraz Ahmad, 25, chimes in, "The choice is any case in between an *andha* (a blind man) and a *goonga* (a dumb one)".

During a recent fire in Bichchaiya, Janata candidate Shastri visited the basti and kept repeating, "Where is the fire? Where is the fire?", claims Sarfraz with a twinkle in his eye.

Sarfraz says that 85 per cent of the 1,500 voters in the basti will vote for the Maharaj, despite his dumb behaviour, because they have served the Raja's family for generations and "have eaten his salt". They cannot now betray him. Most of the crowd around Sarfraz agrees.

Traditional loyalty to the local raja is a major factor in the incestuous politics of northern and eastern Madhya Pradesh which this correspondent has been touring during the past week.

The Maharaja of Rewa stood as an independent candidate supported by the Congress(I) in the 1980 parliamentary election and beat his old Janata Rival, Shastri, by a margin of 2,38,000 votes. No wonder this time the Maharaja's campaign organiser is aiming for a world record.

But it may not be so easy this time for the breeder of the only white tigers in the world. Shastri had beaten the Maharaja of Rewa in the 1977 election, though by a small margin of 4,000 votes. Shastri is a man with a will. He even teaches at a school for the blind in Rewa.

Adjoining Rewa is Damoh constituency, which is centred around the former princely state of Panna, famous for its diamonds since the time of emperor Akbar. The ex-Raja of Panna, Narendra Singh, has always been with the Jan Sangh and the BJP. His main opponent is Dalchand Jain of the Congress(I). Jain is a newcomer and a rich businessman who may win due to the jeep factor. The strikingly beautiful Harshini Kumari, who lives in Panna town and is related by marriage to the royal family of Bijawar, says that Jain with his 50 jeeps is carrying on an energetic campaign throughout the sprawling, rugged, forested constituency of Damoh while the Panna Raja with only six jeeps can hardly push his campaign.

In nearby Khajuraho constituency, C.K. Singh, the nephew of the ex-Raja of Bijawar, had put in his nomination as the candidate of Maneka Gandhi's Rashtriya Sanjay Manch but withdrew at the last moment from the election. He had thought of standing as the RSM candidate mainly due to his friendship with "Dumpy" Akbar Ahmad. Both "Dumpy" and C.K. Singh own farms near Nainital in Uttar Pradesh.

One of the main contenders in Khajuraho now is Uma

Bharati of the BJP, who at 26 is probably the youngest candidate in the current election. The minimum age for a candidate to a state assembly or parliament is 25. The other main contender is an elderly lady social worker, Vidyavati Chaturvedi, who is the sitting MP. It is a close fight in Khajuraho as Uma Bharati has been a religious child prodigy who has toured the villages since the age of six, reciting verses from Tulsidas' immortal classic *Ramcharit Manas.*

In Gwalior, there is the famous battle between the dynamic and clever ex-ruler of Gwalior, Madhavrao Scindia, and the BJP president Atal Bihari Vajpayee. The BJP leader could well loose his party's stronghold due to a mixture of lethargy among the BJP campaigners and the forceful royal cavalcade of Scindia. The queen mother of Gwalior, Vijayaraje Scindia, BJP vice-president, is reluctant to speak out directly against her son who is the Congress(I) candidate.

In neighbouring Bhind constituency, the ex-ruler of Datia, Kishan Singh, is the Congress(I) candidate opposed among others by Vasundhara Raje Scindia, sister of the Gwalior princeling. Vasundhara Raje is the BJP Candidate. Bhind is made up of parts of the former princely states of Datia and Gwalior. The two royals could cancel each other out, leading to victory for DMKP candidate Ramshanker Singh who is reputed to be the most vociferous opposition leader in the Madhya Pradesh legislative assembly where he represents one of the assembly segments of Bhind.

Is there any sympathy factor for the Congress(I) in these constituencies? Ratan Lal, a paralysed old agricultural labourer, weak and bent, answers firmly that he will vote for "*Indira ka bacha*" in the coming election. Ratan Lal lives outside Panna town and he knows all that has happened since October 31. All-India Radio has its uses.

Amazingly the poison gas tragedy of Bhopal has not affected northern and eastern Madhya Pradesh in the least. The lethargic and unimaginative campaigners of the opposition parties have not even bothered to mention the tragedy. Family connections and film heroes may have come to dominate the nation's incestuous politics. That may turn out to be an even bigger disaster than Bhopal.

The Sunday Observer, **December 23, 1984.**

Boatmen at the Sangam Are the Most Accurate Pollsters

Allahabad (Uttar Pradesh)

AT the Sangam, where the holy waters of the Ganga, Yamuna and the mythical Saraswati mingle, the wiliest pollsters on the plains of northern India ply their traditional trade as Mallahas (caste of boatmen) to thousands of pilgrims who come from afar to bathe at the confluence. The devotees talk and the Mallahas listen.

I have great faith in the political wisdom of the Mallahas who only reveal their knowledge after many protestations of modesty. "What do we know? We are poor and unlearned. Who cares about what we think or say?" I persist as they were dead right in their poll predictions when I had last visited them on the eve of the Lok Sabha elections in December 1984 and before that, on the eve of the fateful March 1977 elections which had sent the Gandhi family packing for a few years.

After much prodding, Jagannath Nishad, 45, comments: "BJP ka zor hai. Par ham garibon ki kaun sunega?" (The BJP is going strong. But who is bothered about us poor?). A younger boatman, Ramnarain Nishad, 32, contests Jagannath's statement. Ramnarain says that Saroj Dubey, the sitting Janata Dal MP since 1991 from Allahabad, does listen to the poor and has solved some of the Mallahas' problems.

Saroj Dubey is contesting again this time as the Janata Dal candidate supported by the Samajwadi Party and faces a tough fight against the BJP's leading light, Murli Manohar Joshi. Ramnarain has decided that he will vote for Saroj Dubey and

Jagannath has decided defiantly that he will not vote for anyone. None of the candidates listens to the poor.

Jagannath's angry dismissal of politicians, parties and the electoral process is echoed among several poverty-stricken folk I meet during a trip (April 21 to 24) through Khajuraho and Satna constituencies in north-eastern Madhya Pradesh and Phulpur and Allahabad constituencies in eastern Uttar Pradesh. I had assumed that cynicism about the present political process was a restricted, urban upper-class phenomenon. This cynicism is now apparent among humble villagers even in small hamlets. Mewalal Kushwaha, 65, bare-chested, frail and with only a torn lungi to cover his nakedness, rasps, with fire in his eyes: "Vote-seekers are beggars. They create scandal after scandal." Mewalal has one bigah of land and 15 mouths to feed in the hamlet of Ishipur in Phulpur constituency where the BSP messiah of the downtrodden, Kanshi Ram, is one of the leading contenders. A disgusted Mewalal says he does not know whether he will bother to vote at all.

Seated next to Mewalal on a charpai is Asharam, 21, a confident BA student of Allahabad University. Asharam, who also lives in Ishipur, declares he will vote for Kanshi Ram as during the four months that the BSP was in power in Uttar Pradesh, it did a lot of work for the scheduled castes. Asharam openly proclaims that he is an "SC". Looking on, Audesh Kumar Kushwaha, 21, a B.Com student, regrets that Phulpur will witness a caste-based election and refuses to say who he will vote for. Later, as I distance myself from the open forum at the charpai, Audesh Kumar quietly tells me that educated persons like himself can only support the rational and forward-looking BJP. Though his background is Kushwaha, a backward caste, all literate persons must support the only non-caste party, the BJP.

His views are supported by a fellow student, who is also a Kushwaha, and some other educated persons from backward caste backgrounds whom I meet during my trip. Could this suggest a trend of upward social mobility through supporting and voting for the BJP which has attractive non-caste credentials? Are some literate sections of the backward castes attempting a new, political version of Sanskritisation through the electoral ploy of voting along with the upper castes for the BJP? Just 40 or 50 years ago, some of the so-called middle castes had sought to climb the caste ladder by adopting the social customs and religious rituals of the upper castes, especially that of the Brahmins.

While sections of the backwards or OBCs are attracted towards the BJP and other groups of backwards remain with Mulayam Singh's Samajwadi Party or waver in the direction of its ally, the Janata Dal, the Dalits or SCs are demonstrating a remarkable degree of confidence and cohesion under the banner of the BSP. The BSP's arrogant style is a match for the BJP's machismo. On a dirt-poor wall of a collection of jhuggis in Satna town is an uncompromising slogan scrawled in the bright blue colours of the BSP: "The Bahujan Samaj stands free from the clutches of the Brahmin."

Inside a dark garage, which is the local office of the BSP, the message of the party's election organiser for Satna town, Mohammed Ejaz, is as clear as the blue graffiti on the wall outside: "Other parties talk of providing roads, jobs, etc. We do not mention these at all. The BSP only says it will bring respect and dignity to the people." Ten minutes walk away from the BSP's garage, on Satna's main road is a messy, sprawling bungalow. On its compound wall is a puerile slogan: "Narsinhrao zindabad, Shyama, Vidya zindabad, Digvijaysinh zindabad!" It seems the local Congress office can do little else but wish its various squabbling chieftains a long life. Inside the bungalow are a bunch of demoralised Congress workers moaning about poor resources. Throughout my trip, the popular and constant refrain is that the Congress is finished. Other parties are in the fight but the Congress has lost the will to win.

If the Congress is finished, so it seems are the aspirations of Arjun Singh, one of the top figures of the dissident

Congress(T), who is contesting from Satna. He won on a Congress ticket from Satna in 1991 with a majority of 65,000. This time, he is out of favour with almost every group in his constituency. The general feeling seems to be that he has been too busy grandstanding on the national stage to bother about Satna's local problems such as the severe shortage of drinking water in the town and irrigation water in rural areas. The only group who may stand by him are his Thakur caste companions who number some 50,000 of the total of 11 lakh voters.

There is also similar resentment against Uma Bharati in her Khajuraho constituency where she won twice for the BJP in 1989 and again in 1991, though the intensity and extent of popular anger is not as great as that against Arjun Singh in Satna. She has rarely visited her constituency since 1991 and many in Khajuraho grumble that they have got nothing from her except "Ram ka naam". The owner of a lodging house in Khajuraho town, who does not wish to be named, says he has been a dedicated BJP worker for many years. But this time he will vote for the Janata Dal "to teach Umaji a lesson". She meets only rich and prominent persons in the constituency and has no time for her party workers, the lodge owner claims. Other BJP workers nod in silent agreement.

It is quickly apparent that Khajuraho is an extremely poor and undeveloped constituency, except for the oasis of the tiny town-extended village of Khajuraho where planeloads of chattering French and Italian tourists land to gawk at the erotic temple carvings, while immediately opposite the airfield gates, frail women spend hours in the scorching sun looking for berries which may have fallen to the ground from the roadside trees. They need the berries to save their families from semi-starvation during the long, parched summer months. Uma Bharati has no time for them. She is too busy with issues of national importance.

Laloo Prasad Yadav, Janata Dal chief and Bihar Chief Minister, flies into Khajuraho on April 21 to address a public meeting at Rajnagar village. He says that he wants a "Bharat jis may na rani hai, na mehtarani, na oonch, na neech" (an India where there are no queens nor sweeper-women, no high status, nor low status). Many of the applauding crowd of two or three thousand are party workers of all hues – JD, BJP, Congress, BSP. There is good-natured bonhomie within the political class, regardless of party affiliation.

This is another marked feature of the political landscape: the easy camaraderie and fellowship between the workers and local leaders of the various political parties. They show more concern for each other than for the concerns of the voter. In most small towns, the various parties' election offices are close to each other, grouped around one chowk or all on one road. They are almost like hardware stores or wholesale textile shops, all huddled together, selling wares which are not too different from each other. The only thing that varies is the sales talk.

This political class is present in every town and in many villages. The political class has undoubtedly served a representational and mediatory function of voicing public grievances and controlling the excesses of the local bureaucracy and police. It has, however, grown flabby, self-serving and increasingly remote from the general populace. Part of the reason for its remoteness is that it has not expanded in numbers at the same rate as the growing population of Lok Sabha constituencies or of Vidhan Sabha constituencies.

The Lok Sabha constituencies have grown particularly large in the sheer size of the number of voters. Most constituencies have grown from a rough average of about five lakh voters 20 years ago to about 10 lakh voters now, doubling their size in just two decades. How can an MP represent such a huge constituency?

Satna can be regarded as one such example. Satna was formed as a Lok Sabha constituency in 1967 with 5.25 lakh voters. At the time of the 1971 Lok Sabha election, the number of voters in Satna had increased to 5.71 lakh. The constituency was reorganised in 1977 and the number of voters went up to

5.93 lakh. By 1980, the number of voters had increased to 6.60 lakh. In the 1984 election, the number of voters was 7.30 lakh. In 1989, it was 9.59 lakh. In 1991, it was 9.85 lakh and now in 1996, it is 11.14 lakh. Between 1977 and 1996, the size of the electorate has almost doubled.

The number of MPs in the Lok Sabha over the past 20 years has grown by just a single member from 542 to 543 MPs while their constituencies have grown in the number of voters by almost 100 per cent. An expanded Lok Sabha with smaller constituencies could be an answer. Paradoxically, with the growing popular resentment against politicians, voters might reject the idea of having more MPs to represent them.

Outlook, **May 8, 1996.**

Saffron Juggernaut

Bhuj (Gujarat)

THE lone political personality in Gujarat of any national significance in the Lok Sabha elections is BJP President L.K. Advani, who is contesting from Gandhinagar, bordering Ahmedabad. The Congress candidate, retired Director-General of Police Prabhat Kumar Dutta, is a novice in politics, and constituents of the United Front are almost invisible. The most significant competition for the man who made Hindutva a brand name, comes from Chaitanya Maharaj, an extremist sadhu, shrewdly fielded by Shankersinh Vaghela, BJP renegade and leader of the Rashtriya Janata Party (RJP).

"Effective religious roadblocks" are part of Maharaj's plans to counter Advani. The 34-year-old sadhu has attacked the BJP's religious hypocrisy: "On the one hand they talk about Hindutva and, at the same time, they seek the support of the Muslims....Dharma is not the BJP's exclusive property." Vaghela, known to have a personal animus for Advani, has stated: "Shivaji was a small-statured man but could take on a person like Afzal Khan. We will show that Chaitanya Maharaj will prove to be a Shivaji against Advani."

Advani's strategy is to ignore Maharaj's barbs and never mention Vaghela by name. The BJP supremo has largely left the Gandhinagar campaign in the hands of his superbly organised party cadres as he canvasses across the country. There is some resentment in Gandhinagar – from where Advani won in 1991 with a large margin of 1.25 lakh votes and A.B. Vajpayee in 1996 – that it is being treated as a BJP pocket borough. But the BJP's juggernaut will ensure a comfortable triumph for Advani.

The smooth efficiency of the juggernaut is evident in the BJP election headquarters in Ahmedabad. A clean-cut, young British solicitor of Gujarati origin "helps out" in the management of the BJP campaign. Another, a designer-shirted young man in the party's media unit, monitors Shashi Tharoor's smug column on Hindutva vs Hinduism in a Sunday newspaper, while a third urgently summons a colleague on his mobile. Guppie globalisation of the BJP in Gujarat appears neatly encapsulated. But this is only part of the picture.

The strategy of the BJP, says Yamal Vyas, former Editor of *Dalal Street Journal*, and a key BJP functionary, is to push three issues – stability, law and order, and "Vaghela's corrupt practices". BJP loyalists see Vaghela as a traitor who split their ruling party in 1996 to become Chief Minister with the support of 45 Congress MLAs and 45 defecting BJP MLAs.

While Vaghela – who is not personally standing for election – is a forceful personality, he has little grassroots organisation and has been trying to undercut the political hold of the powerful Patel caste group of rich agriculturists with entrepreneurial talents by promising social and economic welfare measures to tribals, Dalits, Muslims and OBCs. The RJP's only leader with a popular support base is its president, Madhusudhan Mistry, who has done much work for the tribals. Moreover, Vaghela has alienated fellow RJP members. As has the BJP's chief election organiser Narendra Modi who has rubbed his colleagues the wrong way. Yet, in this case, pre-poll skirmishes are unlikely to affect the BJP's solid support base.

Travelling through five Lok Sabha constituencies – Ahmedabad, Gandhinagar, Dhandhuka, Surendranagar and Kutch – it becomes apparent that even opponents regard the BJP as an invincible force. Interestingly, parliamentary and assembly elections will be held together for the first time in Gujarat since 1967. Epitomising the dedication of the BJP activists is Lakhdirsinh, a retired factory manager, who has been working for the BJP for decades in Limbdi, Surendranagar district. Despite being denied a ticket, he has been addressing one exhausting rally after another, exalting the virtues of his party and of Bhavnaben Dave, former mayor of Ahmedabad and chosen BJP Lok Sabha candidate.

Both Rani Snehlataji and Yuvaraj Jaideepsinhji of Limbdi – where the formerly princely family is still respectfully referred to by their titles – who are not supporters of any political faction, have expressed their admiration for Lakhdirsinh's devotion to his party. And on the night bus to Bhuj, the main town of Kutch district, Jaswant Patel, a gas pipeline technician who travels all over Gujarat, also talks of "Bhajpa ka zor" (strength of the BJP).

In contrast, Congressmen in Gujarat, as elsewhere in the country, are lamely banking on Sonia Gandhi's last-minute forays to improve their prospects. Only a few sections of scheduled tribes – 14 per cent of Gujarat's population – and Muslims (10 per cent) are expected to be swayed by Sonia's appeal. Muslims seem to be cynical of the political process as Gujarat's political parties, especially the BJP (earlier the Jan Sangh), have done their best to mobilise Hindus against Muslims through a series of anti-Muslim riots over the past 29 years. Ahmedabad has been the epicentre of these riots which have not as yet destroyed the remarkable cultural and linguistic affinity among the state's Hindus and Muslims.

Yasmin Rehmani, a psychology graduate and member of the 99 per cent-literate Sunni Bohra mercantile community, is still recovering from the trauma of seeing her husband's industrial inks factory looted and burned in 1990, and once again in January 1993, after it had been re-built. With true Gujarati grit, her husband has managed to construct his factory for the third time. In the Rakhial and Odhav industrial areas of Ahmedabad, all the 16 or 17 Muslim-owned factories were destroyed in 1993. Not surprisingly, the Muslims are unlikely to vote for the BJP though the party has recently been making friendly advances.

Cynicism also prevails among the three lakh women members of Gujarat's largest cooperative venture, the renowned Self-Employed Women's Association (SEWA). Bharati Bhavsar, SEWA's co-ordinator for land and water, says: "We have to struggle with each government, regardless of the party, to get results. There is no difference between them".

The only constituency in Gujarat where Muslims form over 20 per cent of the electorate is Kutch, which is also the third largest constituency in area in the country, after Ladakh in Jammu and Kashmir and Barmer in Rajasthan. About 20,000 square kilometres of Kutch becomes a shallow inland sea during the monsoons. In the dry season, it turns into a marshland known as the Rann of Kutch, inhabited only by wild asses, thousands of pink flamingos and the tough men of the Border Security Force, as it borders the Pakistani province of Sindh.

Sitting in the BJP's Bhuj office, khadi-clad and courtly in manner, the soft-spoken Pushpadan Gadhavi, the sitting BJP MP for Kutch, could be mistaken for an old-style, Gandhian Congressman. Gadhavi has been lobbying for the expansion of Kandla port and for ploughing back some of the crores earned from the lignite mine – the port and the mine are two of Kutch's major employers – into the development of Kutch. Gadhavi is confident of returning to the Lok Sabha with an even bigger majority. His reason: the BJP's vast organisation – 11 samiti members in every village, 25 executive members in 13 mandals in Kutch.

In Bhujodi village, 10 kilometres from Bhuj, the Vankers, a traditional caste of weavers, have banded together to sell their brilliant hand-woven textiles directly to buyers in Calcutta, Delhi and Mumbai. They have grown relatively prosperous in recent years, moving from thatched huts into solidly-built houses and have even paid for the construction of a covered drainage system in their village. Dayalal Vankar, a master weaver who has won national awards for excellence in his craft, perhaps typifies the common man's mood in Gujarat towards the elections. He shows little interest in which party comes or goes. The master weaver is far too busy perfecting his skills and earning a decent living.

Outlook, **March 2, 1998.**

Chapter-4

A Fractured Society

THE September 1994 Surat plague, the October 1999 Orissa cyclone, the January 2001 Gujarat earthquake and annual droughts and floods, have occurred one after the other over the past few years. Yet, every time these disasters happen, the response in terms of rescue, relief and rehabilitation is lethargic, chaotic and painfully inadequate. On paper, there are official Central and state disaster management committees and plans but on the ground the implementation process has invariably proved to be a mess. Every time, the army, air force and navy turn out to be the only agencies which respond in an organised manner and with relative speed to these regular disasters. Though NGOs, volunteers from charitable organisations and ordinary citizens invariably react more quickly and caringly than civilian government employees, they are incapable of a coordinated and efficient effort.

There are countless administrative, political and economic reasons for the routine failure to come to the humanitarian aid of our fellow citizens in a systematic way. These rationalisations are peripheral. The root cause of the failure is socio-cultural. Again and again, we demonstrate our inability to work together, to act cohesively and caringly towards each other. Even at moments of great peril, we get diverted into factional quarrels and group rivalries. No social adhesive binds us together and sensitises us to the feelings and lives of co-citizens.

The builders who mixed extra sand with cement and used

low-quality steel girders to construct the high-rise luxury apartments which collapsed like packs of cards in the January 26th earthquake in Ahmedabad and Bhuj are not merely corrupt individuals. They represent a pervasive culture of callousness where the only exceptions who merit caring treatment are members of the immediate family and clan or those who forcefully exert their superior status and wealth. Even within families the weak and defenceless are regarded as expendable. At the holiest of holy occasions, the Allahabad Mahakumbh in January 2001, families after taking a devout dip at the Sangam, abandoned some 10,000 old widowed mothers and grandmothers to their fate.

'Every man is an island unto himself' is an old cliché. Here we have perfected that cliché into a fine art form which we practise every day with mindless ease. Rampant individualism is evident in all our daily functions. The most obvious example of our reckless behaviour is the way we drive without a care in the world about the convenience or safety of anyone else on the road. Weaving, swerving, cutting in, overtaking from any side, honking hysterically, speeding aggressively through crowded lanes, careless even about little children playing on the street. The chronic continuance of fatal school-bus accidents in Delhi and in other cities, despite public outrage and judicial strictures, points to a similar, blithe disregard for any rules and norms. The blatant and inane flouting of protective standards is often carried to a suicidal extent. In some cases, bus drivers were seen to have been driving so furiously that they killed themselves along with the school children in their charge.

Our fatal carelessness is not just an impression. It is a documented fact. According to *The Millennium Edition of Guinness World Records 2000*, India has the most 'unintentional' deaths in the world. *The Millennium Edition* states: "The World Health Organization defines 'unintentional' deaths as road traffic accidents, poisonings, falls, fires, drownings and other accidental injuries (not counting homicide, violence and war). Of a total of 9.34 million deaths in India in 1998, 723,000 – or 1in 13 – were defined as 'unintentional'. They included 32,000 poisonings, 50,000 falls, 135,000 in fires and 92,000 drownings . . . . Indian roads are rated as the most dangerous in the world. In 1998, 217,000 were killed in road traffic accidents."

This suicidal instinct is also reflected in politics. Both the 1998 and 1999 Lok Sabha elections were held after petty factional wrangles and consequent withdrawal of support to the governments headed by Gujral and Vajpayee. Despite members of parliament fully realising that many of them would lose their seats in fresh elections after having served in the Lok Sabha for much less than the their normal term of five years, they were not able to arrange a suitable compromise and to back a coalition government which would complete the full parliamentary term. Similar factional antics by members of the Uttar Pradesh and other state legislative assemblies have led to early dissolution of legislatures, Presidential Rule and wastefully expensive, mid-term state elections. Every political party is riven by group rivalries based on nothing more uplifting than personal greed, personality clashes and caste wars. No wonder we continue to be at the mercy of mis-governance, precariously based on the whims of temporary factional coalitions which misleadingly proclaim themselves as parties.

Talaq! Talaq! Talaq!

WHILE the Republic's official motto may be '*Satya Meva Jayate*' (Truth Alone Triumphs), if the true tenor of our national behaviour were to be taken into account our motto would be '*Talaq! Talaq! Talaq!*' (I divorce thee).

In virtually every sphere of out national life, we have regressed into amoeba-like creatures, constantly splitting, dividing, fragmenting. Solidarity, comradeship, collective effort have become alien concepts overtaken – much like the way we drive – by suicidal individualism and petty irritability towards one another. Factionalism has riven all our important national endeavours and institutions in politics, society, commerce, industry, education, public health, sport, media, the legal profession, the misnamed civil service.

Governance of the Republic has become a tiresome tussle as factions within the political parties and within the bureaucracy grab the plums of office, all the while clothing their greed for power and wealth in the silky gowns of ideology or group welfare. Even those factions which boldly seek benefits for a caste group, usually milk the group to benefit a particular personality or family. Despite all the talk of caste politics, the daily business of government seems to be run for the profit of *gotras* rather than *jatis.*

The classic example of running the country for the glory of the family was the Indira Gandhi phase, especially 1975 and onwards, when she foisted son after son on the gawking Republic. To maintain her personal control, she also promoted the factionalisation of the Congress party and the bureaucracy, though some muted regional factions had existed in both institutions even in Nehru's time. As the reigning mistress of double talk, she split the Congress Party in the name of the poor millions in 1969 and then again in 1978. She made shrill proclamations about national integration even as she engineered the fragmentation of national institutions.

Indira Gandhi was by no means the trend-setter in splitting political parties on the basis of personality and personal gain. Throughout the 1960s and 1970s, Socialists like Raj Narain, Madhu Limaye and George Fernandes indulged in an orgy of temporary alliances and splits, culminating in the this trio being instrumental in the destruction of the Janata Government in 1979 in league with Charan Singh and Sanjay Gandhi. George Fernandes has continued his meanderings with his latest alliance in 1996 with the BJP though his quest for personal fulfilment still eludes him.

As a consequence of the 1962 Sino-Indian border conflict, the Communists split into the CPI and the CPI(M) in 1964. Those who believed in armed struggle rather than parliamentary politics broke away from the CPI(M) under the spell of Charu

Mazumdar in 1969 and started the Naxalite movement which later broke into several personality oriented factions. Personal ambitions have also afflicted the Hindutva groups. Balraj Madhok walked out of the Jan Sangh in 1973, Murli Manohar Joshi and Lal Krishna Advani have barely disguised their suspicion of each other, and Shankersinh Vaghela has broken the notoriously faction-ridden Gujarat unit of the BJP and installed himself as Chief Minister purely on the basis of personal patronage.

Even the separatists who seek to secede from the Republic are afflicted by the Indian malaise of personalised factionalism. The separatist factions in Kashmir, Assam, Manipur and Nagaland are too numerous to be listed here. Sikh militancy had also spawned half-a-dozen Khalistani groups.

Politics merely reflects our social impulse; separatism is rampant at every level of our society. There are uncompromising and angry schisms within communities, within castes and also within families. The lakhs of family property disputes in court throughout the land bear witness to our propensity to push our differences to breaking point. Our sub-continental cousins also have this curious tendency. The most glamorous examples are the Bhuttos of Pakistan and the Bandaranaikes of Sri Lanka. Farther afield in East Asia, Europe and even in the Americas, the general tendency is to resolve social/family disputes through sensible compromise and mutually beneficial give-and-take. Here, the prevailing social norm is the mutually destructive beggar-my-neighbour syndrome.

Big industrialists and trading families whose natural inclinations should be towards consolidating their capital gains are also prone to the national disease. The children of several eminent pre-1950 industrial barons have split their family empires mainly due to sibling rivalry. Professionals – lawyers, doctors, architects, civil engineers – are renowned for their petty jealousies and competitive squabbles. In contrast to the custom of setting up joint practices in East Asia and in the

Western countries, doctors and lawyers here prefer to have individual practices. Partnerships among equals are rare; servile juniors are taken in as dogsbodies.

Journalists can be the most cut-throat of individuals and every major media organisation is riven with conflicts based on personality clashes. The shenanigans within Zee TV are the most recent case of close encounters of the Bollywood kind.

Prior to 1950 and for many years afterwards India's hockey team always came home from the Olympics and other international arena with the gold medal. In recent decades the solitary gold has eluded our team, symbolising, perhaps, our inability to perform collectively. Sports czars, such as superannuated police officers, have also played havoc while choosing team members through personal favouritism rather than merit. Many of the nation's once hallowed universities have become hotbeds of intrigue and in-fighting with professors acting as politicians.

Tight discipline in the armed forces has quarantined them from most of our social viruses but the recent undignified scramble for the post of naval chief indicates that the bacteria of factionalism cannot be totally excluded from the armed services.

Bacteria thrive in particular cultures. Factionalism proliferates in a profoundly unequal and hierarchal society with every individual struggling for a tiny sliver of the economic cake which is expanding ever so slowly. More significantly, beyond the social inequality and the economic distress, lies the grossly inflated male, upper caste, middle class, Indian ego, soppily pampered and spoiled by generations of doting mothers and fathers. This has created a dominant species of self-indulgent and self-glorifying individuals who are out to wreck one another and who could well succeed in wrecking the Republic.

The Hindustan Times, **January 26, 1997.**

Maverick Republic

HELLO?
Hello?
Hello? Kawwn?
Who's speaking? Hello?

VARIATIONS of this enervating charade are repeated thousands of times during the day all over the country. We have no standard etiquette to receive or make telephone calls without hassling each other and raising blood pressure even when the infernal machine does manage to work. Multiply the individual feelings of frustration and anger just over phone calls and all the other daily irritants caused by our mulish refusal to adopt any sensible social norms, and lo, you have the recipe for a society on the verge of collective hysteria. High technology, modernisation, liberalisation, globalisation – all nice trendy concepts – but can they ease our lives if we refuse to adhere to any standards of social behaviour so as to smoothen the path of daily social intercourse?

The crass social tone for the country is being increasingly set by the expanding, metropolitan upper classes with their effortless influence over social trends through personal example and through films, television, radio and the press. Anarchic, whimsical behaviour is apparent even in the most sophisticated offices at the start of the working day. Greeting office or business colleagues in the morning usually depends on personal mood or fancy. At times, this might mean setting a sour note for the rest of the day and damaging the ability of colleagues to work together.

When the boss walks in, there is a distinct change of attitude. The minions rise up with alarming gusto to exhibit their respect in exaggerated tones. Most bosses merely grunt in response, showing their disdain for the lower orders. This is particularly conspicuous in government offices, as well as in the judicial, legal and medical professions. Hierarchy is displayed in its most obvious and vulgar form – arrogance and obsequiousness in equal measure, with no respect for the personal worth of the individual.

Basic *politesse,* regardless of social status, is a necessary lubricant to oil the wheels of daily inter-personal contact, whether in the office, street, market or at a party. Yet, even at parties where, presumably, friends are invited to enjoy each other's company, standards of behaviour have noticeably regressed. While the small, intimate party is *passé,* large parties create a bigger ripple in the social whirlpool.

All kinds of people are thrown together, not because the host or hostess find them likeable or interesting, but because they could prove to be 'useful contacts' at some point of time or they carry the ambiguous 'celebrity' label. Conversations are fleeting and eye contact with the person you are speaking is minimal as he is usually looking over your shoulder with rapid eye movements trying to spot a possible new contact.

Even at the rare small gatherings, we have developed a uniquely Indian style of talking *at* each other rather than talking to each other. Everybody, and especially those who consider themselves to be self-appointed members of the intelligentsia, loves to hold forth and never listen.

These surface social antics may appear trivial but they add up to consequences of volcanic effect. The build-up of daily tensions arising from these thoughtless, anti-social habits is showing up in the form of violent individual and collective actions. A good number of them, usually dismissed as spontaneous acts, are sparked off by the mounting heap of mindless slights and insults which we so casually inflict on each other day after day. Polite words and gentle manners are not pointless gestures: they serve as the invaluable balm to cool tensions.

Lack of norms for daily social intercourse can prove to be irreparably damaging for the moral and political fabric of our society and seriously undermine our ability to work collectively and cohesively in any field of national endeavour. Undefined standards of inter-personal behaviour in our homes, workplaces and streets are a major factor leading to laxity of norms in all our major institutions: parliament, administrative and judicial services, police and armed forces, banks, stock exchanges, hospitals and other public utilities. It is not surprising that individuals and groups with money, muscle or the right patronage can get away with any crime, from purloining thousands of crores in financial scams to such pedestrian acts as rape and murder. It is not the nastiness of the crime that is taken into account but who commits it and on whom.

If that alleged molester, the grandson of the Punjab Chief Minister, had picked on some poor village woman instead of a spirited French one, who had the gall to complain, the whole issue would have been resolved without a fuss. Perhaps, the Chief Minister's grandson's gut feeling was correct. In a social climate without any norms, an act of molestation is a mere wheeze, a jolly bit of fun, if you have the right connections.

In the wider world, we add up to being perceived as 'The Maverick Republic', where any thing goes, and not 'The Largest Democracy' that we repeatedly proclaim ourselves to be. We have satisfied ourselves that holding an election every few years and being able to shout ourselves hoarse in every public place is sufficient to count ourselves among the leading democracies. Does not a deeper sense of democracy also have something to do with some semblance of equality before the law and equal protection of the law, regardless of socio-economic status, and some degree of responsiveness from government functionaries to the woes of the common man?

The Times of India, **November 26, 1994.**

Not Parties, But Factions

THERE is no loyalty in politics anywhere. But in Indian party politics, loyalties can change faster than the time it takes for a politician to nod or wink.

This quick change artistry was most recently demonstrated in the leadership wrangle for the spoils of Oudh. Overnight, sworn enemies embraced and seeming friends parted. Mr H.N. Bahaguna, one of the key leaders of the CFD faction of the Janata Party, joined hands with Mr Charan Singh, faction leader of the BLD in the same party. A few days before the two men had hardly been on speaking terms. But the quest for control of the *subedari* or Chief Ministership of Uttar Pradesh brought them together to ensure the succession to the *gadi* of their new foundling, Mr Banarasi Das. And now to his delight, Mr Das is being kept in power by the tacit backing of the Congress-I. But Mr Das's hold on power is extremely precarious for there is a faction within the CFD faction which is not too happy with Mr Das for having defeated Mr Raj Mangal Pandey who after all also belonged to the CFD faction. So there are factions within factions, leave alone within parties. Every Indian political party from the once mighty Congress to little hill parties in Manipur and Mizoram have a hallowed tradition of in-fighting, defection and factionalism.

Legacy Older than Gandhi

Even under that colossus, Mahatma Gandhi, there were clear schisms within the Congress (founded 28 December 1885), then engaged in the struggle against the British. In May 1934 at Patna, a group of Congressmen formed a party within a party, the Congress Socialist Party (CSP). The formation of the CSP only confirmed the fact that all and sundry were admitted into the Congress from big landowners and personages with impeccable big bania connections to raving socialists and Harijan peasants. Well before independence, the Congress established itself not as a disciplined, dedicated party with a clearly defined strategy of political change but as a disparate group of heterogeneous stock whose limited goal was to make the British quit India. There were some who had very definite ideas about what sort of India should be built after the British were pushed out. One of the most definite in view was Subhas Chandra Bose who was elected President of the Congress in 1938 and again in 1939 despite the open opposition of Gandhi. But the persistent opposition of several members of the Congress Working Committee forced him to resign in April 1939.

With his departure from India on 26 January 1941 and his alliance with Germany and Japan, the formation of the Indian National Army was not long in coming. Even before Bose, there were other Congressmen who splintered away from the Congress and formed their own groups because they were not successful in espousing their causes or furthering themselves in the Congress. These included figures like Motilal Nehru and C.R. Das who formed the Swaraj Party in the 1920s, first within the Congress and then 'half-apart' from the parent organisation. Another unsuccessful figure who broke away completely from the Congress was M.A. Jinnah who was to become the founder of Pakistan.

On Top or Against

These figures may be called the precursors of the post-independence factional leaders. All of them had one marked trait. They founded separate groups and discovered distinct ideologies only after they had failed in their quest for pre-eminence within the Congress Party. The post-independence factional leaders have, however, another trait which men like Bose and Jinnah lacked. The post-1947 generation are more akin to C.R. Das and Motilal Nehru. They keep 'half-apart' from the Congress and keep their options open to float in and out of the parent party at will; a will generated by political opportunity.

The Congress could not possibly say good-bye to factionalism when the country bid good-bye to the British. With the need to retain power by functioning as a political machine, the Congress also had to retain its disparate membership. All the varied groups were encouraged to remain under the umbrella of the Congress which continued its career as a coalition of factions rather than as a united party whose members would be expected to stick to a defined political path. One slight change was made. The constitution of the party was changed in 1948 which forbade any Congress member from belonging to any other party. At this point, members of the Congress Socialist Party left the Congress. But this loss was more than compensated by Nehru playing the father figure and conciliator and keeping the doors open to people of disparate backgrounds and ideologies. He even included Shyama Prasad Mookerjee, with his career in the Hindu Mahasabha, in the Cabinet. Mookerjee was given the important portfolio of Industries and Civil supplies. Mookerjee did not take long to disagree with Nehru on the handling of the situations with Pakistan regarding Kashmir and the East Bengal Hindus. He resigned from the Cabinet in April 1950 and helped found the Jan Sangh. At that time, the right wing in the party, which included Vallabhbhai Patel and Purushottamdas Tandon., had become an important faction in the party, often working at cross-purposes with Nehru. But with the resignation of Mookerjee, the death of Patel in December 1950 and the ouster of Tandon from the Congress presidency, the first of the powerful post-independence factions within the Congress at the Centre faded.

Oh To Be Chief Minister

But in the states, Congress factions began to build up, usually in opposition to the reigning chief minister. Often these factions within the Congress raised their head in demanding linguistic apartheid. The first of these demands was for a separate state for the Telegu-speakers and a number of Congressmen were actively involved in the movement which led to the establishment of Andhra Pradesh. Y.B. Chavan built up his base in the old Bombay Province by, as became a habit with him, sitting on the fence – working for a Maharashtrian homeland but at the same time not totally alienating the Central leadership of the Congress. This was to pay off. He became the first Chief Minister of the new-born Maharashtra in 1960 and was later called to the Centre as Defence Minister. Factional, divisive politics was meant to pay rich dividends and it did.

Why single out Chavan? A number of stalwarts began to form factions in the states whose main purpose was to pressurise the weakening leadership at the Centre. These factional leaders were appropriately named Congress bosses. They included portly and illustrious figures like Atulya Ghosh in Bengal, K. Kamaraj in Tamil Nadu, S.K. Patil in Bombay and so on. These strong, localised factions were to encourage the growth of unalloyed and virulent regionalist parties like the Shiv Sena and the DMK. As became evident later, these regionalist parties, founded on opportunism, were themselves to become the victims of factional oppurtunity. When any leader with a personal following felt he could set himself up in power without the party, he left it and started his own. The classic case is of M.G. Ramachandran, once the hero of the DMK, abruptly leaving the party and forming the AI-ADMK as soon as it dawned on him that he could become Chief Minister.

The quest for electoral victory and ministerial power became the prime motive of which party to belong to. The wavering party member could always clothe his lust for ministership or for a party ticket in a forthcoming election in ideological garb, be it socialism, linguism, nationalism or any other concern which was always meant to benefit the 'masses'.

The Queen of Factionalism

The leader who was to perfect this technique of clothing the garb for power in ideological terms was Indira Gandhi. The most blatant and successful expression of this was the 1971 Lok Sabha election when she promised to *hatao garibi* in return for the vote and she was swept back into power. But before achieving the pinnacle of power she had gone through a thorough schooling in the school of factional politics at the hands of the Congress bosses who had hoped to manipulate her easily when they had first chosen her as Prime Minister in 1966 after the death of Lal Bahadur Shastri, who himself was chosen Prime Minister by a coalition of Congress factions after the death of Nehru in 1964.

Ironically the Congress' factional leaders had become even stronger after the Kamaraj plan of 1963 when six Chief Ministers were made to resign by Nehru to revitalise the party. Most of these figures, who were supposed to generate a new spirit of working for the masses in the Congress Party, spent their time building up their local bases and uniting together as arbiters of power. By the time of Nehru's death, they had acquired the status of a syndicate which controlled the party. Shastri did not live long enough to come into conflict with the syndicate but Mrs Gandhi soon found that to survive as Prime Minister she must become the plaything of the syndicate or break away from them. And using the rhetoric of nationalisation and socialism, she broke away from them and split the party. The split was formalised when the syndicate expelled her from the Congress party on 12 November 1969.

With her great victories in the elections of 1971 and 1972, her party became the Congress and the syndicate rump came to be aptly called the old Congress or Congress-O. Factionalism in the Congress became muted although it was far from dead. Factions now began to give themselves academic sounding names like Socialist Forum while a faction under Chandrashekhar was dubbed as the Young Turks. Alternative seekers of power began to arise in the state units of the Congress Party as in Nehru's time. Attempts by such people as V.P. Naik, Chief Minister of Maharashtra, to assert themselves were promptly scotched and the upstart quickly despatched from office. Some tried to become bosses even during the Emergency but they were smoothly shunted out. These included Nandini Satpathy, Chief Minister of Orissa and H.N. Bahuguna, Chief Minister of UP.

The Janata Khichdi

With the lifting of the Emergency in early 1977, another disparate coalition of factions was formed to oppose the Congress coalition. The Janata coalition succeeded in the March 1977 election. Many of the leaders of the Janata's constituent parties or factions had left the Congress or had been excluded when they found themselves out of the running for the pinnacles of power. These included men like Morarji Desai, Charan Singh, Jagjivan Ram, etc.

The effect of the great defeat on the Congress coalition was electric. Without the perks of office, Congressmen began to desert the holed umbrella with alacrity. Some of them like Jagjivan Ram, Bahuguna and Nandini Satpathy had been clever enough to anticipate the Congress defeat and rush to the new Janata umbrella before the leaky one gave way in the electoral downpour.

In this novel situation of being pushed out of office for the first time since the 1937 elections under the British, the Congress fell to bickering and all its factions began to abuse each other. Indira Gandhi tried the old trick and split the party once again on 2 January 1978. She also renewed her calls of concern in the name of the people, but being without the powers of office, she has so far not succeeded in re-uniting the Congress factions, of which there are at least five, within the Janata Party and outside it – the Congress, the Congress-I, the Congress-O, the Congress for Democracy (CFD) and the Congress dissenters who were arrested during the Emergency.

All the other constituents of the Janata Party, except the Jan Sangh, also have the distinguishing mark of having been Congress factions which expanded into opposition parties. Even the Jan Sangh had as one of its key founders, Shyama Prasad Mookerjee, who as mentioned earlier had been part of Nehru's Cabinet till April 1950. He became the first president of the Jan Sangh when it was founded on 21 October 1951 in Delhi. The other Janata constituents – the Bharatiya Lok Dal (BLD) and the Socialists – have had a much more intimate relationship with the Congress. The major constituent of the BLD when it was formed on 29 August 1974 was the Bharatiya Kranti Dal (BKD) which itself was the brainchild of disgruntled Congress factional leaders who had failed to achieve their targets of power in the mother party.

Election Splinters and Fusions

Whenever elections approach, the struggle to retain or enhance power becomes more acute. On the eve of the fourth general elections in 1967, group rivalries and dissensions within the Congress Party came to the surface. Many Congressmen left the party before the 1967 elections and formed their own parties as they rightly feared the growing mass resentment against their party at that period and felt that a Congress Party ticket would no longer ensure retention of their seats. In order to exploit this opportune moment, the grasping Congress leaders formed their own parties in several states in 1966. These included the Jana Congress in Madhya Pradesh and Orissa, the Bangla Congress in West Bengal, the Janata Party in Rajasthan (only a remote relative of the present Janata Party) and the Jana Kranti Dal in Bihar. These Congress splinters and a number of independents presided over by that veteran 'has been' Congressmen, J.B. Kripalani, met in Delhi on 6 and 7 December 1966. Their only bond was that they were disgruntled Congressmen. A vague 8-point programme was put together and a new party, the Jana Congress, declared, though its formal inauguration was postponed till after the general elections. But after the elections, many of those who had come together informally as the Jana Congress kept away from the attempt to formalise the new party in Patna in May 1967. And only a smaller grouping emerged as the BKD at Indore on 12 November 1967. Only in UP did it become an important force under the leadership of the ex-Congressman, Charan Singh.

After their crushing defeats in the 1971 and 1972 elections, the BKD, the Swatantra Party, the Samyukta Socialist Party and some smaller parties felt the need to unite to overcome their sorry state. They managed to do so only on 29 August 1974, though even then a small rump of the Swatantra chose to remain aloof from the newly formed coalition of factions known as the BLD.

Among these groups, the Socialists must take the cake for having the most notable record of continuous fluctuation between fusion and factionalism. The first attempt at unity was after the 1952 general elections when the Socialist Party and the Kisan Mazdoor Praja Party (KMPP) joined together to form the Praja Socialist Party (PSP) on 12 September 1952. A former president of the Congress, J.B. Kripalani, had formed the KMPP on 6 May 1951 in the hope that his new party would win considerable support in the 1952 elections. But both the KMPP and the Socialists were shocked by the bad results. To overcome this setback, they decided to unite. With such a quick marriage of convenience there were bound to be differences from the beginning. The differences crystallised over whether there should be cooperation with or opposition to Congress rule.

On 28 December 1955, Ram Manohar Lohia and his followers who were completely against cooperation with the Congress left the PSP and renamed themselves the Socialist Party (SP). But there were still others in the PSP who wanted greater intimacy with the Congress. Among them were Asoka Mehta and his followers who joined the Congress in April 1964.

In June 1964, the PSP and the SP joined together. This time the joint party called itself the Samyukta Socialist Party (SSP). This was achieved after long, involved discussions set off by the 1962 general elections in which the PSP and the SP lost many seats, especially in UP and Madhya Pradesh, because they were contesting against each other. But the compulsions of election politics could not paper over the continuing factionalism in the SSP. The Lohia cult and its accompanying anti-Congressism led to the withdrawal of the PSP faction from the joint party at the very first conference of the SSP at Varanasi in February 1965. The separation was to last for some time. The SSP did especially well in the 1967 general elections and eagerly grasped the opportunity of being a weighty faction in the coalition Cabinets in Uttar Pradesh and Bihar. It was only after another electoral debacle during the 1971 Lok Sabha election that the PSP and the SSP came together and launched themselves once again as the 'new-old' Socialist Party on 9 August 1971. Differences arose yet again and the party split once more on 17 April 1972 with George Fernandes, Madhu Limaye, Madhu Dandavate and their group retaining the name of the Socialist Party (SP) while the Raj Narain and Karpoori Thakur groups came to be known as the SSP. When the BKD, Swatantra Party and the SSP and some smaller parties joined together in August 1974, the SP chose to remain aloof.

The SP gave up its independent position only on 20 January 1977 when together with the BLD, Jan Sangh and the Congress-O it decided to fight the 1977 Lok Sabha election as one party under the Janata banner, a tenuous unity brought about by the rigours of the Emergency. A few weeks later the CFD got onto the Janata bandwagon. On 1 May 1977, the Janata arrangement was formalised but, as is evident in daily headlines, the constituents of the party continue to pull in different directions.

Jan Sangh

In UP, the Jan Sangh has been temporarily excluded from the spoils by keeping it out of the state's Janata Cabinet. It may not be long before this group in UP shows the classic tendency of losing some of its members to other groups in their bid to get into the Cabinet. The Jan Sangh has not been a monolithic organisation although certainly less prone to bickering and in-fighting than the other parties. Balraj Madhok, a leading light of the Jan Sangh, left it in 1973 after differences with other leaders of the party and formed his own Loktantrik

Dal. He followed the established expedient of forming yet another party on losing out within the parent party.

When the Jan Sangh was formed on 21 October 1951, apart from the Rashtriya Swayamsevak Sangh (formed 1925), which was its backbone, it had a polyglot Hindu revivalist pedigree. The Jan Sangh's strands consisted of the Arya Samaj (formed 1875), the Hindu Mahasabha (first Hindu Sabha formed in Punjab, 1907) and the Ram Rajya Parishad (the most orthodox Hindu party, formed 1948). To this day, the relationship between the RSS cadres and the non-RSS men within the Jan Sangh has not been resolved.

Swatantra

Another right-wing party with diverse strands was also founded in the 1950s. Its origins go back to two groups who felt that the authoritative and socialist tendencies of the Congress Party must be fought. These two groups were the Forum for Free Enterprise and the All-India Agriculturists' Federation. The moving spirits, as with so many other parties, behind this new grouping were two ex-Congressmen, M.R. Masani and C. Rajagopalachari. This new party was founded on 4 June 1959 and called the Swatantra Party.

Though the brainchild of urban liberals, the party gained electoral appeal by admitting several princes and their personal political parties into the Swatantra fold. In Bihar, the Maharaja of Ramgarh led his Janata Party into Swatantra. In Orissa, the Maharaja of Kalahandi with his tribal following in the Ganatantra Parishad, merged his regional party with Swatantra. The biggest catch of all was "the beautiful and pugnacious" Maharani Gayatri Devi of Jaipur. She not only had a large flock of admirers in Jaipur but several princelings all over Rajasthan followed her lead and joined Swatantra. In the 1962 elections, the Swatantra Party emerged as the largest opposition group in the Lok Sabha, mainly due to the vote-catching abilities of the princes of Rajasthan, Bihar and Orissa. Only in Gujarat did it establish a base which went beyond the charisma of the princes. The princes proved to be no more loyal than any other breed of politician and some like the Maharajas of Ramgarh and Paliwal departed from the party a couple of years after the 1962 elections.

For the campaign in the 1967 elections, the party came to rely more on big industrial houses rather than on the princes. The Swatantra benches in the Lok Sabha after the 1967 elections displayed more industrialists than princes. Despite the backing of wealthy industrialists and vote-catching princes, the party could not develop any grassroots support as it did not bother to pay lip service to the economic aspirations of the poor. In a poor country, openly championing the cause of the rich could not be politically profitable. The party lost out badly in the 1971 and 1972 elections when the Congress rhetoric of miracles for the poor carried all before it. Also, the party had never managed to work as a cohesive group with such disparate interests as armchair liberals and grasping industrialists and princes pulling in different directions in keeping with their personal interests. With its support dwindling, the Swatantra merged into the BLD in August 1974 though a residuary rump under G.K. Sundaram remained apart till it decided to join the Janata Party on 17 April 1977.

Communists

The country's domestic pressures have affected all the political parties. The Communists, however, are much more prone to involvement in international issues. Personal power struggles among the Communists are swathed in the rhetoric of international proletarianism. From the day of independence, the Communist Party of India (founded 26 December 1925) divided into two factions on the question of whether India had really become independent or it continued to be a colonial entity. While P.C. Joshi held the view that the transfer of power was real, B.T. Ranadive and Adhikari advocated the view that real independence could only be achieved under Communist rule. The latter line was initially supported by Stalin in Moscow.

Stalin later changed his views when it suited what he considered to be the interests of the Soviet fatherland.

There were also schisms regarding whether the Telengana armed struggle, which was begun in late 1948, should be continued. Finally, after the brutal suppression of the armed struggle, the CPI formally ended its armed phase in October 1951. But the bitter factional quarrels over Telengana continued to divide the CPI well into the 1950s and factions for and against the Nehru Government were active. The pro-Nehru faction was led by B.T. Ranadive and the anti-Nehru faction by Ajoy Ghosh. After the CPI achieved power in Kerala in 1957 with E.M.S. Namboodiripad as Chief Minister, the CPI's anti-Nehru radicals became muted in their criticism which was to be rekindled when the CPI was unceremoniously bundled out of power in 1959 by the Central Government. At the Vijayawada Congress of 1961, a split in the CPI was narrowly avoided over conflicting attitudes to Nehru and to the Sino-Soviet row. With the Sino-Indian border conflict in October 1962, the factions within the party became more active – one group being sympathetic to China and the other condemning Chinese aggression. In April 1964 at Delhi, matters came to a boil and 32 members of the National Council of the CPI walked out and later in the year formed the Communist Party of India (Marxist).

Both parties were now engaged only in parliamentary politics though there was a small group within the CPI(M) which felt that parliamentary politics could never lead to liberation of the peasants and workers of the country. This group named itself the All-India Coordination Committee of Communist Revolutionaries (AICCR). One faction of the AICCR under Charu Mazumdar advocated immediate armed struggle and broke away from the CPI(M) to from the Communist Party of India (Marxist-Leninist), popularly called the Naxalites, on 22 April 1969. Another group of the AICCR under Nagi Reddy remained aloof from both the CPI(M) and the CPI(ML) on the ground that the time was not yet ripe for armed struggle.

While the Naxalites were carrying out their armed struggle in West Bengal and Andhra Pradesh, differences over tactics and personalities led to the growth of a number of factions. By 1972, the Naxalites had been suppressed and in 1977 a faction under Satyanarain Singh took to the parliamentary path by participating in elections. Other Naxalite factions called the Satyanarain Singh faction a bunch of "renegades". If you look back at twentieth century party politics in India, you may be tempted to call the entire lot of parties a bunch of renegades.

New Delhi magazine, **April 30, 1979.**

Chapter-5

Gorging on the Wretched of the Earth

THOSE with power, authority and influence in this country routinely pick on the weak and the vulnerable. They invariably target those who cannot defend themselves. Traumatised victims of disasters, who are particularly helpless, are ideal targets. Any moment, however ghastly and tragic, is opportune – from the Bhopal gas disaster in 1984 where pregnant women were used as suitable guinea-pigs for medical research on toxicity to the Orissa cyclone in 1999 where recently widowed young women fleeing from devastated villages were preyed on by wealthy men from the big cities.

On a regular, daily basis, most government functionaries, from ministers and police commissioners to petty clerks and police constables, use their positions to exploit and harass any citizen who is not wealthy or influential. However venal these functionaries may be, there is some slight measure of control over politicians and the bureaucracy. Politicians can be dismissed by voters and bureaucrats can occasionally be hauled up, though after a lot of effort, for flouting the rules. There is far less control over private individuals with wealth, muscle power and criminal mendacity as, by the day, the state is increasingly becoming their private estate. Government servants are brazenly seen to be acting as minions of crooked businessmen and criminal wheeler-dealers and not as upholders of the Constitution and the law, and protectors of the public good.

Under the garb of encouraging market forces, the state is

being subverted by unscrupulous and corrupt private individuals who have purloined the law with lucre from their deep pockets. The forces of the state cannot be blamed alone for being corrupted. The state reflects a society where there is a hierarchy of exploitation and deep corruption. Each segment of society squeezes the segments below it. The poorest citizens, who are usually women, tribal people, Dalits and Muslims, are the most exploited.

It is very difficult to identify any islands of fairness and equity. The so-called noble professions – doctors, lawyers and teachers – are as condescending and grasping as the rest. Patients, litigants and students from humble backgrounds are treated with contempt and cheated of their meagre earnings by bullying professionals in hospitals, courts and colleges. Propaganda in the elite-controlled media against the deprived sections is used as a cover for mistreating them. Many of the upper class 'social workers' and NGO operators who appoint themselves as leaders of the downtrodden use their positions for their personal self-advancement and enrichment rather than for any sincere efforts to improve the lot of the deprived.

The top layers of society may believe that they can continue to get away with cynically living off the labour of the lower orders. Their belief is mistaken. There are signals that indicate that they cannot insulate themselves from the disease, poverty, squalor and venality of the society they have wantonly created. When the plague struck Surat in 1994, the city's diamond merchants and art silk magnates had to flee from their marbled apartments along with their illegally under-paid and over-worked employees who live in its festering slums. Most of those who were killed in the January 2001 earthquake in Ahmedabad were from upper middle class families who lived in illegally constructed apartment blocks, knowingly built by flouting zoning laws, floor-space norms and construction standards.

Despite such warning signs, the high and mighty of the land brazenly brush aside all laws and norms with contempt. They make every attempt to sweep under the carpet scandals which have cheated the country of thousands of crores. Their criminal activities are having a demonstration effect on the poor and wretched who are spawning a growing class of petty, violent criminals. The rulers of the nation are adding spice to a recipe for social anarchy.

Bhopal Gas Victims Have Become Guinea-Pigs

BHOPAL keeps reappearing like a terrible ghost. On October 4, many newspapers carried a report from Bhopal. The second paragraph of the UNI news agency item states: "A study on the long term effects of MIC (gas) show that out of a surveyed population of 86,000, 2,712 pregnant women were detected on December 2, when the gas leaked. Of these, 400 foetuses were aborted."

The fourth paragraph of the news item states: "The study also recorded 2,250 deliveries. Of these, 52 were still-births, while 132 babies did not survive long. Nearly 30 cases of malformation were found in the surviving babies, the study revealed."

The news item then provides the names of the distinguished doctors who carried out the first phase of the study and says that the second phase had begun in selected "slum areas" of Bhopal.

It is obvious that the study is not bothered about recommending any medical measures to help the malformed babies or to assist the traumatised Bhopal mothers in ensuring the survival of their newborn babies. The study is plainly one more meaningless statistical exercise to further the career prospects of the doctors and to provide them publicity.

Bhopal has spawned numerous such studies in which the gas victims have become the guinea-pigs. Droves of doctors have descended on Bhopal for a few days at a time to carry out a survey, address a press conference and then fly out as gas experts. In the 10 months since the gas leak took place, only a handful of doctors outside Bhopal have volunteered to come to the city and actually treat the gas victims.

The country's premier medical research body, the Indian Council of Medical Research (ICMR), and its director-general, Dr V. Ramalingaswami, sowed criminal confusion by initially deriding the role of sodium thiosulphate injections in the treatment of gas victims and then changing their recommendations five months later when sodium thiosulphate treatment had become less effective with the lapse of time. At the time of the gas leak last December, local junior doctors in Bhopal had discovered that several gas victims were responding marvellously to sodium thiosulphate. But Dr Ramalingaswami and the ICMR stepped in, together with some local senior doctors of dubious reputation, and effectively halted the sodium thiosulphate treatment. It is not known how many persons died due to this stoppage of sodium thiosulphate treatment. In May, when the ICMR finally decided to recommend sodium thiosulphate, it was no longer that suitable a remedy.

While the ICMR and other medical researchers argue and wrangle about the long-term effects of poisoning, the gas-affected people of Bhopal suffer and die in the short-term.

This excessive Brahmanical intellectualising has also paralysed lawyers, journalists and social workers who have taken up the Bhopal cause. Legal and political bickering and factional quarrels about what 'line' to adopt on the Bhopal disaster have made these groups incapable of practical action to reduce the sufferings of the disaster victims. (Let us ignore those lawyers, journalists and social workers who continue to swoop down on Bhopal like vultures to make a fast buck or a quick reputation.)

A few tiny volunteer groups like Dr Anil Sadgopal's Zahreeli Gas Kand Sangharsh Morcha have persevered and made some serious effort to lessen the pains of a few gas victims. Perhaps because the Morcha is seen to be making a serious effort, it has been attacked by the callous Madhya Pradesh Government and reviled by various intellectual bodies for ideological reasons.

Prime Minister Rajiv Gandhi and the Union Government have dealt with Punjab, Assam and Sri Lanka but have no effective measures to deal with the continuing catastrophe in Bhopal. There are no terrorists or murderous mobs in Bhopal to pressurise the Government or to draw national attention.

In the 10 months since the gas leak, no significant relief or rehabilitation work has been done in Bhopal by Government or private agencies. Bhopal has demonstrated the sheer perversity and utter callousness and rottenness of Indian society.

The Telegraph, **October 16, 1985.**

Indian Worker in the Gulf Is Reviled at Home

THE man ahead of me had a valid Indian passport. The police inspector at the immigration desk flung the passport aside and abused the man. In an automatic reflex and without batting an eyelid, the man gave the inspector the equivalent of Rs 100 in Saudi riyals and was grudgingly allowed to enter his own country. The man was a humble Indian worker returning from the Gulf with his hard-earned wages. The incident took place a few years ago in Bombay but the abuse, extortion and ugly treatment of the Indian working man and woman visiting or coming home continues daily at the hands of every Government functionary and in many ordinary transactions – extending a passport, getting emigration clearance, getting onto an Indian Airlines flight even after having a confirmed reservation or changing foreign money at a bank.

This working man, who is cheated and harassed at every step, is keeping India afloat on the international currency market. Without his thrift and hard work, India would sink into a deep balance of payments deficit and foreign exchange crisis. In the 1980s, he has been India's largest single source of foreign exchange. None of India's major exports – engineering goods, cotton garments, tea – earned the country anything approaching the amount of foreign exchange sent home by the Indian worker in the Gulf.

The latest confirmed figures are for 1982-83. In that year, remittances from abroad, mostly the Gulf, amounted to a net figure of Rs 2,416 crores. Engineering goods earned Rs 786 crores worth of foreign exchange, cotton garments Rs 527 crores and tea Rs 367 crores. Tourism netted another Rs 946 crores. Fears that remittances from Indian workers in the Gulf may go down sharply due to a recession in the Gulf economies have so far proved unfounded. Estimates for 1984-85 and projections for 1985-86 show that India is continuing to earn around Rs 2,500 crores annually from remittances.

The Indian worker is quite distinct from the Indian businessman or professional who lives abroad, mostly in the United States, Britain, Canada or Hongkong. The businessman or professional is forever seeking and getting concessions and incentives from the Union and State Governments in India. Despite this package of favours, the calculating businessman, doctor, engineer, professor or accountant salts away most of his savings in American and European stocks, shares and bank deposits. His family lives with him abroad. So he does not regularly send remittances to India as the Indian worker does.

The Indian worker is not allowed to settle permanently in the Gulf or to take his family there. He retains a stake in India through his wide family responsibilities in his home town or village while the businessman or professional wears his patriotic heart on his sleeve in London and New York. Yet it is the latter who is wooed and welcomed by numerous Government and private agencies while the worker is despised or at best, ignored, from the moment he lands at the airport in his home country. As a Swiss journalist friend with pronounced capitalist leanings told me, we should be erecting statues of the Indian worker in the Gulf for keeping this country solvent instead of reviling and harassing him.

He is harassed both in India and in the Gulf countries which have developed their own perverse caste and class hierarchy based on race. In the pecking order, the Gulf Arabs have placed themselves at the top, followed by Americans, Europeans, other Arabs such as Palestinians and Egyptians, East Asians such as Koreans, and at the bottom of the list, South Asians which includes Indians, Pakistanis, Bangladeshis and Sri Lankans. Wages are also based on this racist classification. An Indian doing the same job as a European or other category gets much lower wages than his counterpart from outside South Asia.

The arrogance of the newly rich Gulf Arab is reflected in his rough treatment of Indians and other South Asians. Gulf employers routinely pay lower wages than promised and demand long working hours. The police there pick up Indians or Pakistanis at the slightest provocation. Rude and offensive behaviour towards Indians, particularly working class Indians, is the norm. The Indian worker bears all this as he is treated no better in his home country and as he earns a higher income than he would ever get at home.

The Telegraph, **October 2, 1985.**

Anaemic Mothers and Olympic Failures

EVERY four years we chant ritual laments at the recurring funeral of our dismal performance at the Olympic Games. The funeral orations are as superficial and depressing as the failures they wail about. The autopsies shy away from mentioning a lifetime of deprivation or excess. The cerebral thrombosis is mentioned but not the careless lifestyle which thickened the arteries and cut off the blood supply to the brain.

We hear of bureaucratic bungling, nepotism, regionalism and sectarianism in selecting the Olympic squad, followed by inadequate training, poor facilities, loss of team spirit and lack of funding. The same tired excuses are trotted out on an Olympian scale after every Olympic disaster.

The more substantial causes of our Olympic failures lie deep in our society. Many are detailed in cold print in the UNDP's 1996 Human Development Report, while others are to be found in UNICEF's studies on the status of children and mothers.

That about 25 per cent – or 229 million – of our 901 million people (1993 figures) have extremely poor incomes is telling. But far more telling is the fact that nations far poorer take better care of young mothers and their children. For instance in Burundi, a country racked by civil strife and with a per capita GDP of $670, 38 per cent of children under five are underweight. In Ethiopia, also ravaged until recently by a brutal civil war and with a per capita GDP of $420, the figure is 48 per cent. The figures for India are $1,240 and 53 per cent.

India also has the horrendous distinction of having the highest proportion of anaemic pregnant women among countries for which data are available. In Bangladesh, 58 per cent of pregnant women are anaemic; in Mozambique, 58 per cent; in Liberia, 78 per cent. In India, 88 per cent are anaemic. The per capita GDPs of Bangladesh, Mozambique and Liberia are, respectively, $1,290, $640 and $843 (at purchasing power parity).

The UNDP report has found that 61 per cent or 554 million of India's people do not have the oppurtunity of living healthy, secure and mentally aware lives. The report refers to this 61 per cent as "capability poor". This is more than double the 25 per cent that are income poor. This means that over 60 per cent of our people are out of the running in the Olympics or any other race.

Add to this the young mothers and female children who, for deep-seated cultural reasons, deprive themselves or are deprived of an adequate diet and basic literacy – 88 per cent anaemic pregnant women and 64 per cent female illiterates – and up to 90 per cent of our young women are unlikely to be able to compete internationally. Anaemic mothers also produce and rear male children whose growth into healthy manhood is thwarted.

What about the 10 to 20 per cent of our population which

could produce promising sports figures? Here again, cultural reasons and social hierarchies intrude. Physical effort or manual labour is frowned upon and left to the lower classes or castes. Physical self-indulgence is the norm, specially among middle class males, who over-eat, drink too much and rarely exercise. Such people do not improve our standing in the Olympic tables but are beginning to show up in statistics which indicate that middle class Indians are more prone to coronary disease than Americans, West Europeans and East Asians of comparable backgrounds.

Then there is the tiny top-income group of social walkers in their Reebok and Nike sports shoes and fancy Benetton T-shirts who do their status-climbing rounds in Delhi's Lodi Gardens or Bombay's Marine Drive and Hanging Gardens. There can hardly be serious sportspersons or Olympic hopefuls among them.

It is no great wonder that such an iniquitous society has produced a solitary bronze medal winner from a sixth of the world's population. Yet our thinkers and intellectuals have shown relatively less concern about the capability poverty of 554 million Indians than about nuclear capability and the CTBT. Perhaps, in a deeply segmented society, self-styled intellectuals form their own rarefied strata with their own hierarchy of concerns. Anaemic mothers and aspiring athletes are at the bottom of this hierarchy. Not surprisingly, even Burundi (one gold) and Ethiopia (two golds and a bronze) performed better at the Olympics while Mozambique (one bronze) equalled India's performance.

Indian Express, August 23, 1996.

Third Sack of Delhi

NADIR SHAH'S vengeful raiders sacked Delhi in 1739. Brutish British soldiery ravaged Delhi in 1857. The city's (and the country's) smug and self-indulgent 'elite' is now mindlessly engaged in the third sack of Delhi. Urban prettification, pollution control and consumerist greed are regarded as sufficient grounds to ruin the economic production base of a city of 14 million enterprising citizens. The economic life-blood of millions of workers and small businessmen is sought to be drained out by a self-seeking, affluent class of entwined bureaucrats, professionals and politicians who have warmly embraced the combined thrust of the World Trade Organisation's (WTO) dictatorial commercial regime, the Supreme Court's insensitive *fatwas* and the Ministry of Urban Development's bulldozer tactics.

Thousands of factories, especially small enterprises, all over the country and in Delhi have already closed down due to cheap, subsidised, foreign goods being dumped on India ever since the Government cravenly surrendered on April 1, 2000, to the new trade regime supervised by the WTO. The recent sealing of yet more factories in Delhi on grounds of pollution control was the final straw for workers and owners seeing their livelihoods being snatched away from their hands. Starvation is apparently being sponsored by the authorities as a substitute for pollution. It should, therefore, come as no surprise that the threatened worker-owners, many of whom are self-employed and operate their tiny industrial enterprises from within their homes, took to the streets during the past week in a mass display of anger and despair. They earned a temporary reprieve on Wednesday with the Central Government's relaxation of 'The Master Plan' to banish factories from so-called residential areas.

Of Delhi's 140,000 industrial units, only 22,000 are in the officially designated industrial zones. The remaining 118,000 units are in tightly compounded colonies where workplaces and homes cannot be distinguished. Insufficient land, lack of basic infrastructure and no provision for financial loans have already made a farce of attempts to relocate polluting factories to the outlying areas of Bawana, Narela, Jhilmil and Patparganj.

In any case, most of Delhi's nasty air pollution is emitted by motor vehicles and not from factories. According to the Central Pollution Control Board, 64 per cent of the city's atmospheric pollution is from vehicles, 17 per cent from its three thermal power plants, 12 per cent from industries and seven per cent from households. Why have the social busybodies who constantly file public interest litigations (PILs) in the courts not sought judicial restrictions on Delhi's multiplying sales of, and recklessly extravagant use of, private cars and government staff cars instead of picking on buses, taxis and autorickshaws which are used by the public? As public health is cited as a major concern, why are the municipal authorities not ordered to provide an adequate supply of clean drinking water to every resident of Delhi instead of pouring water into the vast lawns of the mansions of ministers, senior bureaucrats and judges? Why are the urban development authorities quick to demolish petty hutments and banish cottage industries while being painfully slow at providing low-cost housing?

Judicial pronouncements on public issues do not always help in solving complex social and environmental problems. To take just one example: the Supreme Court order of July 8, 1996, directing the relocation or closure of 168 hazardous and noxious factories in Delhi, actually resulted in 50,000 workers being thrown out of their jobs. Years later, many of them remain unemployed and without compensation, despite judicial directions to factory owners to recompense their former employees. Thousands of ruined families have become paupers.

Desperate teenage male children of some of these jobless workers have taken to burglary and robbery. The recent alarming rise in petty crime in Delhi can be partly accounted for by the Court order which led to throwing thousands of families onto the streets of the capital. Some of the sacked workers have found employment at minimal wages in hazardous, slum-yard metal foundries and units for recycling plastic waste, adding to Delhi's pollution problems. Civic problems should remain in the ambit of politicians and administrators who should clear their own garbage.

The current judicial trend of entertaining too many dramatic PILs also requires self-correction by the judiciary. A number of judges are being swayed by sensational media attention and away from their primary duty of administering even-handed and speedy justice to each defendant and litigant who comes before them. PILs are often foisted on the courts by relatively wealthy publicity seekers who divert the precious time and mental resources of senior judges from their basic task of providing justice to harried and humble individuals.

Public pressure on politicians and bureaucrats is eventually the ultimate weapon in resolving social and economic issues effectively. The ordinary people of this country have over the past 53 years become democratically and forcefully conscious. They are no longer willing to accept mutely the self-serving cant and deceit doled out by elitist charlatans who care more for the lives of trees and dogs than for the lives of their humble fellow-citizens. The street protests of the people who live in the poorer precincts of Delhi are a small warning. If this signal is not heeded and their just demands are not met, revolution is not around the corner. No political group, Communist or other, has had the dedication to organise any significant people's movement. What may be in store for all of us, could be much more terrifying – total anarchy which will be beyond the control of all the forces of the Indian state.

Outlook, December 4, 2000

Suggested Speech for Vajpayee on the Minority Syndrome

IN last month's confidence vote in the Lok Sabha, the Bharatiya Janata Party leader, Mr Atal Bihari Vajpayee, had said that Hindus were a majority with a minority complex. If he were to look forward rather than backward, Mr Vajpayee should now eloquently address the BJP's national executive in the following terms:

We Hindus control every political party in our country except for a handful of hapless one-man outfits. The pride of nationalism so boldly propagated by the sangh parivar has permeated Hindus of every political complexion – from Congress and regional parties to the Janata Dal and even the Communists. Many Muslims have also begun to regard this land as their Bharat Mata. *Garv se kaho, hum Hindu hain* is no longer a slogan. It has become an integral part of our cultural and political life that we are proudly a Hindu nation in spirit. Even the most radical secularists acknowledge their Hindu foundations.

Hindu pride was revitalised on December 6, 1992, with the clearance of the offending structure from Ram's birthplace at Ayodhya. It is now time for us Hindus in the BJP and the sangh parivar to set a dynamic, forward-looking agenda which must not be weighed down by memories of Muslim oppression during medieval times or by the pinpricks of a petty, moth-eaten state that is Pakistan. As for the Muslims of India, they have been further marginalised politically in the recent Lok Sabha elections with the number of Muslim MPs in the Lok Sabha going down by about half despite all the loud noises made by the secularist brigade.

The Muslims are no longer a significant political factor. They are also not a challenge or a threat in any other sphere of the Indian nation's life, economic, social or administrative. There are just two Muslims among the country's top 200 industrialists, and in the highest level of Government administration, the IAS, only three per cent of the officers are Muslims. According to data based on the National Sample Surveys (1988), only 3.7 per cent of all those who received Government financial assistance for starting businesses were Muslims, and only two per cent of those who received industrial loans from the Government were Muslims. In the educational sphere, just 1.6 per cent of all graduates were Muslims and four per cent of those who received high school education were Muslims. (According to the 1991 census, 12.6 per cent of India's population is Muslim, 81.5 per cent is Hindu and 5.9 per cent is composed of Christians, Sikhs, Buddhists and others.)

Such a marginalised Muslim community cannot conceivably pose a credible threat to any quarter of the nation's life. There is no reason for Hindus to feel insecure. The BJP together with all the sangh parivar must lead Hindus in escaping from the psychological trap of being caught in Muslim issues or reacting to every little incident involving Muslims. If Muslims wish to remain entangled in their medieval marriage laws, or if Kashmiris choose to keep Kashmir industrially backward by retaining their exclusive landed property regulations, let them do so till they wake up of their own accord.

The banning of cow slaughter is a non-issue. Most states have already banned cow slaughter and it should further be banned nation-wide. There is no opposition to banning it among Muslims; most of them eat buffalo or goat meat anyway. As for Bangladeshi immigrants, most poor Indian Muslims are against the illegal inflow as it increases the pressure on Indian Muslims seeking scarce jobs and resources. Care should, however, be taken in not wrongly identifying Indian Muslims as illegal Bangladeshis. The Mandir issue is the only serious point of contention. However, if the sangh parivar can provide solid protection to the persons and property of Muslims in the near future, they are very likely to give up any claim to Ramjanmabhoomi.

With these issues out of the way, there is very little left to squabble about except ancient historical and psychological hang-ups. Hindus now clearly dominate this ancient land. We must now act and behave as the confident and assured majority, and not as an insecure minority. If we still have some grievances against Muslims, let us be benignly neglectful and ignore their petty barbs.

The Indian nation and its voters are looking for a nationalist, honest party which can govern firmly and wipe away the tears of malnutrition, ill-health, illiteracy and joblessness which afflict four-fifths of our people. If the BJP can push this economic and social agenda with the same fervour and conviction that it has pushed the nationalist agenda, it would be assured of at least 320 seats in the next Lok Sabha election, doubling its achievements in the recent election.

The Times of India, **June 22, 1996.**

Feminist Leaders Are as Grasping as the Males

THERE is no other capital city in the world where women are quite deliberately burned alive almost every day of the year for a few pieces of silver or for a scooter, fridge or room cooler. Delhi is also the only national capital where "dowry deaths" are classified separately from murders as if the murder of a young bride is understandable and involves mitigating circumstances because further dowry instalments could not be extracted from her or her parents. Though in terms of sheer villainy and brutality, the burning alive of a young woman in the prime of her life should be classified as the worst form of premeditated, cold-blooded murder.

On an average, "dowry deaths" claim two Hindu or Sikh brides per day in Delhi. This gory average has been maintained over the past few years and shows no signs of abating. And these official figures miss out the large number of "dowry deaths" which are not brought to the notice of the police. The all-India figures of such deaths have not been compiled.

In that most modern and cosmopolitan city of Bombay which prides itself on being far ahead of the rest of backward India, the advanced medical technique of amniocentesis is being routinely applied to ferret out and later abort female foetuses, though the original purpose of the technique was to discover malformed or abnormal foetuses.

But then a female child is considered abnormal in this society and is treated as an affliction from the day she is born. Female children are fed less than their brothers are. The illness of little girls is often ignored while little boys are promptly treated. Girls are born constitutionally tougher but after the first week of being born the death rate of girls in this country is consistently higher than that of boys. Female babies are no longer killed off as they were a century ago but a more subtle form of female infanticide through semi-starvation and deliberate lack of care of female infants still persists.

No wonder the sex ratio of India's population is more in favour of males than in any other country of the world. No Latin American, African, Arab or neighbouring Asian country has such a warped sex ratio as India does. According to the 1981 census of India, there were 933 females for every 1,000 males in the country. Though there was some marginal improvement between 1971 and 1981, the number of females per 1,000 males consistently declined from the beginning of this century till 1971. The female ratio in 1901 was 972. By 1951 it had declined to 946, by 1961 to 941 and by 1971 to 930. These figures starkly illustrate that social and religious prejudices against women and girls remain firmly entrenched in Indian society. As the *Atharva Veda* says: "The birth of a girl, grant it elsewhere. Here, grant a boy."

Yet our female *netas* from the upper crust have the effrontery, arrogance, smugness and complacency to proclaim that Indian women are among the most advanced and can set an example to the world. These female *netas* who dominate the women's rights movement belong to the same category of avaricious and unscrupulous social climbers as the males who have succeeded in capturing and perverting so many other progressive movements in this country. There can be no doubt that women are India's and the world's most oppressed and exploited group and any movement for their liberation is conceptually progressive. However, between the concept and the execution of that concept there is a yawning gap. All sorts of rotten apples have got onto the bandwagon of the women's movement here. Most of these rotten apples are from the highly privileged sections of our society and are eager to grab further privileges and perks from the Government which is ever willing to provide financial and administrative backing for any form of progressive rhetoric as long as the rhetoric does not transform itself into reality.

With the ready willingness of the female *netas,* the women's movement has become increasingly involved with ineffective Governmental institutions. The women's movement has become bureaucratised much to the delight of the Government.

Bureaucratic paper-work is of little comfort to the burning bride or the peasant woman who toils both in the fields and as an unpaid slave in her husband's hovel. Of course, the studies, judgements and articles are meant to formulate plans for the upliftment of underprivileged women. But as with other schemes to uplift the "backward sections", the benefits often percolate into the pockets of the forward sections. However, the studies and reports on the status of women will continue to proliferate just like the reports on the definition and extent of Indian poverty and they will be filed away to make way for newer, more current reports.

Social and economic change can be seriously attempted only by dedicated, full-time, social and political activists who are an extremely rare commodity at the moment. Even the handful of radical activists that exist today face increasing Government repression as national politics gets more elite-oriented and more biased in favour of the wealthy by the day.

Meanwhile, apart from some brilliant exceptions, the women's movement here has been hijacked by a gang of macho female *netas* who fit well into the current male-dominated social climate of grab what you can. Many of these female *netas* flew off to the world conference on women in Nairobi recently where they held forth on their great achievements while young brides continued to be burned in Delhi and female foetuses continued to be aborted in Bombay. Despite all the loud-mouthed bally-hoo among the trendy women's libbers in this country, the position of the ordinary Indian woman has worsened over the past decade. The fruits of development have not gone to the ordinary woman or man. The fruits have gone to those who least require them or deserve them which is not at all surprising, considering the class and type of people, both men and women, who dominate and control this society and country.

The Telegraph, **July 24, 1985.**

Chapter-6

India's Little Hitlers

THE poor have only themselves to blame for their poverty. The weak and vulnerable are so because they are unwilling to improve their lot. These condescending put-downs by the high and mighty have become commonplace in a society which has become increasingly insensitive to the plight of the downtrodden. Such rationalisations are as crass and crude as the old innuendo that all violated women have only themselves to blame for having invited rape. Might is right is the current mantra where power and money are worshipped. Among the upper and middle classes, there is amnesia about admitting that some 300 million co-citizens exist in the most abysmal conditions without minimal nutrition, medicine, shelter and education. The new horror is that millions in the dry season now have to struggle to get enough water to drink. Even water that is brackish, slimy, filthy, is being drunk by the thirsty poor while the better off are becoming reliant on bottled water produced by Coca-Cola, Pepsi, Nestle and other multinationals. Despite funds worth thousands of crores poured into the capital city, even Delhi is incapable of providing safe drinking water to many of its inhabitants who become victims of cholera, hepatitis and typhoid in the summer and monsoon months. Dysentery and diarrhoea are endemic throughout the year among the downtrodden.

Two classic and related instruments are used to pre-empt the possibility of united protest by the downtrodden: build up communal/casteist hysteria to target minorities and the underprivileged castes, and encourage the police forces to repress the poor in the most brutal manner while ignoring the criminal activities of the rich. Lal Krishna Advani's *rath yatra* across the country in 1990 and the decade long campaign by the BJP and its *parivar* for the construction of the Ram *mandir* at Ayodhya are masterly examples of strategies to divert public attention away from bread-and-butter economic issues.

One recent example of the blatant police and administrative bias in favour of the rich and powerful is that it took many weeks for the police to detain the builders of the criminally shoddy buildings which had collapsed in the January 2001 Gujarat earthquake. The arrested builders will no doubt be quickly bailed out, the evidence will be fudged and court proceedings will continue for years without any outcome. On the Bofors scandal of 1986, CBI proceedings against the Hinduja brothers are at a preliminary stage 16 years later. On the Rs 5,000-crore securities scam of 1992, some charges were still being framed against the main accused, Harshad Mehta, when he died at the end of 2001. Yet daily, police forces all over the country promptly kill alleged petty robbers in fake encounters without any legal niceties of arrest, prosecution and trial.

In Mumbai, Bal Thackeray, his Shiv Sainiks and several Mumbai police personnel have been indicted by a mountain of painstaking evidence collated in the Report of the Justice Srikrishna Commission for inciting and carrying out attacks on Muslims in December 1992-January 1993. On the role of the police, the Report states: "The evidence before the Commission indicates that the police personnel were found actively participating in riots, communal incidents or incidents of looting, arson and so on. The Commission strongly recommends that Government take strict action against them." There has been very little subsequent action to arrest and prosecute culpable police personnel and sainiks. One of the officers indicted by the Justice Srikrishna was promoted to Police Commissioner of Mumbai. He was ultimately charged in 2001. In sharp contrast, the police acted with unusual alacrity and efficiency in arresting hundreds of suspects within days for the Mumbai bomb explosions in March 1993 when most of the casualties were Hindu. Nine years after their arrest, many of the alleged suspects are still languishing in prison awaiting the completion of their extended trial. Five of the suspects who were bailed out have been shot dead by the Chotta Rajan gang which is reported to work in connivance with police and intelligence agencies.

Brown 'Aryans'

SANE people all over the world celebrated the 40th anniversary of victory over Hitler's barbarians on May 8. Substantial groups of racists in Western Europe and North America continue to admire Hitler for his simple, jack-booted solutions and murderous paranoia against minorities. The skinhead variety of racists openly venerate Hitler while many among Ronald Reagan's and Maggie Thatcher's minions secretly admire the man who caused the death of 50 million persons just 40 to 45 years ago and who reduced medieval barbarians like Genghiz Khan to bumbling amateurs in ferocity.

The presence of Nazi sympathisers in the West is not very surprising, for in Hitler's list of creatures, Jews, Gypsies, Slavs, all Asiatics (which includes all our self-proclaimed Aryans), Africans and other coloured peoples were to be butchered or used as slave labour because they were classified as *untermenschen* sub-humans. Heredity was all that counted in Hitler's cast-iron classification. Genius, merit, diligence, wisdom, were all irrelevant. Albert Einstein would have been sent to the gas-chamber had he not left Germany.

Yet, there are significant members of our upper caste, upper or middle class gentry who revere Hitler and his paranoid priorities and passions. Simple and violent solutions are attractive as they overcome by knife-stroke the tiresome business of controlling the turbulent lower castes and classes through manipulative politics.

Civilised Germans visiting or living in India are baffled,

embarrassed, amazed and exasperated by the fascination and admiration for Hitler often expressed by members of Indian high society whenever they meet a German. Of course, the boorish, *Herrenvolk* type of German who believes he still belongs to the chosen race is also accepted quite easily by our own white-washed Aryans.

One of the most open admirers of Hitler is Bal Thackeray whose Shiv Sena recently won the Bombay municipal elections with a little help from Maharashtra Chief Minister Vasantrao Patil. Thackeray is a respected figure in Bombay's upper caste hierarchy. The Shiv Sena has been periodically terrorising Bombay's poorer, lower caste majority for the past two decades. Yet the Shiv Sainiks are treated as respectable men protected by the Bombay police.

Once in a while, the system which is meant to protect the Thackerays goes berserk and turns like a rogue elephant against its high-riding mahout. The continuing anti-reservation riots in Gujarat have not gone according to plan as the police have this time refused to play ball with the upper caste rioters. Instead, the police have gone berserk, hitting out at all – upper, lower, majority, minority.

On April 22, a most unusual event took place in Ahmedabad. Armed mobs, who in polite society are still referred to as policemen, entered the Khadia and Raipur localities of the city and beat up upper caste boys, made obscene gestures at upper caste women and pulled out plumbing and electrical fittings of upper caste bathrooms.

The very next day there was an agonised squeal which was heard nationwide. Respectable newspapers which regularly downplay the routine mobster and police killings and rapings of scheduled castes, backwards and minorities, went berserk with such inelegant headlines as "Police Bestiality" and "Police Brutality". The sluggish judiciary, which usually passes orders after matters of life have become post-mortems of death, straightaway banned two senior police officers from entering the upper caste localities, a unique precedent, even while the boys of Khadia and Raipur continued to riot and hurl stones and abuses at the police. The BJP, which with other opposition parties had slept through the holocaust when thousands died at Bhopal, immediately rushed a fact-finding mission to Ahmedabad.

Ahmedabad had been having violent convulsions since March with regular upper caste and police atrocities against scheduled castes and minorities. On March 19, Zahida, a 13-year-old girl, was shot dead in her own home in Jamalpur locality. Witnesses testified that police inspector B.K. Jadhav had shot her in the chest without any provocation even as she was spreading her bedding before going to sleep. Several others were also shot dead the same day by the police but they were minorities and scheduled castes and, therefore, expendable.

There was no great uproar in parliament in March, no fact-finding mission, no court orders, no screaming headlines. The situation changed only on April 22, when the police, guardians of the upper castes and classes, foolishly charged into Khadia and Raipur.

In sharp contrast to the happenings in Khadia and Raipur, the deaths of 15 tribals on April 19 in Banjhi village in Bihar were routinely reported with disinterested headlines such as "15 killed in firing on Adivasi mob". The initial reports were totally based on the police version though the truth about police vengeance emerged later. One of those who was killed by the police was a former tribal MP, Father Anthony. But parliament, which was so incensed about the attempted murder of former MP, R.L. Bhatia, in Amritsar, took hardly any notice of Anthony's death.

There is, of course, one major snag in the protection racket run jointly by the police and the higher castes. Police constables are mostly recruited from the intermediate castes, not because of any reservation policy, but because the higher castes are not excited by the prospect of directly doing the dirty work of policing. These recruits can cause complications as happened at Khadia and Raipur.

In Germany, Hitler created classification. In India, we have been classified by birth for thousands of years. And by a twist of historical irony, the police and other security forces are generally manned by castes who have no great love for the governing and business castes. The police work for these castes as paid mercenaries. Mercenaries are never reliable.

The Telegraph, **May 17, 1985.**

Inciting Violence Against Minorities

THE most blatant misuse during 1998 by the press of its right to freedom of expression has been brazenly displayed in Gujarat. Some major Gujarati-language newspapers in that state have concocted entirely false news reports which have not only intensified the atmosphere of hate against Muslims and Christians but have directly instigated violent attacks against the two minority communities.

To give just one specific instance: A 20-member fact-finding team – comprising journalists, Sarvodaya workers, lawyers and academics – which in early July visited riot-hit Bardoli, a town 30 kilometres from Surat, discovered that two daily newspapers, *Gujarat Samachar* and *Dhabkar* had published totally fabricated reports. *Dhabkar* on June 26, 1998, had an eight-column headline: "Bardoli in Flames as Stones Are Thrown from Vhorvad Mosque on VHP rally". On the same morning, *Gujarat Samachar*, a widely-circulated newspaper, had a four-column headline: "Riots Flare Up in Bardoli as Stones Are Thrown from Mosque". These 'news' reports incited the subsequent burning of Muslim houses and shops and led to Muslim families fleeing from Bardoli. In July, leaders of the VHP, RSS and Bajrang Dal admitted to the visiting team that no stones were thrown from the mosque as the police had been sitting inside the mosque on June 25.

On July 18, another major Gujarati daily, *Sandesh*, ran two headlines aimed against Christians: "Hold of Christian Missionaries on Govt. Apparatus" and "Why no Admissions for Hindu Children in Missionary School? Anyone Who Says This Is a Target". 'News' items with such headlines in several newspapers have poisoned the atmosphere in Gujarat and led to attacks on Christian institutions and to incidents of Bible-burning.

Sections of the Marathi press in Maharashtra, notably *Saamna*, the Bombay newspaper edited by Shiv Sena chief Bal Thackeray, have also continued to excite public emotions against the minorities as have some Hindi journals in Uttar Pradesh, Rajasthan and Madhya Pradesh. In 1998, taking the lead from the VHP and the Shiv Sena, these publications enlarged the focus of their attack beyond Muslims to target the Christians conspicuously for the first time.

In comparison, the biases of the metropolitan, English-language press were subtle. Possibly, it was not even aware of its prejudices. Positive news stories about Muslims were often accompanied by stereotypical, file photographs of burqa-clad women or hordes of men constantly kneeling in prayer.

Yadav political leaders, particularly Rabri Devi, Laloo Prasad and Mulayam Singh, were much too often portrayed in a manner which suggested that they were inept clowns or buffoons. Their photographs were taken from angles which made them look faintly ridiculous. While upper caste politicians were usually cast as "leaders", OBC politicians became "chieftains" or "satraps". "Vote banks" invariably conjured images of unthinking herds of Dalit, Scheduled Tribe and Muslim voters. Bloc votes by Brahmins, Rajputs and Banias were never dismissed as "vote banks".

Did this lack of sensitivity, perhaps, have some connection with the fact that there were extremely few Dalit and Adivasi journalists in the press in any language? A couple of years ago, an inquisitive journalist looking through the list of media persons accredited by the Press Information Bureau to cover the Central Government could not find the name of a single

Dalit journalist.

Particularly vile atrocities against Dalits were reported on the front pages of metropolitan newspapers but the continuous daily humiliation of Dalits was conspicuously absent from all pages. This had more to do with the urban, middle class obsessions of the metropolitan press and its general lack of interest in rural happenings rather than any marked callousness towards Dalits. There were exceptions like the series of detailed articles by P. Sainath carried during 1998 in *The Hindu* on the indignities and affronts faced by Dalits in rural areas. *The Hindu* was also exceptional in regularly publishing opinion pieces by radical Dalit writers on its edit page.

Press coverage of the February-March 1998 elections to the Lok Sabha and the November 1998 elections to the legislative assemblies of Madhya Pradesh, Rajasthan and Delhi, relied a bit too heavily on the caste and community configurations of individual constituencies. The results of the November polls clearly showed that the electorate was far less segmented than made out by press correspondents and that most voters were far more concerned about prices and other economic needs rather than about caste and communal issues.

Organised mass killings carried out by Hindutva groups in connivance with the local police of Muslims continued to be blandly called "communal riots". The report of the Srikrishna commission of inquiry on the "riots" or mass killings in Bombay in December 1992 and January 1993 was finally released five years later on August 6, 1998. The main thrust of the report was directed at the involvement of the Shiv Sena and at the anti-Muslim bias of the Bombay police force. This was clearly brought out in a series of excerpts from the Srikrishna report prominently published in August by *The Indian Express.*

Most of the major English-language dailies carried editorial comments condemning the role of the Shiv Sena and Bal Thackeray, though *The Times of India*, in time-honoured tradition, chose to prevaricate and to pontificate in its lead editorial on August 7 about how "All citizens yearn for peace and security". There was not a word about bringing to justice the organisers and the executioners of the massive violence of 1992-93. The editorial also went out of its way to be placatory towards Thackeray by mentioning that, of late, he was being "eminently sensible".

Communal disturbances continued to be reported sloppily and lethargically, often relying entirely on self-serving and biased statements by local officials and police officers. Reporters, especially of the major news agencies, rarely entered the disturbed areas to find out exactly what had happened by seeking the views of the victims. There were some outstanding reports like the June 10 reportage in *The Indian Express* of the Hyderabad disturbances which sensitively noted the pain and suffering of the innocent victims of violence.

The February 1998 large-scale killings of Hindus in bomb blasts set off by Muslim extremist groups in Coimbatore were universally condemned by the press. Most news reports linked these blasts to the Pakistani Inter-Services Intelligence (ISI) agency, though Tamil Nadu police investigators found that the explosions were carried out by local Muslim die-hards seeking revenge for the November 1997 attacks against Muslims in Coimbatore instigated by the Hindu Munnani.

The tendency to link violent acts by Muslim criminals automatically to the ISI was carried to ludicrous lengths in a number of news reports in 1998. Some police officers in Uttar Pradesh made it a point to brand entire districts in UP as ISI strongholds on the sole basis of demography which indicated that they contained large populations of Muslims. Anonymous quotes by these officers were printed without further investigation. Such reports provided instant fodder for those propagandists who wished to paint all Indian Muslims as "ISI agents".

Inflammatory and obviously false statements by irresponsible politicians were printed prominently for sensational effect without bothering about their disastrous consequences on inter-communal and inter-caste relations. Some journals even had regular sections with such confrontational titles as "Controversy" which provided a platform for petty demagogues to fuel dangerous conflicts. A handful of columnists in a couple of metropolitan, English-language newspapers continued to promote enmity between various religious and other social groups, an offence which is punishable under the Indian Penal Code. The number of such virulent writers in non-metropolitan periodicals remains countless.

Vidura, Journal of the Press Institute of India,
January-March, 1999.

Bombay Is the Dying City

I AM a Bombay boy still half in love with the city where I grew up. For the past 10 years I have lived in Delhi, a place which I still find profoundly irritating, a place enveloped by petty-minded bureaucrats and small-time exporters of garments and other such piece goods.

I recently went to Bombay for a two-month stay, vaguely wondering whether I should re-export myself back to that city where people cared for each other without getting in each other's way, where the overwhelming quest for money conferred a democratic equalness to big and small, where people stood in queues regardless of who or what they were.

I returned to Delhi a jilted lover with his illusions crushed. Bombay, I felt, had become a wasteland, not so much of the body but of the mind and the spirit. Far more disturbing was the thought that what Bombay is today, India would be tomorrow.

At least Calcutta or Delhi or even Jaipur or Srinagar had some semblance left of their own soul and spirit. Bombay, I felt, had become spiritless, with a dead soul and a dying mind.

If there was any spirit left in Bombay, it was imported, *ersatz*, totally unsuited and alien to any city of India.

For this state of mindless alienation, Bombay's elite, if it can be called that, is largely responsible. It has rushed headlong, like pack of suicidal lemmings, towards the enticing precipice of a fake westernisation, almost a Californisation of values, styles and goals. Where silicon, plastic, soda-pop and fast food are being used in an imbecile attempt to overcome shortages of mud-bricks, *dal-bhaat* and drinking water.

As no such attempt can succeed, the next line of aggression of Bombay's elite, as already demonstrated by Ahmedabad's elite, can only be an alliance with right-wing terrorist gangs to assault and dissect the miserable majority of Bombay's populace on the basis of caste and creed. By association, Bombay's elite is becoming as criminal as the Shiv Sena and other denizens of the underworld it patronises for its own selfish ends.

A city which was once a melting pot in which all the delicious *masalas* of India mingled to produce a cosmopolitan curry of unrivalled vitality is being reduced to a series of sectarian, hostile ghettos. Bombay is on the verge of social breakdown but nobody in Bombay talks about it or tries to prevent the social explosion which is about to hit the city. A preview of this callousness was apparent last year when Bombay's social and political workers generally ignored and even condoned the brutal riots in neighbouring Bhiwandi and in the poorer areas of Bombay. At least in Delhi, citizens' groups, however small, did come forward to provide protection, succour and relief to the victims of last November's riots after Indira Gandhi's assassination.

This is not to say that citizens' groups in Bombay are unconcerned about their city. They are concerned – but only about the city's physical breakdown and not its social breakdown. The two are of course related, though the social collapse of a city should be far more alarming than its physical congestion.

Crowded slums and pavements, inadequate transport

facilities, power failures, telephones that rarely work, are more apparently a feature of Calcutta than of Bombay. Yet, Calcutta's social fabric is not tearing up or collapsing as fast as Bombay's is. Women and other underprivileged groups are treated more gently in Calcutta than in Bombay. Slum-dwellers are not as forcefully shunted out in Calcutta as they are in Bombay. And police brutality is not encouraged in Calcutta as it is in Bombay.

There is still some social symbiosis, some contact between the classes in Calcutta, Delhi or Madras. This contact between high and humble was Bombay's most endearing feature. It is now visibly breaking down as the city's rich and powerful soar upwards in their skyscrapers, remote and distant from the hovels hundreds of feet below. They live in their mental tower blocks as if they had transported themselves to Manhattan or San Francisco. They are sustained by imported goods, gadgets and gimmicks and by local imitative variants of foreign design, from cigarettes and clothes to trashy high society magazines full of advertisements.

The rich and powerful in other Indian cities are also moving in the same direction but in no other city have they succeeded in making themselves as removed from the ordinary people of the country as they have in Bombay. Most of the 'thinking' people in Bombay – middle class academics, journalists, social and political activists, lawyers – also seem to have distanced themselves from the common man's woes, as if in despair, as if Bombay is too diseased for any cure.

With a cruelly remote upper class, an exhausted middle class and a divided and squabbling working class, Bombay is a dying city, ripe for an open fascist onslaught. Any such onslaught would have to be firmly put down by the Union Government. Otherwise, there would be a chain reaction with parochial fascist goons raising their banners all over the country.

National doom awaits us if Bombay is allowed to become a precursor for the rest of the country.

The Telegraph, **August 7, 1985.**

Nurturing Hate in Mumbai

BOMBAY, that grand cosmopolitan city by the sea, is regressing into Mumbai, a petty collection of squabbling sectarian ghettos. The angry reaction of Dalits to the desecration of the Ambedkar bust at Ramabai Nagar in Mumbai on July 11 is not a spontaneous outburst. It is the end result of the simmering climate of sectarian hate and violence built up over the last 30 years by some of Mumbai's leading political and commercial groups.

Among these, Bal Thackeray and his Shiv Sena deserve top honours for diverting Bombay's vibrant energy into Mumbai's dark alleyways of parochial mayhem. Over the past three decades, the Shiv Sena's Supreme Leader has hurled crude obscenities at women, at distinguished Maharashtrian literary and social figures, at the so-called South Indian clerks and, repeatedly, at Muslims. There have been mild murmurs of disapproval by the social elite of Mumbai, which has generally regarded him as an endearing, warm-beer-drinking eccentric.

Thackeray and the Shiv Sena were initially encouraged by Mumbai's textile mill-owners and later by the city's building contractors. Cowardly, upper caste Communist trade union leaders retreated when faced with Shiv Sena threats and busied themselves organising seminars on class consciousness.

Maharashtra's Congress satraps, starting with Y.B. Chavan and V.P. Naik, followed by Vasantdada Patil, S.B. Chavan, Sudhakarrao Naik and Sharad Pawar, have all at some point displayed a soft corner for the Shiv Sena. Despite repeated violent outrages by the Shiv Sainiks, Congress Governments in Delhi and Mumbai have avoided taking firm action against the Shiv Sena. Even in January 1993, when the Shiv Sena was the prime engineer of the holocaust in Mumbai, Maharashtra Chief Minister Sudhakarrao Naik, Defence Minister Sharad Pawar and Prime Minister Narasimha Rao strained every optical nerve to look the other way while hundreds of the city's Muslims were murdered. The holocaust was a political disaster for the Congress and by March 1995 the Shiv Sena was in power, with the BJP hanging on to Thackeray's blazing saffron kurta.

Many wishful thinkers had hoped that power would turn the Shiv Sena overnight into a disciplined and restrained organisation. While there have been no volcanic eruptions since 1995, the Sena has continued its low-intensity war against anyone who dares to cross its path, whether it is the late Ramesh Kini, the sacked (now judicially reinstated) G.R. Khairnar, social reformer Anna Hazare, dissident editor Nikhil Wagle, Congress leader of the opposition Chhagan Bhujbal or the Dalits.

The conflict between the Shiv Sena and the Dalits began way back in 1988 with the controversy over Ambedkar's book, *Riddles of Hinduism.* It widened in January 1994 when the Sharad Pawar Government announced that Marathwada University would be renamed in honour of Ambedkar. Shiv Sena cadres were infuriated and in the subsequent violence 11 Dalits were killed and 41 of their settlements torched in Marathwada. On January 27, 1997, the murder of a Dalit youth by a Shiv Sena corporator in Aurangabad sparked off large-scale riots. On March 16, 1997, another Dalit youth was killed when violence erupted at Shrirampur in Ahmednagar district, following the desecration of an Ambedkar statue. The July 11 incident in Mumbai was a sequel to these earlier episodes.

The Shiv Sena's acts of vandalism and violence are invariably ignored by the Mumbai police, as was evident on July 13 when the homes of Congress leaders were ransacked. During the January 1993 violence, some sections of the Mumbai police had even proudly declared that they were Shiv Sainiks in uniform and till now, not a single Sainik has been prosecuted by the Mumbai police for involvement in that month's terrible incidents.

The Shiv Sena, together with its partisan administration and police, is relentlessly fragmenting Maharashtra's and Mumbai's once cohesive society. As each section of society defensively confronts the other, Maharashtra is moving towards becoming a Bihar with a difference. In Bihar, the upper segments of its economy and society are bitterly apposed to Laloo Yadav and his followers. In Maharashtra, the upper segments continue to humour and cajole Bal Thackeray and his cohorts.

Indian Express, **July 22, 1997.**

Rape and Torture

'LAW AND ORDER' seems to have become a euphemism for 'rape and torture' over much of the baking hot Indo-Gangetic plain this summer. Baghpat, Durg, Lohlara, Morena and Unnao are among the places which have become nōtorious dens of infamy. Ramtek in Maharashtra and Sealdah in Calcutta can be added to the list. In a majority of these incidents, police officers, and not their constables, have taken the lead in rape, torture or shooting people in the back. In the Unnao outrage, two police sub-inspectors entered the house of a Harijan and raped his 16-year-old daughter while two police constables stood guard outside!

If our society had any sense of justice, such officers would have been speedily tried and sentenced to hard labour for life. Instead police officers are recommended for 'bravery' awards of Rs. 1,000 by their superior officers for shooting unarmed alleged dacoits in the back and are protected by the Union Home Minister by the commonplace device of instituting a judicial inquiry.

As invariably happens, the judicial inquiry takes ages, public commotion dies down and the offending policeman gets away scot free. So the charade goes on, with the opposition parties demanding a judicial inquiry and the party in power gracefully acceding to the request. And so all are happy. The police have been able to get away with rape or murder, the opposition has been able to do some flag-waving, depicting themselves as the saviours of the people, and the ruling party has once again established itself as a paragon of justice.

The plain fact of the matter is that the police, the opposition parties and the party in power act in unison and are part of the same gang. In public, these factions of one gang noisily blame each other but in reality they are completely dependent on each other. Witness the great peasant prophet of the people, Charan Singh, currently shedding crocodile tears over the Baghpat outrage. Two years ago when he was the Union Home Minister, the Pantnagar massacre took place. Scores of landless peasants were shot dead without any provocation and some of the wounded were crushed to death in the fields by tractors.

Charan Singh then protected the sadistic police officer who ordered the massacre and the vice-chancellor of Pantnagar Agricultural University who inspired the operation. By now the police officer has probably earned a couple of well-deserved promotions and Mrs Gandhi, who had then shed crocodile tears and visited Pantnagar, has conveniently forgotten the whole episode, now that she is in power and has to hush up more recent happenings like Baghpat.

Police sadism is not restricted to small towns in northern India. It is routine all over the country. Even in the supposedly civilised city of Bombay, people living next to police stations complain of hearing ghastly screams night after night from their uniformed neighbours' torture chambers. Yet these good citizens do very little but grumble during private conversations. Why should they bother to do anything more? Rape and torture have, after all, become a part of our way of life. So, why worry? Even the present Union Home Minister has blandly stated in parliament that "rape has been committed in the past and will continue to be committed".

It has become a national trait to ignore brutality much as we ignore the convenience of others in our daily lives – in how we work, talk, walk, eat, drink, catch a bus or drive. All these daily functions are executed with maximum callousness and minimum concern for the other fellow unless he happens to be a bigwig.

In this sort of society where callous individualism is the norm, the weak have no chance. They are mown down like the peasants at Pantnagar by those who wield the power provided by politics, money and the big stick. The rape of the weak by the powerful is inevitable and natural in such a society. The rape of a Harijan or tribal woman by landlords and contractors in parts of Uttar Pradesh, Madhya Pradesh and Bihar is considered a right, not a crime. The police officers only imitate their masters!

But let us not be too complacent. The weak will not always remain weak and quiescent. They can hit back and in the most nasty fashion. The terrible killings of innocent Bengali villagers by the tribals of Tripura are part of the wild indiscriminate rage of those oppressed for far too long.

Even after the pot has boiled over, as in Tripura, the rulers send in more of the same, namely, more callous administrators and police officers plus the Border Security Force and the army, who do not have the background or the training and patience to win the hearts and minds of the alienated tribals. More rape, loot and murder follows, as has been happening for years in Nagaland and Mizoram.

And there are fears, expressed even by members of parliament, that the tribals of Bihar, Madhya Pradesh, Orissa and West Bengal, who live in a region forming a continuous belt, could rise in revolt if their humiliation continues. Under the British, hundreds of tribal revolts were sparked off by colonial arrogance and interference in tribal affairs. The mentality of our present day rulers has not changed much. It is the same old attitude of the rulers being superior to the ruled, particularly to the 'inferior' tribals.

In fact the social spirit and organisation of the tribals is far superior to that of the rest of the country. The tribals are cooperative and collective in their values. They practice relative sexual freedom and gender equality, widow re-marriage and divorce. They do not have a caste system, child marriage or bride burning for dowry. As they are not sexually repressed or socially organised in a rigid hierarchy, rape is extremely rare among them.

It is time that the smug and complacent ruling class of this country realises its own backwardness and begins to exercise some control over its criminal elements in uniform who have been running amok for a long time. The tribals of the north-east have already shown that they will not take atrocities lying down any longer. The fears of some MPs that the rebellious spirit of the tribals may spread are entirely justified. But the Zail Singhs and the Charan Singhs will continue to condone rape and murder as they have become dependent on the very people who commit these crimes. The criminals may soon realise that they might as well take over from those who are dependent on them. We may then be ruled directly by criminals in conflict with perpetually rebellious tribals.

An impossible scenario? It has happened in many Latin American countries and it could happen here. But this is not South America and we are a civilised society. Are we really?

Business India, **July 21, 1980.**

We Get the Cops We Deserve

AMONG established democracies why do we have some of the most brutish and bumbling cops in the world? The usual excuses trotted out by senior police officers are inadequate. Overwork, underpay, insufficient training, judicial laxity, political interference, do not fully account for the lathi blows to the head, kicks in the groin and other gruesome forms of brutality so casually inflicted on hapless Indian citizens. Often, the brutality is totally mindless and pointless, as the recent bashing administered to Martin Massey by the Delhi police for mistakenly driving through Prime Minister Gujral's security cordon so graphically demonstrates.

The key to understanding the escalating police violence lies in the social attitudes and psyche of the great Indian middle classes who tolerate, and even encourage, violence so far as it is directed against the lower classes and castes. A servant suspected of petty theft is a soft target for his master's violence or, even better, some rupees provided to the local police *thana* can ensure a more professional softening up. After that, even an innocent person will confess to a crime he did not commit. The end result of mindless brutality is that the real culprit is often not caught while the innocent is trapped.

Of course, there are mighty public uproars against police violence but these occur when businessmen are shot in a police encounter in the centre of New Delhi or when a business executive is roughed up. Most executives, professionals or even lawyers in their Marutis do not turn a hair when they see a traffic cop thrashing a milkman on a bike for crossing the white line at the traffic lights.

In remote rural areas, the most despised and dreaded personage is not the local landlord, hoodlum or politician but the local police *thanedar* or *daroga.* Contrary to the usual image of the political species, the local party *neta* often serves to curb the excesses of the local *thanedar.* Politicians generally act as a buffer between the police and the common man, though there are political mavericks like Bal Thackeray who openly encourage violence by the police.

In any advanced democracy, the Shiv Sena's remote controller would be hauled up for incitement to violence but here he is treated as a messiah above the law. In our democracy, encounter killings and incidents of torture are excused if the victims are faceless and nameless street people.

We like to believe that we now have a sophisticated and highly educated upper and middle segment comparable to the middle classes of the western world. By flaunting our technical qualifications and our superficial social tastes like designer dresses, red wines from France or white wines from Australia, cuisine from Mexico and bathroom fittings copied from Italy, we can con ourselves into believing that we have developed a world class elite.

Our society has a veneer of sophistication. It utterly lacks the deeper sophistication of the Scandinavian, British, French or German middle classes who generally have strong convictions about the sanctity of every human life; of the right of every individual, regardless of social status, to be handled within the bounds of the law; of the right of alleged criminals, not to be physically ill-treated; of tolerating the most eccentric views of peaceful individuals; of lawfully prosecuting those individuals, however high and mighty they may be, who incite or encourage unlawful violence. These societies provide mass support for human rights groups. Every Western society does not have such deep convictions. The US is a glaring example of a society which tolerates routine police brutality.

It should be no consolation to us that the US tolerates its brutalities or that we are much above the horrors inflicted on the terrorised peoples of Serbia, Saudi Arabia or Zaire. Surely, a mature Indian nation should have infinitely higher moral standards than those imposed by a fanatic ethnic dictatorship, by a tribal robber-baron kingdom or by a greedy and murderous buffoon who is on his way out after 30 long years of ruinous domination.

Indian Express, May 17, 1997.

Chapter-7

Self-Promotion and Self-Service

TOO many journalists and TV jockeys have become as bloated with self-importance as other high-flying balloons of the establishment – Cabinet ministers, secretaries to government, Supreme and High Court judges, reputed writers and academics. They are constantly engaged in feeding their own egos (which is the highest form of moral corruption). Their consequent flatulence has led them into believing that they are infallible and peerless. They resent being questioned. Balloons are notably thin skinned and they burst out with indignation and anger if they are pricked by the slightest criticism. Some of the high-flyers employ their powers to try and suppress valid criticism. Recently, judges have become prone to launching contempt of court proceedings against individuals who comment adversely on their judgements. Witness the Supreme Court's contempt proceedings against Arundhati Roy for criticising the Narmada Dam judgement. In turn, Arundhati Roy and other eminent writers and professors react with hysterical verbiage on being faulted.

Journalists often comment without basis on anyone and everyone but the mildest criticism about their own unprofessional hypocrisies, manipulation of news and politicking with power brokers invites their indignant wrath. In retaliation, stories are planted against individuals who may have crossed the path where journalists strut. Journalists and other personages make no attempt to rectify their own faults first, before pronouncing judgement on the concerns of others. For instance, the courts have made no serious attempt to speed up justice and clear the backlog of lakhs of criminal and civil cases pending before them for years but have enthusiastically entertained public interest litigations (PILs) and passed strictures on external issues like air pollution, public transport and traffic regulation. The Delhi High Court used a PIL to order the Ministry of Urban Development to provide the best government bungalows for its own judges. (Thankfully, the order was subsequently struck down by the Supreme Court.)

Easily puffed up with self-importance after acquiring any vestige of influence, every segment of the elite uses its powers for personal and sectional profit or gain. The most glaring symbol of self-serving privilege is the country's capital, New Delhi, a pampered ghetto created by the elite for themselves. For their own comfort and delight, politicians, administrators, judges, commercial tycoons and other members of the elite have grabbed large annual financial grants from the national exchequer for New Delhi. These subsidies pamper New Delhi's eight lakh inhabitants who form less than six per cent of Delhi's total population of 138 lakhs. The city within a city has its own exclusive administrative machinery to care for it in the form of the New Delhi Municipal Council which is distinctly aloof from the pedestrian Delhi Municipal Corporation. With its well-maintained boulevards, gardens, shopping malls and other amenities, New Delhi is the most manicured tract of real estate in the country. It is a swanky showpiece standing out in the general landscape of urban blight and squalor.

The elite also protects its own lawbreakers. When it becomes apparent that 'the pillars of society' are deeply implicated in a major disaster or scandal, the standard political ploy employed to take the heat off them is to set up a commission of inquiry which takes years to complete its task. By then, other issues and disasters have cropped up and the pillars of society are absolved of all blame and criminal liability. Condoning perjury in the courts and employing Section 197 of the Criminal Procedure Code to disallow prosecution of officials are among the other legal ploys used to protect pedigreed criminals. Yet another simple method of allowing privileged offenders to go free is to delay crucial decisions, a mode perfected by that master of inaction, P.V. Narasimha Rao, when he was Prime Minister from 1991 to 1996.

Even those who speak in the name of the underprivileged poor, the Communists, have been corrupted by the governing system of privilege. In their strongholds of West Bengal and Kerala, the aging leaders of the CPI and the CPI(M) have given up the harrowing task of mobilising the great mass of people against glaring economic and social iniquities. The Communist leaders have succumbed to the temptation of taking the easier path of using the bureaucratic machinery of government in the hope of bringing about social and economic change. That hope has been belied as the Leftists have become entangled in the cobwebs spun by bureaucrats.

New Delhi Is the Country's Best Maintained Ghetto

A STRANGER from an alien land arriving at the dead of night at Palam airport would come to some strange conclusions while driving into the heart of New Delhi. He would pass the neat cantonment area with its green golf course and pretty park with an ornamental pond. Onto Sardar Patel road with the gleaming Taj Palace and Maurya luxury hotels on the right and the lush shrubbery and woods of the ridge on the left.

Further on, the villas of merchant princes and diplomats, followed by the serenely white residences with acres of verdant lawns of ministers and senior officials on Willingdon Crescent. Circling two or three manicured roundabouts, aglow with roses or pansies if it is winter, the stranger would pass by the imposing mansion where Jawaharlal Nehru lived, through avenues of regal trees, to the central vista of Rajpath.

Flanked by the stately domes of Rashtrapati Bhavan and the Central Secretariat, the stranger's gaze would take in the splendour of the spacious lawns and pools flowing towards the floodlit India Gate. Turning onto Janpath, he would pass a few more luxury hotels and the colonnaded Roman facades of the Eastern and Western Courts, before entering Connaught Place which can be regarded as the heart of New Delhi. The tourist limousine carrying him will be guided on its smooth path by rows of sodium lamps which make the night shimmering bright. There will be very little traffic on the drive from Palam to Connaught Place.

If the stranger has arrived without any prior knowledge of India, he would easily assume that he has arrived in one of the most affluent and beautifully maintained lands of the world. He could also assume that India was an underpopulated country with an abundance of trees and water and no shortage of electricity (if there has been no abrupt power blackout during his drive).

On his first night in India, the stranger would not realise that he has arrived in one of the richest ghettos in the country. New Delhi is the best maintained ghetto in the country simply because more public money per square foot is spent on it than on any other property in the country.

New Delhi, as the capital city, symbolises the domineering power structure of the country in an obvious way. New Delhi also symbolises the more significant reality of plenty in the midst of poverty.

Just across the river Yamuna, or *Jamnapaar* as the locals say, are the shanty-towns of the poor. There are also some hidden pockets of the dwellings of the poor within the New Delhi Municipal Committee's area, but these are under constant threat of being demolished and their inhabitants being banished to *Jamnapaar,* as happened on a massive scale during Sanjay's heyday. The poorer inhabitants of *Jamnapaar* and other such areas have to commute miles every day to work for and to service the privileged denizens of New Delhi.

New Delhi is the most obvious example of what is happening in all the major cities of the country. Though not in as clear a way as in New Delhi, in all the big cities the rich are building ghettos for themselves surrounded by the squalor of urban India. In Bombay especially, and also to some extent in Calcutta, the ghettos are in high-rise towers glowering over the hovels at ground level.

The physical apartheid breeds a nasty psychological disdain among the rich for the plight of the poor. The rich, which includes the middle classes, become more contemptuous of the poor by the day as they fortify themselves in their urban ghettos.

These ghettos will not breed revolution. They may well breed creeping fascism to control the inhabitants of the hovels at the foot of the tower-blocks.

The Telegraph, **June 27, 1986.**

Indira's Petty Use of Power

"I AM the least powerful head of government in the world. I have much less power than the Prime Minister of Britain or the President of France."

So claims Indira Gandhi in a characteristic outburst published by *The Guardian* (London) on May 7. Is this her usual mod Gandhian hyperbole or does it have some substance?

The legal wrangles about the constitutional limits of power, as divided between Government, parliament, judiciary and the states, hardly touch the day-to-day working of the head of Government. It is not the constitutional tangles that speed up or slow down the daily grind of the wheels of power in India – or for that matter, in Britain, France or elsewhere – but the social aura and bureaucratic ethos within which the Government works. And probably the most significant element which inhibits or expands the Government's power is the working style of the particular head of Government, in our case Indira Gandhi.

The social aura enveloping any Indian Prime Minister, and

particularly Indira Gandhi, is of knee-bending, forehead-to-the-floor obeisance. Look at any photograph of Indira Gandhi with other members of the species Indian *homo sapiens* (look especially at cabinet colleagues bidding her *bon voyage* or welcome back before and after her glamour tours abroad) and you can see the fearsome awe in which she is held. Her peremptory and arbitrary manner of functioning might have something to do with this halo but that is too trite an explanation.

The social aura that surrounds her has much more to do with our feudal urge to placate and pamper any person in authority – from Postmaster to Prime Minister. For the poor and the wretched of the Indian earth, this a necessary remedy for survival. (Just watch any two paisa babu in any Government office dealing with an ordinary bloke and you will see what I mean.) But for the moneyed upper classes to indulge in this disgusting feudal obeisance is an obvious sign of their lack of vitality and character. Getting their rights and rewards through grit and gumption is too much of an effort for the Indian upper classes. It is much easier to suck up to anyone with power and influence. Making useful 'contacts' is the fulltime occupation of a large section of our dissipated upper classes. And our politicians, from the Prime Minister downwards, are more than delighted to become the stars of the feudal firmament.

Even more servile than the social environment is the ethos of our bureaucracy. With the exception of a few individuals, the bureaucracy (which includes the police) is willing to contort itself into the most undignified postures to do the bidding of the politician. Even where there is no apparent pressure, the administrator or policeman will rush in to wield the big stick to earn laurels from the political master. Witness the recent alleged knife-throwing incident which involved the now well-known Lalwani and the Prime Minister. The police went all out to discover a conspiracy but fortunately two independent minded magistrates were not willing to go along with their discoveries. The Baroda magistrate was promptly transferred for his pains.

The aftermath of the Lalwani incident aptly illustrates how independence and integrity are minus points for any cog in the machinery of Government. From the moment a young recruit to any Government service steps out of the ivory towers of the training academies, his spirit of independence is squashed by his superiors in the bureaucratic hierarchy. Honest mistakes which would be forgiven in any reasonable bureaucracy are promptly recorded as black marks in the service record of the young administrator.

The lesson is clear. Be cautious. Play safe. Pass the buck. The fewer decisions you make, the better your service record.

The reluctance to take decisions, coupled with the encyclopaedia of official rules, regulations, permits, licences and by-laws which govern every aspect of social and economic development in this country, gives the Government enormous powers. Due to the 'play safe' bureaucratic ethos, many of these powers end up in the hands of the Prime Minister. No British Prime Minister or French President or the head of any other 'democratic' country is so burdened with taking decisions which could easily be disposed of by some minor functionary. This incredible centralisation of power in a huge sub-continent jams up the works. Plans, policies, programmes are churned out on paper but can never be implemented, at least partly because of the paradox that the Prime Minister is so powerful that she has made her bureaucratic instruments powerless.

She does not have much time to concentrate on the greater national issues as she is so tied up with trivia – making minor appointments and transfers, unscrambling red tape, helping out with licences, permits and even with such petty matters as providing Government housing for persistent hangers-on.

Such is Indira Gandhi's style of functioning that she encourages hangers-on. Independent individuals are distrusted. In her 11 years of power, she has unerringly cut down all other centres of power which have emerged within her own party. Dummies are favoured as Chief Ministers of Congress-

I ruled states and any Central Cabinet minister with verve and initiative is invariably dropped.

This combination of a feudal social climate, a servile bureaucracy and the personalisation of power in her own hands and those of her son, makes Indira Gandhi one of the most powerful leaders in the world. Yet very little can be done with all that power to move India into an era of dynamic and modern growth as Mrs Gandhi after all functions as an empress of old, engaged in durbar manoeuvres and manipulations rather than in the formulation of important national policies.

Business India, **May 26, 1980.**

Sonia's Totalitarian Background

Orbassano (Italy)

CONTRARY to the common myth, the Indira Gandhi family's Italian connection in this industrial slum town shows no signs of great prosperity.

Down a dingy lane in this grey northern Italian town on the outskirts of Turin (the centre of the Fiat empire), the Maino family, Mr Rajiv Gandhi's in-laws, live a modest life in a moderate-sized bungalow.

Mr Stefano Maino, 62, stocky in build and rough in dress, is not too happy with his daughter Sonia's Indian ties.

He resignedly notes: "After the Sonia marriage, everyone thinks that we have got rich and made free trips to India. But we have paid for everything ourselves. Sonia's marriage has been an expensive thing for us."

Nadia, 24, Sonia's petite and pretty younger sister, is "very upset" about the newspaper reports stating that the Mainos have made a lot of money through India.

As for the hotel supposedly owned by him, Mr Maino would like to know where it is? And from all that we can see, there is no evidence that Mr Maino is a rich man.

He is a self-made man, a building worker, who after years of effort now has a small construction business. He still works on building sites with his rough hewn hands. He built his own bungalow, working at weekends and in the evenings.

He has very definite views on life and politics, reflecting his petty bourgeois progress. Sitting in the dimly-lit, front room of his house amidst a clutter of decorative volumes bound in artificial leather and a collection of uniformly unattractive pseudo-modern paintings, Mr Maino declares his unwavering loyalty to Benito Mussolini and Italy's "admirable" fascist past.

The present Italian Government, he states, without batting an eyelid, is composed of traitors who betrayed Mussolini and the Fatherland.

He is all for compulsory sterilisation of Italians. From the corner of the room, Mrs Indira Gandhi with her grandchildren, Priyanka and Rahul, smiles benignly out of a silver-framed portrait.

"She is the only person in India who can do good things for India", says Mr Maino, looking appreciatively at the portrait. Her recent arrest worries him, but not much. He is mainly worried about the future of Priyanka and Rahul.

In the integrity of his son-in-law, Rajiv, he has absolute faith. He is "absolutely confident that Rajiv has no connections in the Boeing or any other deal. Rajiv is not in the least interested in such matters".

As for corruption charges against Sanjay, "he is just a boy and businessmen and politicians may have used him". Mr Maino adds that "Sanjay is a young politician and not very experienced. That is why he has not been successful".

Has Mr Maino's Gandhi family connection been successful or profitable? "Sonia's marriage has been an expensive thing for us", he murmurs again, as we leave his home (14, via Bellini) and go back into the slushy lane outside.

Indian Express, **October 26, 1977.**
(Jointly written with Bharati Bhargava.)

"Narasimha the Sleep-Walker"

EARLY this month, Mr P.V. Narasimha Rao was reported to be working furiously on his computer to find the perfect mix of Congress politicos for his Cabinet reshuffle. Personal loyalties, factional factors, caste, communal and regional pulls, all must have featured in the permutations and combinations fed by the Prime Minister into his friendly computer. But by June 10, when the long awaited Cabinet reshuffle was finally announced, the poor computer must have been tearing its electromagnetic hair for the most vital input could not be keyed in. That key ingredient is decisiveness. Even the most sophisticated super computer cannot provide that human input which is missing from the operator – the ability to take clear, firm decisions.

In the event, Mr Narasimha Rao, after his usual painful dithering, fudged his reshuffle by recycling three discredited former Chief Ministers as Union Cabinet Ministers, two of whom had led notoriously corrupt state administrations in Bihar and Maharashtra, and one who had failed to inspire any confidence in Kerala. They have been slotted into ministries in such a way as not to disturb any sitting minister. Not one of the present inept or plainly incompetent ministers, ministers of state or deputy ministers has been weeded out.

Even Mr Narasimha Rao's departure for Europe was a painful exercise in prevarication. He had earlier wished to go to Britain to receive an honorary degree from the University of Hull. At the last moment the Indian High Commission in London was asked to arrange a meeting on a proposed date with the British Prime Minister, Mr John Major. While attempts were being made to fix the appointment, the date was changed by the Prime Minister's Office in Delhi, and finally the British leg of the journey was cancelled, causing a lot of embarrassment to Indian diplomats in London. These are just two instances of Mr Narasimha Rao's wayward style of functioning which has been repeatedly passed off as a deliberate exercise in masterly inactivity. This explanation is wearing a bit thin now, if one looks at his record during his four years as Prime Minister since mid-1991. His record exhibits a litany of crucial decisions avoided or fudged, leading to disastrous consequences.

The most monumental indecision was over Ayodhya when he let matters slide to such an extent that thousands of Central police personnel looked on as a handful of kar sevaks wrecked the Babri Masjid. The police personnel had gathered the correct impression that the Prime Minister would continue to look on passively even as blatantly illegal and violent acts were carried out. If the top leader is openly seen to be a sleepy onlooker, state-level political leaders, bureaucrats and police officers are quick to take the cue from him, as happened most conspicuously when the administrations in Bombay and Surat watched as Shiv Sena and Hindutva goons ignited massacres of the minority community following Ayodhya.

On Kashmir, the muddle and mishandling have been even more conspicuous because the Prime Minister has been unable to lay down a clear chain of command between the PMO, the Home Ministry and the Jammu and Kashmir Governor. From the beginning of the Rao administration in 1991, there was public warfare between the Home Minister, Mr S.B. Chavan, and the Minister of State for Internal Security, Mr Rajesh Pilot, on tactics and policy in Kashmir, till Mr Chavan was provoked to criticise the junior minister on the BBC from London in October 1994. Only then were the two feuding ministers deprived of interference in Kashmir. Mr Narasimha Rao took direct charge of Kashmir affairs but the bureaucrat in charge continued to be the Union Home Secretary, Mr K. Padmanabaiah. In between, Mr K.R. Venugopal, Secretary in the PMO, was put in charge of development projects in Kashmir, till he took early retirement.

The Chrar-e-Sharief fiasco in May led to recriminations between the Union Home Secretary, the Jammu and Kashmir Governor and the army. Again, the Prime Minister had failed to take command or to place someone in full command of a key area like Kashmir, allowing petty renegades like "Major" Mast Gul to cock a snook at the Government.

At one time in January 1995, Mr Narasimha Rao was the minister in charge of 24 Government Departments. For a man who is congenitally averse to taking decisions, to hold up 24 Government Departments amounted to keeping substantial blocs of the Government of India in suspended animation like insoluble particles floating around in a chemistry experiment gone horribly wrong.

This includes blocs such as the Defence Ministry which portfolio continues to be held by Mr Narasimha Rao. One of the consequences is that vital decisions, including the Indian Air Force's urgent requirement for advanced jet trainers and the regularisation of major army formations, have been kept hanging.

Over the past three months, even that relatively autonomous and fast-moving darling of the Government, the Finance Ministry, has found some of its files being held up by the Prime Minister. It could be that with Lok Sabha elections due within the next 11 months, pregnancy pains caused by that important baby, the poverty-stricken electorate, have begun. Globalisation and liberalisation of the economy have largely benefited foreigners and local fat cats, including politicians and the upper crust, craving for the latest consumer goodies. There has been no visible improvement in the lives of the humble hundreds of millions who await some slight advances in health care, basic education and employment at a living wage.

Despite all the hype over the past four years about Mr Narasimha Rao pushing India into the golden age of market-led growth which would turn the country into a springing tiger on the world economic stage, it is doubtful that he or his financial factotum, Mr Manmohan Singh, have ever had a carefully thought out, deliberate strategy to open up the economy. Both of them were expedient votaries of Mrs Indira Gandhi's version of socialism when that was the prevailing wind in the early and mid-1970s. Neither of them is a man of deep convictions.

When the mid-1991 foreign exchange reserves crisis, brought on by the profligate spending of the Rajiv regime, burst forth on the new Government, Mr Narasimha Rao and his economic advisers had little choice except to bow to the dictates of the international moneylenders led by the IMF to open the economy to commercial interests abroad and at home. The IMF's dictation pad was cleverly converted into the new mantra promising riches for all and sundry, just like the mantra of socialism had promised a similar miracle in the 1970s.

Mr Narasimha Rao had not sought out this new vision. He had stumbled into it just like he had stumbled into becoming Prime Minister, being acceptable to all the Congress factions as the least offensive candidate. As the Narasimha Rao era looks like coming to an end in the impending Lok Sabha elections, we should, like historians of old who coined appropriate suffixes for their kings and queens, begin to find suitable titles for our Mr Narasimha Rao and our other recent rulers. Going by his record, the most appropriate title for Mr Narasimha Rao would be "Narasimha the Sleep-Walker".

The Pioneer, **June 24, 1995.**

Can V.P. Singh Give Capitalism a Human Face?

IS finance minister V.P. Singh the future face of capitalism in India? Dedicated, determined and ruthless. So far, capitalism has been a portly figure ambling along quite comfortably, bribing the tax-collector, procuring for the politician, manipulating the law, cheating the consumer and kicking the labourer. Both the native capitalist and the foreign capitalist operating in India have played their games in tandem, bickering occasionally, but cooperating for mutual gain usually. Dexterity has been the hallmark of both, along with ruthlessness when required. Dedication and determination to fight the competitor in the open market have never figured as capitalist attributes in this country. Nor were these qualities necessary as the market has never been open. Will Mr V.P. Singh and Mr Rajiv Gandhi change the face of capitalism in India? Even if they wish to, can they?

Lower taxes, liberalisation of imports and some degree of de-regulation of industry during the past year are meant to encourage the dynamic growth of capitalism in this country. But old ways die hard. Bribery, manipulation and cheating continue, though not as merrily as before, because Mr V.P. Singh is doing something highly 'irregular' in the Indian context: he is enforcing the law. He also believes that nobody is above the law, not even the chairman of a large company like Orkay Silk Mills. Mr V.P. Singh is an exceptional politician. His actions are related to his words and beliefs. In a recent interview, he has plainly stated, "The culture of Indian business has to change."

The Finance Minister's statement implies that excessive corruption, favouritism, pandering to friends and relatives, and selective bending of rules, damage the basic capitalist thrust which is to maximise profit. The social consequences and disasters (remember Bhopal and Union Carbide) caused by the capitalist thrust are of no great concern to the Finance Minister or to the Government he serves. The onward march of capitalism cannot be halted just because it leads to further misery for a few more million Indians.

It should not be forgotten that Mr V.P. Singh is the same man who gave a blanket order to the Uttar Pradesh police to wipe out dacoity from UP when he was the Chief Minister during 1980-82. He was not bothered in the least by the fact that his order caused the death of hundreds of innocent humans from the poorest and most defenceless rungs of society. The UP police, which has a fair proportion of criminals employed in it, went on a shooting spree with great abandon, killing some dacoits and many innocents in the usual 'encounters'. Dacoity did not end and Mr V.P. Singh resigned as Chief Minister on June 28, 1982. After handing in his letter of resignation, he told newsmen in Lucknow, "My conscience does not permit me to stay in office with my ministry having failed to end the dacoit menace. If my Government cannot give them (the people of UP) protection from dacoits, I have no right to stick to office."

Well said. But not a word of conscience about the hundreds of innocents who died in the process or even a hint of the bare truth that the people of UP require protection from the UP police as well as from the dacoits. Mr V.P. Singh is making the same mistake again as Finance Minister. The culture of Indian business cannot be purified with the rotten bureaucratic instruments at his command or in the feudal social climate that still prevails in this country or in the opportunist atmosphere generated by his Congress Party colleagues. Mr Arun Nehru, the Minister of State for Internal Security, is reported to be attempting to grab the Finance Ministry's economic and revenue intelligence units so that he can use them for his own purposes, which could include the harassment of political opponents through tax-raids. With such constraints imposed by the retrograde Indian social and political structure, Mr V.P. Singh cannot succeed even in his limited task of whitening the ugly face of capitalism.

The Telegraph, **December 4, 1985.**

Fiery Bahujan and Frozen Communist

BOTH are tubby figures. Both are seemingly committed to fighting those who repress vast sections of the Indian people. There the similarities end and the stark contrasts begin. Mayawati and Indrajit Gupta could not be more dissimilar in their backgrounds, their political behaviour and their administrative styles.

During her recent six-month spell as UP Chief Minister, the diminutive Mayawati had IAS bureaucrats and senior police officers quaking in their polished boots because she was so obviously and imperiously in command of UP's administration. She would brook no opposition from mere pen-pushers and *babus.* There was no malingering, no hesitation in issuing orders and seeing that they were carried out. She knew exactly what she wanted to do. She wanted to empower the Dalits and unite them behind her own Bahujan Samaj Party and to direct the state's resources towards improving the social and economic condition of the Dalits.

Mayawati's determination to uplift the oppressed should not be underestimated as she is driven by a burning resentment, a deep fury against the social tyranny of the caste-ridden UP village of her childhood. Now that she has given the Dalits of UP a scent of power and a sense of political importance, however ephemeral, Mayawati and UP's Dalits can no longer be taken for granted.

A man who is taken for granted in his domain is Union Home Minister Indrajit Gupta. Officials in his ministry routinely ignore, block and contradict his plans. He seems in awe rather than in command of his ministry's bureaucrats.

The Communist leader who used to make thundering speeches in parliament about the rights of the oppressed now regularly opts for the overblown security scenarios presented by his bureaucrats rather than for the pleas for protection from police brutalities made by the humble citizens of this country. He has been co-opted into becoming a bureaucrat himself. Coddled as an apparatchik within the conformist democratic centralism of the CPI for over five decades, Indrajit Gupta's transition to a bureaucrat could not have been too difficult.

Like so many other CPI and CPI(M) leaders – including Jyoti Basu, Somnath Chatterjee and also some of the relatively younger ones – from upper-middle class backgrounds and educated at Cambridge or London Universities, Gupta has smoothly slipped into being part of the conservative establishment of the country. He has been such an upright Home Minister that Bal Thackeray's mouthpiece, *Saamna*, has written editorials in praise of him.

Politics through bureaucratic intervention has become so much of a mainstay for the Communist Parties that their leaders make very little effort personally to seek the support of the masses, particularly in the rural areas. However symbolic and superficial their tours may be, veterans of other parties do make a greater effort to 'keep in touch' with the general populace. L.K. Advani, during his paranoid and incendiary *rath yatras*, splutters and coughs while inhaling the dust of the Indian road but persists in rousing the sectarian instincts of some of the crowds he addresses in remote hamlets. Catch a Jyoti Basu or an Indrajit Gupta doing something so uncomfortable and undignified to counter Advani's rustic rallies. It is much more comforting to fly between Delhi, Calcutta and London to confer with pink trade unionists and students.

No wonder the oppressed castes and classes turn to a Mayawati, to a Laloo Yadav or a Mulayam Singh Yadav, who do provide an emotional salve, if nothing else, for the long-standing social brutalities of this nation. Mayawati and the Yadavs may be corrupt and self-seeking but they echo the hurts of the Dalits and the OBCs. There is a fire in the belly of these leaders and an emotional commitment to battling against social indignities. The Guptas, Basus and Chatterjees have no emotional driving force, no fire in the belly to convert their intellectual commitment to social justice into a people's movement.

Indian Express, **December 3, 1997.**

CPI(M) Is Becoming a Geriatric Ward

THE Communist Party of India (Marxist) and the Janata Party seem to be the only national and sizeable liberal parties left in the country. All the other national parties have become politically insignificant or have become engulfed in the rising tide of middle class greed and right-wing chauvinism. Compared to the crime-prone and corrupt rabble who make up the other parties, the cadres of the CPI(M) are paragons of virtue and discipline. The leadership of the CPI(M) is relatively clean and still cares for the common man and woman in contrast to the avaricious and cynical *netas* of the other national parties. The regional parties are a mixed bag of vice and virtue. Many of the regional parties are of recent origin and their workers and leaders have not had the time to be corrupted.

The recent victory of the CPI(M) candidates in the Bolpur Lok Sabha and Nanur Assembly contests in West Bengal confirms the extraordinary sophistication of the Indian voter who remains committed to any Government which is reasonably humane, clean and concerned about the common man. The continued loyalty to the CPI(M) and its Left partners shown by the people of West Bengal merely means that the CPI(M)-led state government is still regarded as clean and caring. And nothing more.

Next door in Assam, the CPI(M) has failed dismally. It has managed to secure just two miserable seats in the 125 Assembly contests despite a tailor-made situation which could have yielded much greater electoral dividends to the CPI(M). The terrified and socially deprived Bengali Hindu and Bengali Muslim voters in Assam were looking desperately for a party which would voice their feelings against aggressive Assamese Hindu chauvinism and which would be able to offer some degree of protective security. In the campaign leading up to the Assam election, the CPI(M) failed on both counts to inspire the confidence of the Bengali voter who has clearly become the underdog in Assam. Instead, the Bengali Hindu voter chose to cling to the discredited Congress(I) while the Bengali Muslim voted for the United Minorities Front which was cobbled together just a few weeks before the election.

The dismal failure of the CPI(M) in such a potentially favourable situation suggests there is some deep rot within the body of the CPI(M). Part of the explanation for this deep rot lies in the lack of renewal of the party leadership with fresh blood and brain cells. Age, experience and hierarchy count for much more than ability and dynamism in the rungs of the CPI(M). The result is the failure to recreate and recast Marxist thought towards winning the political struggle against the country's crudely exploitative classes. The tired old ritualistic jargon spouted by the tired old Indian Marxist leaders does not educate or inspire a people seeking a path out of their misery.

Even worse, the lack of fresh blood has led to a woeful lack of fighting spirit in the CPI(M) hierarchy. Assam is one more demonstration of the fact that Marxist cadres and leaders do not have the will and the courage to face fascist goons. (Some of the most demoralised people I met during the Emergency years in Delhi were CPI(M) members.)

Convoluted theoretical formulations are always readily available as substitutes for fighting spirit and organisational ability. The standard ploy for shying away from the stark realities at home is to point fingers and tongues at 'Imperialism' and 'The Great American Satan'. Supporting the distant struggles in South Africa and Nicaragua is far easier than fighting the Indian cousins of US imperialism. In his inaugural address last week in Calcutta at the 12th Congress of the CPI(M), that great jelly-brain of the party, Mr E.M.S. Namboodiripad, continued to give unstinted support to Mr Rajiv Gandhi's "fight" against imperialism even as Mr Gandhi's Government was busy opening India's doors to Western capital. Are Mr Namboodiripad and his party both deaf and blind?

The Telegraph, **January 3, 1986.**

We Need Journalists, Not Showmen

THE recent public mud-slinging match between Khushwant Singh, former editor of *The Hindustan Times*, and N.C.

Menon, the present editor, is hugely entertaining. The melee has also raised some issues which are probably beyond the comprehension of both the entertainers.

These issues revolve around the behaviour of journalists. The first of these issues is whether journalists, specially senior journalists, should become too chummy with Governments, political parties and political personalities/top bureaucrats. There is always the rationalisation that big news can only come through big contacts. This is an archaic argument peddled by those fading glories who believe that most worthwhile news emanates from the corridors of power. Some old glories like G.K. Reddy and Nikhil Chakravartty may still tramp around the corridors of power, picking up some news crumbs, but it should by now be clear as daylight that the most dramatic and the most interesting news stories come from the man in the street who is at the receiving end of the vagaries of political and administrative power.

There are, of course, those journalists whose purpose is more specific and mercenary, which is to pick up some crumbs of officc, such as Rajya Sabha nominations, thrown at them by their political mentors in the shape of a Sanjay Gandhi or a Surjit Singh Barnala. Such mercenaries can hardly be taken seriously when they attempt to analyse serious crises like the Emergency or Punjab.

Another issue on which no professional journalist should compromise is that of using his media platform to project himself as a public personality. Instead of skulking around as sporadic journalists, the Arun Shouries of the media world should more honestly join a political party or a film unit, assuming that some party or unit will welcome self-seeking image-builders even after knowing that such stars can never work as part of a team.

Such self-seekers easily succumb to the temptation of using the press as a vehicle to launch themselves as messiahs by concentrating on emotional questions and topics. Complex questions are then deliberately reduced to simple and sensational formulas which yield instant dividends in the form of public acclaim for such rabble-rousing scribes.

There is yet another breed of deviant journalists who have been bred largely by the glamorous society magazines of Bombay. This breed has the rather limited goal of climbing to the top of high society through high visibility at trendy parties, wearing garb more suited to peacocks. Publicity is ensured through photographs and write-ups in glossy magazines whose editors love to scratch each others' backs.

This bring us to the third issue of whether professional journalists should be known by the content, wit and elegance of their writing or by the parties they attend, the clothes they wear, the flirtations they indulge in and the cocktails they mix. To anyone who is not an illiterate peacock the answer should be obvious.

These issues are important for journalists and readers alike as the press still has some credibility in this country where other institutions like the executive, the legislature, the judiciary, radio and television *(then monopolised by All-India Radio and Doordarshan)* have largely lost their credibility. To retain its credibility, the press must expose the deviant journalists within its fold.

The press has two great advantages which enable it to expose the deviants within its fold. It does not have a monolithic character and it does not function as part of a hierarchical structure as other national institutions do. It is probably the most open and decentralised institution in this country. It has many faults and regularly commits many sins. But there is always some section of the press which is ready and willing to expose the faults and sins of another section. Long live journalists who are critical of everything and everybody, including themselves, especially at a time when the brutish and arbitrary power of other established institutions is growing by the day.

The Telegraph, **June 13, 1986.**

Perjury Is as Indian as Chewing *Paan*

WHILE the President of the United States may lose his job for having committed perjury (and not for having committed adultery), our legal system has shown an apparent tolerance of perjury or wilful lying under oath during a legal proceeding. Patently false depositions are commonly made at every stage of our legal process.

In a great number of cases, policemen and lawyers openly tutor witnesses to tell blatant lies in court. Many police thanas even have lists of stock witnesses whom the police can routinely call upon to make false depositions under oath. It appears that if adultery is as American as eating apple-pie, perjury is as Indian as chewing *paan*.

The courts see and hear falsehoods uttered before them daily as witnesses are routinely coerced or tampered with. Yet these acts of perversion of the process go unpunished. A judge sentencing anyone to imprisonment for perjury is virtually unheard of.

The law clearly allows for stiff sentences for acts of perjury. An entire chapter (XI) of the Indian Penal Code (Sections 191-229) minutely details crimes and penalties concerning "False Evidence and Offences against Public Justice". Section 191 stipulates that "Whoever, being legally bound by an oath or by an express provision of law to state the truth . . . makes any statement which is false, and which either he knows to be false or does not believe to be true, is said to give false evidence".

Section 192 similarly deals with fabrication of evidence in records and documents. Section 193 lays down that uttering or fabricating false evidence during a judicial proceeding "shall be punished with imprisonment of either description for a term which may extend to seven years, and shall also be liable to fine".

Why does the judiciary largely ignore the lies uttered by witnesses in court and the false documents presented in court?

One of the rationalisations by the legal fraternity is that strict punishment of perjurers may lead to witnesses becoming even more reluctant to appear in court. Another excuse is that judges do occasionally pass contempt of court sentences to discipline perjurers.

These excuses are inadequate. It seems that the judiciary has through long inertia come to accept perjury as part of the legal system much as the public has accepted monetary corruption and nepotism as a part of the system. Perjury is corruption and upright judges must begin to fight it as boldly as other forms of corruption.

Sections 217 to 223 of the Indian Penal Code specifically deal with crimes by public servants to pervert or obstruct justice by acts of omission or commission. These sections have been deliberately subverted by politicians and civil servants who have provided large escape-hatches for themselves by bringing in legal procedures which stipulate that certain classes of public servants can only be prosecuted after getting the permission of the state.

Section 197 of the Criminal Procedure Code specifies that "no court shall take cognisance of such offences except with the previous sanction" of Central or State Governments. "Such offences" refers to crimes allegedly committed by public servants in the discharge of their official duties. Section 197 effectively negates Sections 217 to 223 and other sections of the Indian Penal Code as, not surprisingly, Governments routinely refuse to sanction prosecution of their officials.

Equality before the law and equal protection of the law are the bedrock of democracy. They are the touchstones by which citizens measure and retain their faith and loyalty to democracy, buttressed by the belief that justice will be rendered without fear or favour. These touchstones are more important for democratic functioning than elections every few years.

It is incumbent on a vigilant Supreme Court to question the entire concept of exceptional legal lacunae for public servants which allow them to get away just because the state can – and often does – withhold permission to prosecute erring police officers, bureaucrats and ministers.

Another, more recent, legal trend which requires self-correction by the judiciary is that of public interest litigations (PILs). Sections of the judiciary are being swayed by mass appeal and away from their primary duty of administering even-handed and speedy justice to each defendant and litigant who comes before them. PILs are often foisted on the courts by relatively wealthy social busybodies and publicity seekers who divert the precious time and mental resources of senior judges from their basic task of providing justice to harried and humble individuals.

Judicial pronouncements on public issues do not always help in solving complicated social and environmental problems. To take just one example: the Supreme Court order of July 8, 1996, directing the relocation or closure of 168 hazardous and noxious factories to save Delhi from growing pollution, resulted in 50,000 workers being thrown out of their jobs. Two years later, most of them remain unemployed and without compensation, despite judicial directions to factory owners to recompense their former employees. Thousands of ruined families have been reduced to semi-starvation.

Desperate teenage male children of some of these workers have taken to burglary and robbery. The recent alarming rise in petty crime in Delhi can be partly accounted for by the Court order which led to throwing thousands of families onto the streets of the capital. Some of the workers have found employment at minimal wages in hazardous, slum-yard metal foundries and units for recycling plastic waste, adding to Delhi's pollution problems. Judges ought to be more cautious about striding into labyrinthine alleyways which even environmental and social angels fear to tread.

The Supreme Court and High Courts should also be wary of political petitioners who are out to involve them in messy political disputes such as which factions constitute a true majority in a legislature or whether a State Government has been rightly dismissed. It is for politicians to clear their own garbage. Judges must not allow themselves to be used as municipal sweepers for other people's rubbish heaps.

Indian Express, **October 16, 1998**

Commissions to Delay Justice

THE presidential ordinance to prevent parliament and state legislatures from knowing the contents of inquiry commission reports may well be a blessing in disguise. Judicial inquiries have become rituals to wash away or to forget repeated sins of omission and commission. Setting up an inquiry commission has become a standard ploy for the Union and State Governments to postpone any action against the criminal acts of their ministers and officials.

The retired judges who are usually provided employment in inquiry commissions take so long to complete their task that the disasters under inquiry are forgotten by the time the report is completed. Or, similar disasters occur in the meanwhile, pushing the earlier disaster into the hazy past. That is the intention of callous and corrupt ministers and officials.

Lethargic and equally callous opposition and social busybodies also participate in the charade by demanding an inquiry and then comfortably sitting back. A prolonged political struggle or painstaking measures to assist disaster victims are thus avoided. Once in a while the ritual inquiry does not serve its purpose as in the case of the Thakkar Commission to inquire into the Indira Gandhi assassination and related security lapses. The Thakkar Commission completed its work too fast, much to the embarrassment of those who till recently controlled or meddled with the Union Government's security apparatus. Some of the Gandhi family retainers, who continued to mess around with Indira Gandhi's personal security arrangements and with the Punjab situation long after their formal retirement from the Research and Analysis Wing (RAW), are most likely to have been indicted along with ex-Home Minister Narasimha Rao for their incompetence by the Thakkar Commission.

It is for the protection of such loyal, though incompetent, family bodyguards that the Union Government seems to have suppressed the expeditiously completed report of the Thakkar Commission by hurriedly promulgating the May 15 presidential ordinance. The completion of the Thakkar report before the full judicial process of the Indira assassination was completed, added to the distress of the Government.

There is, of course, the argument that even when inquiry reports are habitually completed many years after the event, they are helpful as part of the learning process, thereby preventing the recurrence of similar mishaps and disasters. The evidence shows that our political and bureaucratic mentors, like the Bourbons, learn nothing.

Take, for instance, the remarkable Madon Commission report on the 1970 Bhiwandi riots in which scores of innocents were massacred. The Madon Commission in precise detail documented the genesis and development of those riots and clearly indicated that there was collusion between the Hindu fanatics of the Shiv Sena and the Maharashtra State Government and police in encouraging the riots. The Madon Commission report was ignored and in 1984 there was a repetition in Bhiwandi of the horrors of 1970. The pattern of the 1984 riots was almost a carbon-copy of the 1970 riots.

The Telegraph, **June 6, 1986.**

Chapter-8

Bureaucracy's Wheels Grind On

THERE could be no greater misnomer than calling an Indian bureaucrat a civil servant. He is arrogant and uncaring and usually regards his own lower staff and the general public as servants. He is civil only to his superior officers and servile to his minister. Yet, like so many in the upper and middle classes, he is curiously dependent on the very 'servants' he despises. The personal assistant, the section officer, the peon, the driver of his staff car, are his crutches without whose ministrations he is paralysed. These are all paid for by a generous state milking an indigent society. If he employs any other servants at his own expense, he makes sure that they are paid half the market wage as he allows his servants' extended families to live in the garage attached to his subsidised government accommodation. If he is posted abroad, he carries his retinue and his attitude with him, projecting an abysmal image of the nation he represents.

He is a cog in the vast official hierarchy which perpetuates and encourages the continuing social climate of medieval contempt for the lower orders and boot-licking towards the upper crust instead of moving society towards a modern culture of respect for individual dignity regardless of social status.

Negativism is the bureaucrat's forte. Positive projects and programmes are held up for petty procedural reasons or because they require too much persistence and effort. Demolition is far easier than construction. The cheap route to applause from the well-heeled for every second-rate municipal commissioner or district magistrate is to erase the self-made homes of the impoverished, otherwise known as slums. Providing low-cost housing is a far more difficult exercise than sending in a couple of bulldozers and destroying humble dwellings without following any legal procedures.

He can get away with breaking the law and bending the rules. The rule of law is only for lesser mortals. He is effectively above the law. To prosecute him even for the most blatant criminal offence is almost impossible. Under Section 197 of the Criminal Procedure Code, prior government permission is required to book him. Government rarely grants permission as it is largely run by and for him.

He is also a huge financial burden on the tax–payer. According to a survey in *India Today,* each Secretary who is the top dog of a Central Government Department costs the exchequer eight lakh rupees a month while an Additional Secretary costs six lakh rupees a month. Between 1979 and 1999, the number of Secretaries and Additional Secretaries at the Centre escalated from 162 to 258 despite the functions of many Departments having become redundant due to economic reforms. Many of the Secretaries were involved in privatising or downsizing public sector units but there was no attempt to downsize their own clan or their retinue of 'personal' staff. Each Secretary is serviced by a principal private secretary, a personal assistant, an upper or lower division clerk, a peon at the inner door of the office, another peon at the outer door, and a chauffeur to steer the official car (which is routinely used for family chores). In addition, serving under the Secretary, are countless officers and their factotums, strictly ranked in a rigid hierarchy from joint secretary downwards to section officer.

The total number of civilian employees on the rolls of Central Government Departments and their subordinate offices amounts to 37 lakhs. This awesome figure does not include some 20 lakh uniformed personnel of the defence forces, Border Security Force and Central police organisations. Due to then Prime Minister Inder Kumar Gujral's abject surrender to bureaucratic whining and wheedling, the Fifth Central Pay Commission's recommendations made in 1997 to hike wages were accepted. As a result, the total pay and allowances of Central Government civilian employees jumped to Rs 37,457 crores in the financial year 1999-2000 from Rs 28,903 in 1998-99. Over 20 per cent of the Centre's revenues are swallowed by the pay and allowances of its civilian employees. These increases were followed by hikes in payouts to uniformed personnel and to the employees of state governments. The Pay Commission's recommendation to reduce the size of the bureaucracy by 30 per cent has been ignored.

No Servants in Antarctica

ANTARCTICA is populated by millions of hardy penguins and a few acclimatised scientists from the West, the Soviet Union and Japan. There are also a handful of scientists from India. Complaints by some of the Indian scientists, including those made in letters to the Prime Minister, indicate that they have not been able to acclimatise themselves to the rigours of Antarctica. It is not the freezing blizzards or hazardous ice-fields which have upset the Indian scientists but the harsh social climate: there are no servants in Antarctica to do the dirty work.

One scientist, disgusted with the physical chores of setting up camp on the ice-continent, complained that "most of our time on the expedition is devoted to loading and unloading cargo". Other scientists were even more wary of physical work. They continued to stay on the expedition's ship instead of shifting to tents at the experiment sites.

Why pick on the scientists in the snows? They are only pining in Antarctica for a lifestyle and culture so familiar back home in India where every official, professional or individual in an office chair is dependent on a personal assistant, *chaprasee* or some other servant for fetching even a glass of water.

The slightest physical effort is considered an affront to the social status of the man in the office chair. Deputy secretaries and above in Delhi are entitled to an electric bell at their feet so that they do not even have to lift their little fingers to summon a PA or a peon. Officers commonly fling Government files on the floor after signing them. A lower fry then bends down and picks them up for transmission to some other vulgar officer in the hierarchy.

Such attitudes are not only unseemly but they also create sloth and inefficiency. One of the major unstated reasons for the many failings of the Indian intelligence and security services is that delicate and dangerous missions are usually assigned to some semi-literate, poorly-paid, lower rank rather than to an experienced officer. Senior Indian intelligence officials try and ape the style of classy British secret agents but they ignore one essential feature of British security stories. The most dangerous missions are always carried out by the British officer himself and not by some lower rank. If the security of the Indian state is to be preserved, the task should not be left to the servants but to the masters.

The masters are, however, getting more slovenly and lethargic by the day due to their dependence on the servants. Key Government documents are increasingly drafted by the lowest official, the section officer, who is also the repository of detailed knowledge about departmental rules, regulations and precedents. The senior officer constantly looks to the section officer for help and guidance. The chain of authority and discipline breaks down and the section officer or the PA becomes the petty tyrant. The powerful petty tyrant also becomes a barrier between the senior officer and the citizen seeking redress.

Some may hope that this topsy-turvy turn of affairs within the Government system is an ingredient of the coming social revolution. It is nothing of the kind. It is an indicator of the decay of the Indian ruling classes and a pointer to social anarchy.

The Telegraph, **October 30, 1985.**

Taking the Country for a Ride

FIVE months ago I went for a country ride. For a city-bred person like me it was an eye-opener.

Seventeen months ago I had also gone for a ride. The euphoria of the imminent Lok Sābha election and the open nastiness of the Emergency regime had then obscured the dull, plodding brutishness of a system which has existed for decades if not centuries. Those who operate the system have not changed but the victims of the ruling system, the common people of the land, have changed, I was to discover on my more recent trip.

On my first night out my car breaks down in a remote village surrounded by an eight-foot high crop of sugar-cane. The only place where I can seek refuge in this village, about 150 kilometres north-east of Delhi in Muzaffarnagar district, is the cinema hall with its ritual romance on for the night show.

Outside the cinema hall is the symbol of Government authority, the beflagged jeep of the SDM (sub-divisional magistrate) with its complement of two peons and a driver. Inside the hall, the SDM, along with some excise officials, is entertaining himself on the house.

The wizened old chaiwallah and the solemn-faced paanwallah are summoned to send up half-hourly supplies of tea and paan to the "afsars". There is not a word about payment. The cinema show is also free for the "afsars". An obscure rule about inspection of possible fire hazards in the cinema hall can always prove handy for the officials if anyone dares to object.

The manager of the cinema hall shrugs his shoulders and sighs: "*Yeh to rivaj hai*" (This is the custom). The chaiwallah is beyond caring. The paanwallah is visibly agitated. His little shop keeps losing money due to these officers. Why should he keep giving away free paans? Will there never be an end to this freebooting by the "afsars"? Emergency or no Emergency, it is always the same. He protests to the cinema manager who repeats his customary dirge.

The manager, a beaten-looking, kindly man, throws up his hands. He knows the ways of officialdom. He spends half of every working week satisfying the egos and pockets of officials at the district headquarters to keep the business running. The Emergency was not very different from the years before or the year after except that sales for the night show have gone down recently due to the increasing number of road robberies. He advises the paanwallah to keep quite. But the paanwallah is not to be quietened. He continues to mutter.

On the way to the Pauri Garhwal hills, a strapping farmer asks for a lift to the next village. He is selling off his crop of sugar-cane from 10 acres at a loss. Sterilisation or not, at least during the Emergency, the price of cane was higher. If the farmers in his village have to keep selling their cane at a loss, they will vote for Indira again.

The rotund, talkative owner of a family-run sugar mill is all praise for the local newspaper which has dismissed allegations of under-weighing of sugar-cane brought in by the peasants. The sugar mills continue to pay the peasant the Government-stipulated price for cane even though they cannot afford it. Yet they are accused of under-weighing and under-paying. Yes, the Emergency days were good. No nonsense. No false accusations. He is an Indira supporter and always was an Indira supporter.

Kotdwara, the green gateway to the sub-Himalayan hills of Pauri Garhwal. An unidentified man-eating animal has been roaming the hills, killing 13 children over the past year. But the wildlife official, sitting behind his files, is more keen on prosecuting the local hunters who have mistakenly shot suspected maneaters than on tracking down the maneater. Innocent animals are being killed. The innocent children are not mentioned.

Nestling 5,000 feet up in the hills among terraced fields, the village of Birmoli. Population, five hundred. Only thirty men, the rest women, children and unemployed youth. Most of the men are away in the plains working as servants, peons or soldiers and sending their petty cash home.

The youth have all been to school but now even the market for soldiers and servants is drying up. The terraced fields provide little employment. So the teenaged boys play football all day on the deserted road and the young women fret away hoping for rich husbands to take them away.

At night behind locked doors, as the maneater is on the prowl and has dragged away and killed a village girl a few days back, a village elder and his retired chum from the army inevitably turn to politics. It is not the airy-fairy politics of Delhi drawing-rooms but the politics of bread and a little butter.

Both the village elder and his friend are sitting up stiffly against the wall. Why don't they sit more comfortably? Their backs still ache due to the crudely performed, forced sterilisations they had to undergo during the Emergency. But what now, they ask? They brought the Janata Government to power. They created the Janata Government. Were it not for them, where would all the Janata leaders be?

But for them and the people of the village nothing has changed. There is not one little benefit from the Janata Government for the village.

What does the village need? It needs a storage tank to catch the water from the spring which trickles away wastefully when the village women are not queuing up for hours to collect it in their brass pitchers. All the major quarrels among the women are over the spring water. They have pleaded with the local administration for a metal or cement storage tank for 10 (or is it 15?) years but the water still trickles away. They cannot get a water tank for themselves as nobody has a rupee to spare.

Look at the village boys. They cannot even join the army now with the recruitment rules which have raised the minimum height requirements and are unfair to the short pahadhis (hill people). Has anything been done by the Government for the village over the past few years? Yes, a road was built. But without any bus service on it, why build a road? It is never used except by an occasional forest contractor's truck. The nearest bus stop is still miles away and nobody walks on the road. They all use the shorter mountain path. A total waste, this road.

Nobody cares for them or their village. If the villagers are given half a chance, they will vote for the Indira Congress again. Why? There is no other party to vote for and the Janata Government they created has done nothing for them. Have they forgotten their own forced sterilisations? The village elder's eyes glow in the light of the dying pine-cone fire. Wait a while and the Janata Government will also resort to sterilisations. What else can Governments do except sterilise the people?

The morning dawns early and bright in the hills. We go into the fields behind the village. The village elder points out the black, tell-tale droppings of a panther. Could have been the maneater watching over the village at night. To top all their problems, there is now this animal, the elder mutters quietly. Now at night, no one can go into the fields to protect his crop from the rodents and other creatures.

I bid good-bye to Birmoli. As I leave, an intelligent looking young man stares blankly at me. What does he do? Nothing. What will he be doing? "Well, what?" he says with that peculiar intonation which means "We can't go on like this".

Kotdwara again. The rice-miller's son, a technical student, gets acquainted. It's a wretched town. Nothing much to do here. What local news? A nurse in the local hospital disappeared recently. Another nurse was carrying on a trade. The nurses get used by the local bigwigs. The students do not like these goings-on. There was a riot. The police beat up some students.

His father. Everyone comes to him. The politicians, they always want donations. Before it was Congressmen. Now it is Janata politicians. Excise officials, they always want to go to

Delhi in father's car. Father never says no. The local SDM? An honest, fresh young man. He does not ask for anything. But he won't last.

Back to Delhi. The intellectuals, the MPs, the editors say that the common man has no attachment to democracy. Despite the hearings of the Shah Commission, the common man is going back to Indira Gandhi.

The newspapers are full of Emergency "excesses". But there is nothing about the daily, dreary little excesses being committed every day by officials, politicians, sugar mill-owners in a thousand little Kotdwaras and Birmolis. A thousand Shah Commissions will not be able to unravel the excesses committed every day which are a part of the "rivaj", the custom.

The Emergency only centralised the custom in the hands of Indira, Sanjay and Bansi Lal. Or were the "excesses" just gross and ugly symptoms of a ruling system gone corrupt and rotten?

The 1977 elections removed the gross symptoms but the system remained. The symptoms are arising again. A rotten system will throw up rotten, corrupt or just plain brutish leaders, be they Sanjays, Indiras, Raj Narains, Charan Singhs or Jagjivan Rams.

The people who are at the receiving end can feel the system physically. They do not have to think about it. On the eternal Ganga 15 months ago, as the day was awakening, three boatmen rowed me to the Sangam near Allahabad. The March 1977 election was a few weeks away.

Whom would they vote for? They would vote Janata but what difference would it make to their wretched lives, they asked cynically? Politicians only thought about themselves or about making money for their own families.

A bloated, bleached corpse floated by on its long journey to the sea and to eternity.

Sunday magazine, **June 25, 1978.**

Foreign Service Uses Bonded Labour

INDIAN Foreign Service officials in Europe and West Asia treat their Indian domestic servants as bonded labour.

A number of bureaucratic stratagems are used to keep these servants in bondage to their masters while they are leading a wine-and-roses high life. It is almost standard procedure to impound servants' passports. This clearly illegal procedure is effected as soon as the servant has been flown in and he does not get his passport back till he goes home with his master which is usually after three years.

If the servant "misbehaves" or is a "trouble-maker", it is made known to him that any future application for an independent passport will receive an official "black-mark". With such bureaucratic power unleashed, most servants meekly serve out their three-year terms at wages which amount to little more than cigarette money in expensive countries.

The Indian domestic employees whom I met recently in several European countries and West Asian capitals are particularly bitter about the huge gap between the paltry sums they earn and the wages of the local domestic staff occasionally employed by embassy officials. An educated young man from Delhi who works as a cook-cum-bearer for an IFS officer in a Central European capital is angered by the knowledge that his monthly wage is equivalent to two or three evenings' earnings by local waiters brought in to serve cocktails at the Indian ambassador's residence.

He wants to go home but he has neither the money nor his passport which is tucked away in an embassy safe. He earns the equivalent of Rs 200 per month at the official exchange rate. In terms of actual buying power in Europe, this is enough only for some bus rides and a few packets of inferior cigarettes. He does not complain openly as one day he hopes to get a passport in his own right and come back to the West to live affluently as the locals do. If he makes too much fuss he has been told that he may never get another passport.

A woman cook from Uttar Pradesh employed by a young IFS officer in another European capital is extremely lonely and also wants to return home but she has to serve out her three-year term. She does not speak the local language, she misses her friends and relatives in India and has no contact with local people or happenings.

There are countless such unhappy persons eager to tell their histories of neglect and bondage in Indian missions abroad. The official rationalisation trotted out ad nauseam is that the air fare, both ways, is paid for by the Government of India and free boarding and lodging is also provided for the domestic servants in the homes of the officials. Therefore, the servants must stick out their three-year terms with their masters. This reasoning has a familiar ring about it. It is still used by money-lenders and landlords nearer home who keep agricultural labour in bondage to repay an old debt.

Indian Express, **December 30, 1977.**

Diplomatic Impunity

INDIA is not a banana republic. Yet, some of our diplomats treat it as if it were a banana republic – behaving outrageously and then seeking diplomatic immunity abroad or patriotic excuses at home as covers for their wanton acts. Banana republics and medieval sheikhdoms indulge their offending diplomats and consider them to be above the law. Civilised democracies promptly withdraw diplomatic protection and allow the law to take its course against their erring officials.

The latest alleged incident involving an Indian diplomat in Paris is particularly horrifying. A French NGO, the Committee Against Modern-Day Slavery, and a distinguished French physician have established that Lalita Oraon, an orphaned servant-girl from a Scheduled Tribe in Bihar, was allegedly maltreated for a sustained period and mutilated with a blade in her genital area in the home of Amrit Lugun, First Secretary at the Indian Embassy in Paris. Having fled from Lugun's residence, she was found wandering in the streets of Paris in a suicidal state on September 5 and was put in the care of a monastery by the French police. She, again, tried to commit suicide at the monastery by jumping off a high wall.

Instead of allowing police and legal investigations to proceed against the First Secretary, the Indian Embassy in Paris launched a cover-up operation through the favoured PTI news agency, accusing the French police of being involved in a "campaign of disinformation and defamation" against the Indian diplomat and accusing the girl of not having worked satisfactorily! The Embassy also demanded the return of the seriously injured girl to its custody. In Delhi, some air-headed Indian Foreign Service officials are reported to have even threatened to expel a French diplomat of equivalent rank from India in retaliation for any possible French request that the offending Indian official be withdrawn from Paris.

This is not the first instance of an Indian servant being mistreated by Indian diplomats during their postings abroad, though it is the most horrific to have come to light so far. In the past, incidents of servants being ill-treated by Indian diplomats have been reported in Britain and Switzerland. Such matters have usually been hushed up under the garb of diplomatic immunity and for the sake of maintaining good bilateral relations between Governments. Every time such an incident happens, the image of India takes a severe beating. Ironically, the very same diplomats who constantly mouth platitudes about promoting the honour and dignity of India, damage the country's image by insisting on diplomatic protection for those colleagues who have committed criminal acts. It should be said that wealthy private Indian individuals living abroad often also over-work, under-pay and mistreat their Indian servants. However, if caught, they face the full vigour of the law. An Indian doctor living in London was sentenced to several years in jail by a British court for illegally confining and beating his servant.

Indian diplomats must be made to subscribe to higher standards of moral behaviour than that of the usual humdrum, fat NRI businessman. Many of our diplomats are fine people but there are still far too many others who arrogantly think that as twice-born officials chosen to represent the country, they can get away with the most abominable behaviour, particularly towards their own countrymen and women. This manifests itself not only in the treatment of servants but also in how Indian embassies and consulates deal with ordinary Indian citizens who may require some mundane service from an Indian legation. Rudeness, delay, harassment are the common experience of Indian nationals living abroad who may require as simple a transaction as attesting a legal document or adding a few pages to a full passport.

When a major problem occurs or when there is a major mishap involving Indian nationals, our diplomats tend to look the other way instead of coming to the help of their fellow citizens. For instance, in the Gulf our legations tend to be passive in reacting to patently offensive acts of physical abuse against Indian labour (especially maids) by their Arab employers. Strong representations to the host Government to take legal action against such employers are generally avoided as these may upset the authorities of the Gulf states. Our diplomatic motto seems to be: protect your colleagues but not your countrywomen or men.

This ethos of contempt and disdain for the ordinary citizen marks not just those in the Indian Foreign Service (IFS) but a whole lot of other bureaucrats including those in the IAS or the IPS, though there is a difference. The officers of the IAS and IPS are under constant pressure and surveillance by public opinion, by politicians and by the media to be accountable for their actions. IFS officers are still a rarefied and protected species, wrapped in a silk cocoon, placed on a high pedestal, distant from the heat and dust of their mother country. But some officers are more privileged than others. Within the service, there is a palpable caste (and racist) hierarchy. Senior

IFS officers belonging to the reserved category of Scheduled Castes and Tribes rarely make it to the top slot at our coveted embassies in the white, Western countries. They usually end their service days packed off as ambassadors to countries in black Africa which are regarded as hardship postings.

Under the cloak of national interest, IFS officials have carved an elitist niche for themselves and have so far managed to remain relatively unaccountable. On the specious ground of maintaining the nation's status abroad, they have been pampered. Note the grand and sparkling residences of Indian ambassadors abroad and contrast them with the neglected state of their smelly and messy embassy office buildings. Under threat of being branded anti-national, journalists have been discreet about their inquiries into the workings of the IFS.

The IFS remains the last bastion of the brown sahib and the last remnant of the Indian Civil Service (ICS) of colonial times when the natives were despised and kept at a distance to avoid offending the prim sensibilities of their masters. Times have alas changed and the IFS will sooner or later have to change and come down to earth and become answerable to the Indian people whom they are expected to represent abroad.

Outlook, **September 27, 1999.**

Chapter-9

The Emergency – Durbari Melodrama

THE wisdom of hindsight indicates that the Emergency drama of 1975-77 will just be a blip on history's screen of continuing misrule in the country. At the time, particularly among those of us who were reporting for the ndian E press, the newspaper which singularly defied the dictates of the Indira-Sanjay regime, many of the incidents of that period were certainly regarded as gruelling and nasty. News reports about those unsavoury events could not be published due to official censorship. But looking back at the man-made disasters and degrading brutality the people of the country have serially suffered before and after the Emergency, those years seem melodramatic rather than uniquely cruel.

Petty vendettas and arbitrary commands were the order of the day, especially in Sanjay Gandhi's domain, which did not extend much beyond Delhi and its hinterland in the neighbouring districts of Haryana, Uttar Pradesh and Rajasthan. Sanjay's orders were carried out by pliant officials who became the main tool of oppression. Politicians and the Congress Party's district committees became largely irrelevant. In the administrative units of northern India, the powers of the district magistrate were often usurped by the district superintendent of police due to the requirements of the Gandhi family's centralised rule and crude concentration of power and corruption. Thousands of persons were detained without trial and lakhs were forcibly sterilised in primitive and medically unsafe conditions.

Till today, those conditions have not changed greatly. Government hospitals remain filthy and callous charnel houses for the common patient and lakhs continue to be effectively detained without trial for years. Even after the trials begin, they proceed at a lackadaisical pace for some more years till the verdict of conviction or acquittal is announced. Only 20 per cent of those held in Delhi's Tihar jail, Asia's biggest prison, are convicts. Eighty per cent are undertrials, a majority of whom will be found innocent when their verdicts are pronounced years later. Arrests by the police of those who are penniless or without influence are often arbitrary or because the law-enforcer has not received the customary piece of silver on his palm. These innocent victims who have committed no crime, except being from the wrong background, can be termed as political prisoners as the political and law enforcement systems specifically target them. Some, though not all, of the Emergency's detainees were different. They were from 'respectable' and comfortable backgrounds and were detained as they were perceived to be opposed to the ruling regime. They were political prisoners in the more obvious sense.

Another aspect of the Emergency was the obsession with cosmetic beautification through the demolition of the tin, tarpaulin and thatch homes and workplaces of the poor. Demolition drives against 'unsightly slums' by administrators have continued after the Emergency, usually without providing any alternative accommodation.

The Emergency regime miserably failed to suppress news despite media censorship and detention of opposition politicians and some journalists. The regime did not realise that in an oral culture where people are volubly talkative, news would travel and be exaggerated when the media was censored. Word-of-mouth transmission was so effective that news of every major incident that the regime tried to suppress was known throughout the country at astonishing speed. Travellers and telephone conversations carried the news almost as fast as the free media used to. Minions of the regime and of the Indira-Sanjay household were the first to tell secrets in confidence to their friends who in turn repeated the confidential stories to their friends, relatives and colleagues. The bush telegraph was so effective and accurate, though slightly exaggerated, that the Shah Commission which later investigated the excesses of the Emergency period, confirmed each and every incident that was commonly talked about during the years of censorship.

Every incident was publicly known soon after it happened: Police shootings of people resisting forcible sterilisations and the demolition of their homes, Sanjay's humiliation of ministers and officials and his reckless mode of piloting his aircraft, the names of the governing coteries around Indira and Sanjay, Swami Dhirendra Brahmachari's land grabbing assaults for his ashrams and private airfield, Rukhsana Sultana's bejewelled forays into Delhi's walled city to grab victims for sterilisation, the Defence Ministry's referral of decisions on senior officers' appointments to Sanjay, draconian night raids on villages by the Haryana police to take away truckloads of men, young and old, to fulfil sterilisation quotas.

The sad part of what followed the Emergency was that many of the victims of that period remained uncompensated and some of its real heroes remained unsung while many who had obsequiously bowed and scraped before the dictatorial regime claimed to be defiant heroes.

Premonition of Dictatorship

"THE Queen is a certified crook! Long live the Queen!" So runs the doggerel in the minds of all those hundreds of Congress MPs and other courtiers who have been lounging around within the portals of power by courtesy of Indira Gandhi.

In the morning (June 12) she was unseated by the Allahabad High Court verdict for having used officials and official machinery during her election campaign. In the afternoon busloads and truckloads of municipal employees and factory workers were cajoled into congregating outside her residence at Safdarjang Road to demonstrate "popular" support for her "dynamic leadership".

The trucks belonged to the New Delhi Municipal Committee and the buses to the Delhi Transport Corporation. Many of the hustlers who organised the demonstration were local government officials. As added inducement, some of the demonstrators were offered five-rupee notes and others were given bread and milk.

To most Congressmen it is quickly obvious that it if she is made to step down from the seat of power they might have to follow as they have no political base of their own. Most of them were hand-picked by Indira Gandhi in 1971 or 1972. Now in this emergency situation, their dependence on her has become a bond.

In this circumstance, legal 'quirks' like not using officials and official machinery for personal and party ends are nuisances which can simply be ignored – in the afternoon as in the morning. In the violation of legality, some of the Chief Ministers have a wealth of experience. Two of them, Siddhartha Shankar Ray and Bansi Lal, who have revelled in the politics of terror in West Bengal and Haryana, are drumming up support for Indira Gandhi. Truckloads of 'captive' workers and peasants were brought from Haryana for the show of strength organised by Bansi Lal. Strongarm men like Lal and Ray are the most frightened at the prospect of Indira Gandhi's resignation. Deprived of Central protection and with only a police base in their states, they might be the first to be sent packing if the Prime Minister resigns. Compared to the state bosses of the early 1960s, Chief Ministers now have no substantial political machines of their own.

The only man who has recently tried to build his own political machine, Chief Minister Bahuguma of Uttar Pradesh, was regarded with instant suspicion by Indira Gandhi and reprimanded in no uncertain terms. Being the Chief Minister of the Congress heartland places him in a key position. He is the only Chief Minister who will not be unhappy to see Indira Gandhi go.

This does not mean there will be a smooth transition in New Delhi, like after Nehru or Shastri. Once she steps down, the immense centralisation of political manipulation she has effected is bound to fall to bits: The dirty linen will come out in laundry-loads.

Jagjivan Ram is regarded as the front-runner with the unassuming Swaran Singh as an interim Prime Minister. It might just so happen that the empty symbolism of having a Harijan Prime Minister in the portly and stable shape of Jagjivan Babu would suit the Congress mentality. He would be regarded as useful at a time when the Harijans are not only beginning to get militant but are showing some slight signs of developing a class ethos in Bihar and Uttar Pradesh, again in the Congress heartland.

This revolt of the minorities is also erupting in Gujarat, where the ever faithful Scheduled Castes and Tribes and Muslims are no longer slipping in the Congress ballot. The election results from Gujarat have shown that Indira Gandhi's helicopter trips are not very charismatic these days. As all the non-CPI parliamentary opposition leaders have repeated parrot-like, this has been a great day for democracy and for justice. Whose democracy and justice for whom are irrelevant issues at a durbar where personalities are primary and where economic issues are mere fodder for the speech-writers and the journalists.

Whether she comes down or not, the country is no longer going to be as sleepy as it has been for the last three decades. The starvation induced inertia will continue but it will be fitful. There will be ever more gheraos, morchas, police-firings and lathi-charges.

The vast tragedy will continue alongside the durbari melodrama. The melodrama has reached the second act. The durbar has got entangled within its own postures of propriety. The final suicidal act has yet to unfold. There is as yet no directing party which is capable of precipitating the final act.

All the same, this day has been momentous. The future may regard it as the moment when a ritual drama turned into a living confrontation.

Economic and Political Weekly, **June 14, 1975.**

Resistance at Turkman Gate

New Delhi

ON this day, a year ago, the people of Turkman Gate resisted the destruction of their homes. Many gave their lives so that we may breathe free. This is their story told in their words.

A single bulldozer started eating up homes in the area on April 13, 1976. Its first morsels were the houses of the "transit camp". The camp had been there on Asaf Ali Road since 1965. Its residents, like hundreds of thousands of others in Delhi, had no options. Their homes were churned into rubble. They were carted out in trucks and dumped in the wilderness where the only comforts were the bold yellow boards of the Delhi Development Authority (DDA) marked "facilities".

The fate of the people of the transit camp, which was almost opposite Turkman Gate, was noted with dread by the people of the area.

Some local leaders went to see H.K.L. Bhagat, then Union Works and Housing Minister, on April 16. The Minister told them no houses – permanent structures which had been there for generations – at Turkman Gate would be destroyed. But the bulldozer kept moving towards the Gate.

On April 19, from seven in the morning, people started collecting on Asaf Ali Road, in front of the whitewashed Dargah Faiz-e-Elahi. They were told to stage a sit-down demonstration to prevent the bulldozer from moving onto Turkman Gate. By 10 am several hundred men and women and some children had gathered in front of the Dargah and sat down peaceably on the road, as had been suggested by Subhadra Joshi, then a Congress MP.

In front of the Delite cinema and the Hamdard Dawakhana, two other groups gathered to lodge their protest. Most of the people in these two latter groups lived in the streets of the area and had no proper homes. They did odd jobs and somehow managed to earn a living. Some had no roof over their heads while others were temporary tenants of the householders who had gathered in front of the Dargah.

Till one in the afternoon the three groups sat it out in the heat of a summer day, the temperature soaring up to 108 degrees Fahrenheit. It was then that lorry-loads or riflemen of the Central Reserve Police Force (CRPF) had begun to arrive along with some from the Delhi Police.

Just after one pm some persons in the group squatting in front of the Dargah got up to walk away. A few were tired, others wanted to say their noon prayers. The police shoved them back and told them to sit down again.

The pushing and shoving continued for a few minutes. Then someone hiding in the police ranks threw a stone. More stones were thrown, initially all from the police side and into the group of squatters. After a slight lull the squatters retaliated.

Mohammed Yunus, who then had a tin shop in Turkman Gate, was face-to-face with the front rank of the police. He saw a Sub-Divisional Magistrate (SDM) ordering a lathi-charge at about 1-30 pm. There was pandemonium. Screams, shouts, people running helter-skelter. The police moved into the group and by 2 pm had arrested several hundred men after brutally hitting them on their heads with lathis "as if they were rats to be exterminated".

Most of the crowd that remained were women. Seeing their men being dragged off, more women came out from their houses armed with kitchen implements like rolling-pins. For a moment the police were pushed back by the enraged women.

Mohammed Yunus found himself pushed almost into the SDM's arms by the surging crowd behind him. Right next to Yunus was Abdul Malik, a young man of 22. Malik bared his chest in the SDM's face and shouted: "Kill me or stop the demolition." The SDM ordered a policeman to shoot him at point-blank range. Yunus, whose voice still quivers with emotion to this day, saw Malik fall dead, a bullet in his chest. Yunus ran from the scene of horror. He kept moving for the next four months like a demented fugitive, to Moradabad, to Lucknow and then to Bareilly. Even today his eyes look haunted.

More shots were fired by the police and the bodies of those defending their homes began to fall along with those of several bystanders. The firing continued sporadically from 2.30 pm to 5 pm when a curfew was imposed.

Mohammed Qadir's nephew, Zahuruddin, a young man of 18, was killed instantly by a bullet as he was running away from the horror. He had come to Turkman Gate from Chitli Qabar to take away his female relatives. He could not reach them.

Mohammed Hanif, who used to own a meat shop before it was bulldozed, was not in any of the groups of demonstrators. He was sitting in his shop when the tear-gas canisters started descending on the crowded lanes of the Gate. He tried to gather up his children who as usual were roaming around in the street. He caught sight of Anwar. Just then, his six-year old son's mouth was bashed in by a six-inch long tear-gas grenade. The boy died instantly, his mouth a pool of blood.

Another son, Shabir, who would now have been nine, has not been found to this day. Nobody has seen him or heard of him since April 19, last year. Hanif says, in all the confusion, he could only run with the body of Anwar in his arms.

Together with the firing, the bulldozers were also moving in like unstoppable mammoths. Many were to die that day from police bullets or lathi blows or tear-gas canisters. Some were crushed under the rubble of falling houses torn asunder by the 14 bulldozers which had replaced the single old bulldozer. Hanif does not know whether Shabir may have been crushed under the rubble.

Nobody really knows how many died that day or during the nasty 45-day curfew that followed. *Indian Express* reporters counted 12 bodies in the Irwin hospital morgue, all identified by relatives from Turkman Gate. *Express* staff saw five or six bodies being brought under police escort on April 20 to be returned to the earth in the burial ground behind the *Express* Building.

Beating and killing were accompanied by looting by the CRPF and other representatives of the raj. Ram Devi, 52, was returning home on the evening of the 19th when a policeman hit her with a lathi on the leg and demanded to know what she was carrying. Her month's salary, which she had just collected, was snatched away and when she got to where her home was, all she found was a heap of rubble.

Allah-rakhi's house was not destroyed as it was across the street from the area which was demolished. But her house was entered into by 10-12 riflemen of the CRPF. They entered the small, dark room in which eight women and girls were hiding. They kicked the frail, wooden door aside and dragged Allah-rakhi out. The skin on her forehead is still blotched and the bridge of her nose disfigured due to the rifle-butt with which she was hit in the face. Her earrings were also snatched away.

Her neighbour who had been hiding in the same room, Ahmadnissa, 35, was dragged out by her hair. A rifleman tried to grab her. She jumped down from a 15-foot high parapet, leaving him holding her dopatta.

Rehmatunissa, a bright-eyed 25 year-old, was also dragged out and dishonoured ("*beizzati hui*"). Another girl shouts that her sister was . . . . But she is quickly shut up. None of the survivors of Turkman Gate talk of rape. But a number talk of being dishonoured and stop there.

The aftermath was, perhaps, worse. Lachmi, 40, says she was alone when the bulldozers came. She spent two days on the road and was then trucked to Trilokpuri where there was nothing but wasteland, also flattened by bulldozers. All her possessions had been crushed by the bulldozers at Turkman Gate. Her husband found her in Trilokpuri after roaming around for several days.

Kirori, a sad-eyed, gaunt-looking 85, used to be happy in those distant days before his home in Moti Gali was destroyed on April 19. He used to own three rickshaws and looked forward to a mellow old age. Now he has little except a flimsy brick structure which he shares with five others.

Here there are no proper tenements, no filtered water to drink, no jobs, except miles away. To get to the walled city, which everyone poignantly refers to as Delhi, the wait for buses is interminable. Some persons have been given bank loans of Rs 2,000 but no one can build even a singe solid room with that. A year after the happenings at Turkman Gate, the yellow boards of the DDA marked "facilities" are still surrounded by barren land.

At Nandnagri, the other wasteland where the survivors of Turkman Gate now live, the conditions are even worse. There is still no proper drainage system and it will soon again be flooded knee-deep as it was during the last monsoon. The mosquitoes create hell every night as they do in Trilokpuri. Many of the men have still not been able to find jobs. Many were self-employed at Turkman Gate and were house-owners. Now they have lost everything.

Yet, you can sense a calm pride among them. And among the women, there is a new-found, almost arrogant, assurance. All the women who lived through that fateful day of April 19, last year, talk to you with a self-assurance and directness which is astounding. Does it reflect an inner consciousness that they have resisted and faced tyranny and nothing can now destroy their spirit?

Do the oppressors have moments of remorse? It seems not. Three hundred former residents of Turkman Gate went to visit Indira Gandhi last June after taking an appointment. She was not there. They insisted on meeting Sanjay Gandhi. After making them wait for two hours, Sanjay met their spokesman, Bashiruddin Shafi, and a few of Shafi's colleagues.

Shafi asked for some facilities for the victims of the April 19 incident. Angry about the facts that these people had related to Sheikh Abdullah and his strong condemnation of the incident, Sanjay told Shafi and the others to go and get a certificate praising the DDA from the Sheikh. "Then we will give you facilities", he said.

Sanjay also wanted a signed list of 800 persons to be arrested under MISA for having attacked the police on April 19. (About 550 were already under arrest.) He said: "You people have been thrown out for attacking the police. You are liars. You have made false complaints to Sheikh Abdullah. You must now suffer for this."

Indian Express, **April 19, 1977.**

Morarji Calls for Freedom from Fear

New Delhi

MR Morarji Desai, Congress-O leader and former Deputy Prime Minister, stated here today that the nation could not be strong without freedom from fear. Speaking to this newsman five hours after his release from detention since June 26, 1975, Mr Desai said: "Individuals will come and go but the nation has to be strong and fearless."

Referring to the election announcement made this evening by the Prime Minister, Mrs Indira Gandhi, he said that this sudden decision after an authentic denial only a few days back, gave very little time for election propaganda and was very unfair to the opposition, putting it under a great handicap.

Mr Desai said that the Prime Minister had the right to fix the date of election according to her best judgement which had to be exercised in fairness to all concerned. He wished that right had been exercised fairly.

However, he said, the election decision had to be faced. It would be a test of the capacity of the people to understand their real interests consistently with the interests of the nation and irrespective of individual interest.

He hoped that the Government would be just and fair in its conduct of elections.

Mr Desai flatly denied that there had been any feelers from the Government for him to join its fold. He said that even if there were ever such feelers, he would not touch them.

He said that since he had just been released, he was not in a position to talk about opposition election strategy and prospects.

Mr Desai looked cheerful and spoke very clearly. In answer to a question, he said he was in very good health.

Mr Piloo Mody, BLD leader and MP, said that he was very happy about the coming election which was long overdue.

He said that he hoped the Government would lift the Emergency and press censorship and put MISA in cold storage. He expressed surprise that the elections had been called before all detenus had been released. He believed that there were still 10,000 inside, including some MPs.

Regarding opposition prospects in the election, he said they were "very good".

Indian Express, **January 19, 1977.**

Congress Debacle Around the Corner

Varanasi

THE Congress heartland, eastern and central Uttar Pradesh, has by all indications been won over by the Janata Party. With the sole exception of Rae Bareli, Congressmen at all levels do not consider even one of the 46 seats of this area absolutely safe for their party.

With the great majority of this big chunk of seats going over to the opposition the overall defeat of the Congress in the country may be around the corner.

There are four major factors which make a Janata victory in eastern and central UP almost certain. The first factor is overwhelming support for the Janata Party in all urban areas of this region. In big cities like Allahabad, Varanasi, Lucknow and Kanpur, popular feeling is so anti-Congress that the ruling party shies away from holding street meetings and processions. Lanes and by-lanes in the poor and crowded sectors of these cities display Janata flags and Congress symbols are hardly ever visible.

The second factor is that rural Muslim support, which for the last three decades has been the monopoly of the Congress Party, has shifted massively against the Congress. Muslims in this region have become solidly and vociferously anti-Congress as they feel that they have borne the brunt of forcible sterilisation drives and the consequent police firings at places like Sultanpur. This rural shift is more than the urban shift as the towns have always had pockets of opposition support which first came to the fore in the 1967 election.

The Muslim shift is a new phenomenon. Put together the urban and rural Muslim vote accounts for about 35 per cent of the electorate. If, as looks likely, most of this block votes for the Janata Party, Congress chances in UP would be extremely dim.

The third factor working against the Congress is the scale of electoral enthusiasm this time. A high turnout of voters invariably means a protest vote which will go against the Congress.

The key and final factor is that the opposition is united this time.

At the height of the Congress wave in 1971 the Congress won 73 of the 78 seats it contested on a majority vote of 48-56 per cent of the total votes cast in the state. This time the opposition votes will not be divided and even a small swing of about 10 per cent of the Congress vote away from that party would probably ensure a large Janata majority in this part of the country.

This does not mean there is going to be a landslide vote in favour of the Janata Party in this region. After an extensive tour of several eastern and central districts of UP it is apparent that the rural voter retains some degree of loyalty to the Congress despite his anger over sterilisation and enhanced land revenue. There is also fear and awe in the villages about the "sarkar" and what would happen to the villager if he voted against the Congress "sarkar".

But at the same time there are many villagers who are willing to take the risk of openly saying that they will vote for the Janata.

In this atmosphere, even the seats being contested by Congress notables like Mr K.D. Malaviya (Domariaganj), Mr V.P. Singh (Allahabad), Mr K.N. Singh (Sultanpur), Mr Chandrajit Yadav (Azamgarh), Mr S. Prasad (Bansgaon) and Mr Sanjay Gandhi (Amethi) look shaky.

Seats which look more hopeful for the Congress are being contested by figures who have feudal, princely or taluqdari connections with their constituencies. These are Balrampur (Maharani Raj Kumari Devi), Pratapgarh (Mr Dinesh Singh) and Bahraich (Mr Joginder Singh). Machlishahar is another constituency which is still considered loyal to Congress candidate, Mr Nageshwar Dwivedi.

Reports reaching Lucknow and Varanasi indicate that the four seats of the Bundelkhand region have become fiercely against the Congress. Ruling party MLA's from that area openly say "Sanjay Gandhi ne chaupat kardiya" (Sanjay Gandhi has ruined things).

Mr Sanjay Gandhi is reported to have alienated the electorate in that region by having called them traitors during the course of electoral meetings.

Indian Express, **March 14, 1977.**

Sanjay's Flighty Election Style

Amethi

THERE is a world of difference in the campaigning methods till now of Mr Sanjay Gandhi and Mr Ravindra Pratap Singh, the Congress and Janata candidates, respectively, from this eastern UP constituency.

Mr Gandhi, much before his official nomination as the Congress candidate, has been flying into the neighbouring old World War II airfield at Amhat, spending the day, making public speeches, meeting local personages and visiting some development projects, and then usually flying out the same evening. He has made several such flying visits over the past year.

Mr Pratap Singh, since he was released from jail in early February, has been going round from door to door with folded hands, at times even touching the feet of the humblest voters, saying that he spent 19 months in prison for their sake. He says that he could have earned Rs 50 a day as an advocate but gave this up for their sake.

The two most pressing issues on the minds of voters in Amethi and in the neighbouring areas invariably come up and Mr Singh promises that if his party comes to power there will be no forcible sterilisation and no forcible collection of enhanced land revenue. He also promises that land revenue rates would be lowered.

Apart from his five-point programme, Mr Gandhi has been extolling the virtues of hard work and progress and he repeated his call at two public meetings in this area yesterday.

Mr Gandhi has also encouraged voluntary work such as road building by Youth Congress workers from outside the area. He has also fostered Government investment in an industrial estate and a giant textile mill in his constituency.

But the talk in wayside teashops continues to centre round forcible sterilisation and forcible collection of land revenue.

Even among those who are angry about these issues, there are people who say they will vote for Sanjay because they feel their area will benefit from a lot of Government assistance once it becomes a confirmed VIP constituency.

Yet others deride this view and point to the roads and canals which are started every election time and left incomplete. As for the Youth Congress camp last summer near Amethi town, there is a feeling that outsiders came in for a short while, did some token work and then disappeared. One influential farmer in the area referred derisively to the Youth Congress boys at the camp as "hippies".

The contrast between the young canvassers of the Congress and the Janata Parties is clearly visible to any observer. The Congress boys are going round in jeeps shouting, "Sanjay Gandhi zindabad", while the Janata boys are moving from village to village on bicycles with only *chana* (dried gram) in their pockets to sustain them.

Neither side is as yet making any caste or community appeal as it may not work this time.

Indian Express, **February 20, 1977.**
(Jointly written with Bharati Bhargava.)

Sanjay Waterloo

New Delhi

MR Sanjay Gandhi has lost (March 20), despite the mammoth resources poured into his Amethi constituency, because he thought he could browbeat and bully all the people all the time. In the end he only deceived himself.

His contemptuous attitude towards voters was amply proved by his campaigning style in Amethi. He addressed dozens of meetings in the constituency, many of which were well attended. But most of the people in his audiences were "persuaded" to attend his meetings. They listened to him in awe and fear but seem to have gone away and voted against him, trusting in the secrecy of the ballot.

In his speeches, he told them that the forced sterilisations were false stories even while many in the crowd had suffered this humiliation themselves. He blamed the "few excesses" on officials and said they would be punished. Many in the crowd already knew that he was the one most responsible for insisting on forceful and rapid fulfilment of sterilisation targets.

Mr Gandhi told the voters that Mr Charan Singh, the Janata leader, would sterilise them. But what about those who had already been sterilised? They listened in silence and appear to have gone quietly and voted against him.

He told the youth of Amethi that the future belonged to them. But it was the youth of Amethi who most resented the presence of the brash, upper-class boys from Delhi and other big cities who used to come to Amethi and treat the outing as a picnic while doing some token work, building a road or two in the name of the Youth Congress.

Many local young men resented the fact that while they were unemployed and under-fed, these healthy-looking outsiders were being brought in to build roads in their villages.

During his padyatras or jaunts through the villages, he thought he could impress the "simple" villagers by almost running through them without talking and listening to individual persons. The few times he did stop and try and talk, it was a fiasco. The villager would be tongue-tied with fright and Mr Gandhi did not know what to say and how to comfort him.

In stark contrast, the stocky Janata candidate, Mr Ravindra Pratap Singh, not only spoke individually to thousands of voters but slept many nights on a bed of hay in countless village barns while Mr Gandhi drove back in his jeep convoy to specially reconditioned rest houses.

Indian Express, **March 21, 1977.**

Divergent Pulls in Indira's Constituency

Rae Bareli

THERE is a wave of indignation and fear about the Emergency in this constituency. But these feelings are more than neutralised by the calm assessment that being the Prime Minister, Mrs Gandhi, has brought tangible material benefits and could bring further gifts for the electorate.

The teacher of a village primary school told us how he had been forced to get sterilised under the most unwholesome pressures but he would still vote for the Congress as the area had been developed greatly over a period of several years. The kisans around him owning three to six acres of land said that they now reaped three crops a year compared to a single crop some years ago, due to the tubewells they had installed with Government loans. There was no doubting that the area had progressed.

Yet the same villagers expressed cynicism about such election-time happenings as electricity for their tubewells being on for 24 hours, compared to 10 years of sporadic performance. They also repeated how sterilisation cases were demanded by the Government for anything from licences to secondary school places for their children.

An advocate in Rae Bareli town said that the family planning drive "has done wonders for the opposition."

Most of the town's lawyers, college teachers and students appear to be ardent supporters of the Janata Party but are doing no active canvassing. The Janata Party campaign manager is a sincere old Socialist backed by a number of former Jan Sangh student activists. They seem impressed by the rhetoric of Mr Raj Narain, the Janata candidate who draws large crowds when he is in town. The admiring crowds may not all be Janata voters. The Congress campaign here is led by seasoned sevaks of the Congress Seva Dal.

Nehru, Feroze Gandhi and Indira Gandhi are not mere names here but are known and revered by the veterans of the

Seva Dal. The local Seva Dal chairman proudly shows you the room next to his where Feroze Gandhi spent many months when he represented this constituency.

A number of officers of the Intelligence Bureau of the Central Government and of the Uttar Pradesh CID are in town, for what purpose one does not know. Local lawyers allege that some of them are being harassed in petty ways by the local intelligence unit of the CID.

State ministers also find time to visit Rae Bareli frequently. The district administration, consequently, is constantly tied up with such visits.

Indian Express, **February 21, 1977.**
(Jointly written with Bharati Bhargava.)

Where the Gods Failed

New Delhi

THE gods came bearing gifts. The humble humans graciously accepted the gifts, smiled knowingly and voted away the gods who had reigned so long in Rae Bareli and elsewhere. For the humans knew that the gods had also borne the big stick not very long ago and wielded it on them as if they were sheep.

This is not a fable. It is the story of the experiences and fortitude of the people of Rae Bareli.

Over the past decade, Mrs Gandhi's Government lavished much care and expense over the first lady's constituency. Some people did benefit. Parched fields turned green and began to yield three crops a year in place of one. Bank loans, tubewells and electricity made this possible. Those who had fields prospered.

The landless rural labourers who did not own any patch of earth continued to live in poverty.

An industrial estate was set up near the town of Rae Bareli

with a huge complex of the public sector Indian Telephone Industries (ITI) as its centre-piece.

The ITI factory provided many jobs but the locals felt that most of them went to outsiders. A mistake had been made. The telecommunication industry needed skilled workmen. Rae Bareli lacked the skills. A more basic industry would have made the locals happier. But again the planning had failed even in the serious game of gaining votes.

The district administration helped distribute the gifts, but in the process of pandering to the whims of the droves of VIPs, who insisted on paying a pilgrimage to this sacred constituency, it could not keep up with the demands of day-to-day governance.

Then came the Emergency and thinking that it would be "a thousand-year-reign", the bureaucrats and the local Congress busybodies decided they must ruthlessly implement the holy word that came down from Delhi and Lucknow on sterilisation, on forcible land revenue collection and on arbitrary irrigation rates.

And all protest was muffled under the mask of MISA, although the machinery of repression was much less callous than in other, less fortunate, areas which did not have the Prime Minister as their mentor.

In mid-January, elections were announced and the lid was taken off the brew of simmering resentment. But the people did not boil over. They still talked in hushed tones. They watched and waited and listened patiently to the explanations of Mrs Gandhi and other Congress leaders. They listened to her talk about the excesses of others, about the fruits of the Emergency, about the promising future and about the sacrifices her family had made.

Through all this, they kept their own counsel and some wisely pretended that they would vote for the Congress. On March 16, the people of Rae Bareli quietly went and cast their lot – against Mrs Gandhi.

They no longer believed her.

Indian Express, **March 23, 1977.**

Indira Resigns after Wild Swings of Fortune

New Delhi

Mrs Gandhi was sworn in as Prime Minister for the first time on January 24, 1966, succeeding Mr Lal Bahadur Shastri who died of a heart attack in Taskhent. She resigned this morning (March 22) at 11 am after being Prime Minister for 11 years and two months.

She was also sworn in as Prime Minister after the elections of 1967 and 1971 when the Congress Party's popularity swung from one extreme to another and has swung yet again in 1977. With Mrs Gandhi at its helm in 1971 the Congress won 352 of the 518 Lok Sabha seats

These wild swings reflected Mrs Gandhi's great capacity to take risks and bold decisions. In 1967 she went to the polls at the head of a disunited party and did badly. She made up for this by fighting the established "strongmen" of the party and splitting the Congress in November 1969. She ruled the country at the head of a minority Government, supported by the CPI and the DMK, till the snap election of March 1971.

Then with the slogan of "Garibi Hatao" and some populist measures like the nationalisation of banks and an initially thwarted derecognition of the princes to bolster her, she stormed the hustings and the people gave her their support, love and loyalty.

Her greatest hour was yet to come. It was not in domestic political decisions that she achieved her glory but in foreign policy. The cool and calculated handling of the Bangladesh crisis and the final victory over Pakistan on December 16, 1971, was her finest hour.

Drought and the economic crisis, culminating in the railway strike of 1974, were to follow together with the resurgence of popular feeling with Mr Jayaprakash Narayan at its head.

To top all this, she was unseated by the Allahabad High Court on June 12, 1975. She refused to resign under pressure and only four Congress MPs dared to stand up to her and openly ask for her resignation.

They and thousands of her other opponents were arrested in midnight swoops on June 25-26, 1975, and the Emergency was proclaimed the following day. This clandestine method of operation, aided and abetted by the growing importance conferred by her on her son, Sanjay, was to become the hallmark of the Emergency.

Propaganda was another feature of the Emergency. This was greatly encouraged through censorship and control of the press, the radio and TV. The propaganda centred around the 20-point and 5-point programmes and around the "indomitable and faultless" personalities of Mrs Indira Gandhi and Mr Sanjay Gandhi.

There were no attempts to gauge objectively the public reaction to such unsavoury programmes as forced sterilisation which became particularly unpopular. There was serious resistance at places like Turkman Gate. But all this was pushed under the carpet.

In late 1976, prices began to go up again after a notable lull of two years, the monsoon was not expected to be bountiful once again and the opposition had been passively in jail for 19 months.

In this atmosphere, Mrs Gandhi decided to go to the polls on January 18, 1977.

Since then a historic political drama has unfolded through the reassertion of the popular will.

Indian Express, **March 23, 1977.**

People Angry With Janata

Rae Bareli

MR Raj Narain asks for a glass water at an official lunch. He is promptly offered three glasses of water plus a glass of orange juice by officials bending over in supplication.

Mr Raj Narain, MP from Rae Bareli and Minister of Health, seems puzzled and embarrassed but takes it all in his stride. He can hardly shout at these 'humble' officials doing all they can to be courteous.

Asked why he is not looking too happy on a day (March 20) which marks his electoral victory over Mrs Indira Gandhi a year ago, Mr Raj Narain manages a tired smile and says, in his husky voice, "I am unwell".

All is not too well with his constituency either. Lawyers and students, the barometer of political change, are now as angry with the Janata as they were with the Congress when I last visited Rae Bareli, 13 months ago. The class of fawning officials who offer orange juice to the Minister, are not averse to offering the big stick to lesser mortals at the slightest hint of trouble. And Janata rule has become associated with official rule. So, where is the difference between the Congress police raj and the Janata police raj, some agitated young advocates of Rae Bareli want to know?

They cite a recent incident at Lalganj-Bainswara where students were severely beaten up by the police for insisting on registration of an accident in which a Harijan student had fallen off a bus and injured himself. Mr Raj Narain, who a year ago would probably have launched a demonstration against police brutality, is now irritated with the whole episode. If someone fell off a bus, why did the students have to kick up such a fuss, Mr Raj Narain wants to know?

The arrogance of power is not yet openly apparent in Mr Raj Narain's voice, but it is creeping in. The victor of Amethi over Mr Sanjay Gandhi, Mr Ravindra Pratap Singh, is also in Rae Bareli for the opening of a sophisticated, ultra-modern telephone equipment factory. On questioning, he agrees that such plants are not the answer to the problems of poverty and unemployment in a backward district like Rae Bareli. He claims that the Janata Government is doing something to develop villages, but is rather vague about it all.

Are the people getting discontented with his party? Mr.

Pratap Singh parties the question and humbly suggests that nobody and no party is elected for all times. He does not rule out a change of ruling party after a few years but does not say who will then come to power.

The telephone factory, on which Rs 19 crores of public money has been spent, is a mechanical marvel but it has to date provided only around 1,400 jobs to the local populace with another 600 going to outsiders who, due to their skills, get the better paid jobs. The people of Rae Bareli were unhappy about skilled jobs at the factory going to outsiders during the Indira Gandhi days. Their complaint is still valid. With an outlay of Rs 19 crores, the factory has provided one job (counting only the locals employed) per Rs 1,35,714 of capital investment.

Another factory coming up in the district will produce carpets at automated speed, at half the cost and double the output of traditional weavers. This is being done with Danish collaboration. The net result will be to throw more carpet-weavers out of work from a skill which has been theirs for centuries and without help from Denmark. All the Janata talk of small-scale industries and labour-intensive programmes is being negated by policies which have not been able to cut themselves off from the projects initiated under Congress rule.

No wonder the wizened, old chairman of the Congress Seva Dal – who owns Laxmi Hotel in Rae Bareli town where Feroze Gandhi's old room is still revered – is convinced that the people would vote for Mrs Gandhi again if given the chance. It is clear that if they do it will not be for her or the Congress but against the Janata, just as last year they had voted against the Congress. Would it be wrong to presume that the people want a change which will bring them some material gain? But it never comes.

Indian Express, **March 23, 1978.**

Fighting Spirit at *Indian Express*

THE smell of fear, the musty odour of fear-induced sweat, pervaded the Emergency. It was an unknown, new odour for the upper and middle classes, most of whom had no perception of the midnight knock and had never considered even the remote possibility of being whisked off, unknown and unsung, to some dank cell. This may have been the reality for the voiceless and penniless wretched of the Indian earth through history, before and after 1947, but for the post-Independence articulate classes it was a new experience to fear that loose talk and unbounded expression could land them in a prison. Relatively very few were picked up but the smell of fear hushed the vast majority of the babbling classes.

At the *Indian Express*' musty offices in Delhi, there was the smell of dust but no odour of fear or, perhaps, only a whiff. Fear is more infectious than a virus. The disease-ridden vector was missing at the *Indian Express*. Its proprietor and many of its key staff showed no fear or, at least, hid it successfully from their colleagues. Some of them may have had their faults – avarice, politicking, parochial prejudices, hubris – but at a time of universal panic, they proved they were true men (which was not a pejorative term in those days). Ram Nath Goenka, B.D. Goenka, S. Mulgaokar, V.K. Narasimhan, Kuldip Nayar, Ajit Bhattacharjea, H.K. Dua, Virendra Kapoor, 'Piloo' Saxena, S.K. Verma, Abdul Rahman, Rajendra Bajpai and many other *Express* men and women in Delhi and others in *Express* offices all over the country, especially S. Krishnamoorthy in Bombay, displayed rare fighting spirit and professional pride in their work.

With such unruffled and steady companions, most correspondents, reporters, sub-editors and also the business and managerial staff began to feel an *esprit de corps*, a sense of mission to counter an evil and autocratic regime. *Express* men and women used little tricks and put in snide or subtle anti-establishment reports and comments which could be picked up by discerning readers, played down the glorious and glowing propaganda reports put out by the news agencies, and played up foreign reports which pointed out the gross failures of dictatorships and ruling dynasties abroad.

When one morning, the Government abruptly cut off all news agency wires to *Express*, the paper relied on its own network of correspondents all over the country and its two or three foreign correspondents to try and fill the gap. The foreign news gap was, however, too wide to be adequately filled. The solution was simple and effective. I remember staying up till two in the morning for about three weeks, monitoring broadcasts from all over the world on Ram Nath Goenka's massive old shortwave radio set in his guest suite. The noise of static often disrupted hearing but the reports we were able to publish the same morning, datelined Moscow, Washington, Peking (now Beijing) and London, were all from the old man's guest room at Bahadur Shah Zafar Marg, New Delhi.

When Indira Gandhi announced on January 18, 1977, that there was going to be an election, I went off to interview Morarji Desai the same wintry night. He had just been released from isolated captivity in a Government guest house in Haryana and driven down to his old residence on Dupleix Road. His cheeks were as rosy and fresh as a baby's. I asked him if he would be forming a united opposition. His reply was characteristic: "How can I think of uniting the opposition when I have not even had time to go to the bathroom?" I persisted and got an interesting interview from him which *Express* published next morning on the front page. Most other national newspapers continued to remain fearful and were reluctant to publish news about the opposition as the Emergency continued to be in force till the election results were announced on March 20 and 21, 1977.

Bharati Bhargava, a colleague at *Express,* and I asked to be sent to cover the beginning of Sanjay Gandhi's election campaign in Amethi which he had nurtured during the Emergency. *Express* promptly packed us off to Amethi and to

Rae Bareli, Indira Gandhi's constituency. The first person we met at the railway station near Amethi, a rickshaw-puller, told us that he would not even think of voting for Sanjay Gandhi or his party as the district administration had treated people brutally during the Emergency months, pushing them out of their homes and arbitrarily picking up people and dragging them to be forcibly sterilised. Sanjay kicked off his campaign with a sneer on his face, referring in his first election speech at Amethi to the opposition leaders as "*keedhas*" (insects) who should be crushed.

One riddle remained unresolved. The Emergency regime had used its full bag of underhand tactics to try and bring *Express* down to its knees: cutting off electricity, withdrawing all Government and public sector advertising, cutting all credit from financial institutions, initiating numerous cases in the courts, threatening its proprietor and editors, creating newsprint shortages and snapping news agency wires. Why did Indira Gandhi not use the ultimate weapon and arrest Ram Nath Goenka whose bold leadership of *Express* had been such a major thorn in the flesh?

One day just after the Emergency was over and Ram Nath Goenka was in a relaxed and expansive mood, I asked him this very question. He gave an interesting explanation. At one time much before the Emergency, he had employed Feroze Gandhi, the estranged husband of Indira Gandhi, in the *Express* group. At that time, both Feroze and Indira Gandhi had been fairly close to him and regarded him as a sort of father figure. They were going through a difficult patch in their marriage and both of them wrote a bunch of letters to him accusing each other of a range of personal misdemeanours. Ram Nath Goenka had filed away these intensely personal letters. According to Ram Nath Goenka, Indira Gandhi had convinced herself that if she had arrested him, these personal letters would have immediately been published worldwide in the foreign press. Ram Nath Goenka told me that Indira Gandhi's perception had been totally wrong. He would have never publicised these letters, come what may, as he could not even consider carrying out such an act of grave personal betrayal.

There were other figures of the same mould as Ram Nath Goenka whose journals defied the Emergency despite threats and harassment. Those who come to mind from the English language press are C.R. Irani of *The Statesman*, A.D. Gorwala of *Opinion*, Romesh and Raj Thapar of *Seminar*, Nikhil Chakravartty of *Mainstream* and Krishna Raj of *Economic and Political Weekly*. This is by no means an exhaustive list.

The Emergency regime was rough with the press but was much more nasty and brutish to the general populace of the poor and underprivileged in northern India while trumpeting its feigned concern for them through its twenty-point programme – a hypocritical tradition which has continued since then, regardless of the party or Prime Minister in power. Oppression of the poor was uniform and without much communal and caste bias. The result was a short period of genuine emotional harmony between communities and castes during and immediately after the Emergency.

Indian Express, **July 7, 1995.**

Chapter-10

Second-Rate Yanks

OUR information technology (IT) software sector employs four lakh persons while small-scale industry directly and indirectly provides work for seven crore persons. In the fiscal year, 2000-01, software exports are estimated to have earned the country $ 6 billion while our humble migrant workers, mostly in the Gulf, sent home double that amount, $ 12 billion, from their meagre earnings. The IT software sector is pampered with a host of incentives and tax holidays provided by an enthusiastic Government while small-scale industry is under attack from all sides and the Indian worker in the Gulf is ignored or derided. In a remarkable display of surrendering the national interest, the Government allowed unrestricted imports of 714 categories of foreign goods into the country from April 1, 2000. Many of these foreign goods are subsidised by the producing country and sold here at unbelievably cheap rates. Such imports have caused the closure of thousands of small-scale industrial units and devastated the livelihoods of lakhs of workers. The Government is also withdrawing reservations under which specified goods could only be produced by our small-scale factories.

From April 1, 2001, the agricultural sector, which is the country's largest employer, has also been under attack by enhanced imports of farm products from the United States and the European Union which pamper their farmers with hundreds of billions of dollars worth of direct income support and subsidies. Simultaneously, the same countries brazenly demand that India and other developing countries should withdraw the relatively measly concessions given to their poverty-stricken farmers.

Capitulation to commercial pressures by the United States and other wealthy countries – which now disguise their trading interests under the garb of a one-sided globalisation – does no harm to the upper layers of our society. Selective and biased globalisation only destroys small farms, small industries, small businesses and small people. The sons, daughters-in-law, nieces and nephews of senior politicians, bureaucrats, business executives, lawyers, doctors and other professionals benefit from high-paid jobs in the IT sector, in banks and in multi-national companies which sell everything from diamond-studded watches to fizzy drinks to satisfy the consumerist cravings of India's upper crust. Their sons and daughters also constitute the new wave of NRIs in Los Angeles, Long Island and London, many of whom fervently support the fanaticism of the BJP and its parivar with funds and fanciful propaganda from the fleshpots of the West.

There is no mystery about the BJP-led Government looking towards the United States as its role model. The Government and the bulk of the great Indian upper and middle classes long for the power and glory of leading a great nation, second only to the United States. The Indian reality humiliates and frustrates them. They drug themselves with delusions and myths. The latest myth, encouraged by an orgasmic national media, is that India is about to explode onto the world stage as a super power, solely on the basis of churning out computer software and software operators. Twenty crore Indians thirst in summer for a satisfying gulp of drinking water and thirty crore Indians suffer daily from malnutrition as they cannot afford to eat nutritious food, but hold on, the IT whiz-kids will convert us overnight into the Bill Gates of the world. Delusions of grandeur and shortcuts to instant greatness abound.

The wild applause all over the country which greeted the May 1998 nuclear explosions at Pokhran was mainly a warm massage for our national ego. The explosions were meant to show the world that we had achieved great power status with a few expensive bangs. The world remained unimpressed by our show of bombs and missiles. The United States was particularly angered by our nuclear pretensions. We placated the Americans by signing an agreement in December 1999 to grant them premature trade concessions and followed that up with an opulent and obsequious welcome for Bill Clinton in March 2000. We were charmed by every little gesture and smile of the Big White Father just as we are captivated by every technological gizmo, consumer goodie and cultural artefact from his country. Every English-speaking, middle class teenager seems to model himself/herself on American fads, fantasies and fashions, from Nikes and Levis to Heavy Metal and Rap, from Revlon to Calvin Klein. Adults from the same class are almost as bedazzled as their children. American culture is good for American commerce. In our yearning to become second-rate Yanks, we are selling our souls and our remaining family silver.

Selling the Economy Down the Ganga

ON March 19, US President Bill Clinton will be arriving in Delhi. On April 1, All Fools' Day, India will be embarking on a process of unhampered import of 1,429 items from the United States. Very quietly and without open debate, on December 16, 1999, Susan G. Esserman, US Deputy Trade Representative, and N.N. Khanna, Special Secretary in the Ministry of Commerce, signed an agreement which lifts all quantitative import restrictions on 714 items by April 1, 2000, and on the remaining 715 items by April 1, 2001. The December agreement has also pre-empted the February budget. In addition, under other protocols, India's rights to impose countervailing customs duties on the imported items will be severely constrained. Similar agreements, to be supervised by the World Trade Organisation (WTO), have been negotiated with the European Union and other key economic powers. These agreements could lead to the ruination of the livelihoods of tens of millions of our labouring people and to the destruction of hundreds of thousands of our small farms and business enterprises.

Allowing in generally unrestricted imports on such a large scale and in such a short time span will have a disastrous impact on domestic industry and agriculture. The trade agreements will also make us dependent for our basic food requirements on foreign countries, causing the loss of our food security which is the most crucial ingredient of national security, more fundamental than even the defence forces. Foreign investment in India and privatisation of the public sector are issues of relatively marginal consequence compared to the opening up of the Indian market to 1,429 foreign items, ranging from basic necessities like rice, bajra, potatoes and milk to textiles and footwear. Millions of the poorest agricultural labourers, subsistence farmers, fishermen, dairy-women and small-scale producers of shoes, sandals, garments, rubber goods, electrical fuses and wires, and hundreds of other local products could become unemployed and lose their enterprises in the next few years as our markets are flooded with the deviously subsidised produce of highly automated farms and factories of developed economies. This is not an alarmist scenario: Russia, other constituents of the former Soviet Union and several African countries have already been denuded of major sectors of their industry, agriculture and enterprise, and their peoples pauperised as their Governments were pressurised to surrender their national economic sovereignty by Western-dominated financial institutions.

It is unintelligible that a nationalist Government is selling Bharat Mata's economy down the Ganga and the opposition parties, including the Communists, are pre-occupied with the job prospects of lethargic insurance clerks and corrupt employees of state electricity boards rather than with the impending threat to the sustenance of the lives of major segments of our populace. The BJP, whose agenda is being increasingly set by its partners in the Sangh Parivar, is dazzled by the prospects of purifying the country's culture and mesmerised by threats to internal security. The Sangh Parivar's purification rites at the ghats of Kashi, in the Valentine gift shops of Kanpur and in the corridors of the Indian Council of Historical Research enthral the BJP-led Government. Kashmir, terrorism and the ISI agitate the Government. Yet, these are not sufficient reasons for the Government of India to surrender our national economic sovereignty in a fit of hazy forgetfulness.

The answer to the riddle seems to lie in the grand obsession of the Government, the opposition and the great majority of opinion-makers, including the media, for India to be acknowledged as a major strategic power sitting at the world's high tables. As we are not yet a modern, advanced country, the short cut to world star status is perceived to be through entertaining the commercial and economic wheedling of the major G-7 powers (which also dominate the WTO) while retaining our nuclear standing. We will not sign the CTBT but are signing away our economic heritage in agreements with the major powers and the WTO. The stealth and unseemly hurry in which the December trade agreement was signed points to a willingness to placate the United States and other developed countries and, hopefully as a reward, to win a place at the tables of the major powers as a strategic partner. In the event, we might win this place but as a lesser partner, much like an economically emasculated Russia, tolerated as an extra on the fringes of the G-7.

The Russian experience is a salutary warning. One of the prime reasons that the Soviet Union surrendered its economic sovereignty in 1991 was that the cadres of the ruling Communist Party, corrupted over long years of a monopoly of power, sensed an opportunity to become instantly richer. They grabbed their main chance by converting themselves into robber-baron capitalists, throwing open the domestic market overnight to imported goods and selling off their country's huge natural resources to the West. The Russian economy is now largely controlled by Communists-turned-mafiosi supported by the West. In this rush to economic suicide, the

Russian people were never consulted and did not have any democratic experience or organisations to resist the cataclysmic changes.

Fortunately, India is not the Soviet Union. India is an open society with a large and enterprising entrepreneurial class. In disregarding these positive factors, the BJP is acting strangely against its own self-interest. By hurriedly agreeing to open Indian markets to an invasion of foreign goods, the BJP-led Government has opted to follow the lead of big businessmen and industrialists represented by their associations – CII, FICCI and Assocham. The Government has ignored the interests of thousands of small entrepreneurs who form a vital component of the political support base of the BJP and its partners in the Sangh Parivar. Of India's half-million joint-stock companies, both public and private limited, only 8,000 are openly listed on the stock market and only about 1,500 of these have regularly traded shares. Of the total of half-million companies, over 400,000 are private limited companies. These 400,000 companies and countless business partnerships – and not the over-glorified 1,500 – are the backbone of the nation's small-scale commerce and industry which employs millions of workers. Capital-intensive big industry swallows a lot of credit and employs relatively few workers. Thousands of dynamic, wheeling-dealing, business families have a direct stake in their private limited companies and partnerships. Most of them are dependent on the domestic market; relatively few are export-oriented. Big industry can always sell out at a handsome profit to foreign competition when it gets too hot but large segments of the small-scale sector will just be wiped out.

The impact of the trade agreements on the small-scale agricultural sector would be even more disastrous. Millions of peasants (many of whom are tribals), cultivating small, dry-zone plots, and selling their tiny surpluses of bajra, jowar, ragi and maize at a strictly local level, could be driven off their lands and into urban slums due to imports of cheap grain from big farms in North America and Western Europe assisted by disguised subsidies. For instance, the US Government gives direct income support payments to American grain farmers and stubbornly maintains that this is not a form of subsidy. At the Seattle WTO meeting, US support payments were a major bone of contention with the European Union which doles out subsidies in other devious forms. The crucial importance of national food security has been ensured by the Americans and Europeans while we are on the verge of divesting our security in basic food supplies. The RSS has repeatedly and pointedly stressed that it wants the Government to focus on rural development, small-scale industries, tribal welfare and national security. The Government has shown an abiding commitment only to an extremely narrow concept of national security. It is time the RSS and its brothers in the Swadeshi Jagran Manch and the Bharatiya Mazdoor Sangh spent more of their energy in preventing the Government from attempting economic suicide at the cost of rural development, small industries and the tribal peoples.

The Times of India, **March 4, 2000.**

The Foreign Bug Bites Deep

OUR opinion-makers, NGOs and political leaders are increasingly entrapped by the tawdry glamour of cutting a dashing figure on the world stage while crucial issues affecting the lives of millions at home are sidelined. A pretty face, firm breasts and bottoms, and smart repartees to inane queries "goes to prove that the next millennium belongs to India", if the leading editorial comment of one of the country's major dailies is to be believed. This dizzy height of journalistic pap was mounted on the occasion of yet another Indian girl being awarded the tinsel crown of Miss World. Most of the sensitised world now looks upon international beauty contests as crass circuses which demean women but our middle classes persist in lapping up such winning shows as demonstrations of India's universal prowess.

There is a slight problem of perception here in that much of the rest of the world continues to regard India as the land of emaciated babies, illiterate peasants and massive disasters such as the Orissa cyclone despite our bombs, missiles and Miss Worlds. It is naïve to expect our middle and upper classes to take a clear-eyed view of our own national realities and not to get carried away by every little tinsel-town achievement on the world stage. Looking inwards rather than outwards has become difficult to achieve as almost every opinion-making leadership group and institution has been bitten by the foreign bug. A feverish greed for foreign, usually Western, funding or foreign acclaim or even foreign jaunts has distorted the vision of a wide spectrum of our political, business, academic, scientific and intellectual 'elites'.

Shrill leftists and nationalist radicals are the most hypocritical along with Hindutva *sevaks*. Vishwa Hindu Parishad leaders regularly visit the United States and Western Europe to seek dollars, pounds and marks even as they extol the virtues of Bharatiya *sanskriti* and *swadeshi*, and abuse Western-Christian interference. Well-known leftist intellectuals and nationalist radicals rant about American and Western hegemony even as they eagerly seek and grab invitations from Western NGOs and universities. Seminar and lecture circuits in the fleshpots of the West keep these radicals happily occupied for several months every year while providing a welcome cache of dollars passed off as tax-free expenses. The thrill of foreign flights and applause from fringe Western audiences has become an addictive drug for many whose mental horizons are attuned to cutting a dashing figure on the world stage rather than painstakingly building a firm support base at home. Several prominent Indian intellectuals and 'activists' – whose fulsome theories are composed on the basis of railing against the conspiracies of the West – have little support here but attract cult followings among Western anti-establishment academics. Their 'activism' consists largely of getting onto a flight bound for Amsterdam, Stockholm, Oslo, New York, Toronto and, increasingly, Tokyo, now that the Japanese are expending large funds to hold dialogues with Third World groupies.

The dilution of our resolve to resist Western blandishments where it matters was recently most evident at the World Trade Organisation (WTO) conference in Seattle. Despite Commerce Minister Murasoli Maran's claims about resisting the Americans on their intrusive attempts to foist labour and environment issues onto trade negotiations, it was the tiny Caribbean countries and the African bloc which finally refused to be bulldozed by the United States into instant consensus agreements at Seattle. It is Caribbean and African resistance which has temporarily halted American commercial triumphalism and not Indian ambiguity.

Many of the American and European NGOs and labour unions who were protesting on the streets of Seattle had their own genuine concerns about job losses and wage depletion among their own people and equally sincere but selfish concerns about environmental issues. Our NGOs and unions ought to be just as seriously concerned about the interests of our own workers and small farmers. It should be apparent that the WTO is being used by Bill Clinton and other Western politicians to further pauperise the people of the poorer countries through the 'dumping' of agricultural and industrial products from the United States and Western Europe. Such tactics have already ruined small-scale agriculture and industry in several African countries.

There has been no significant mobilisation here by NGOs and unions to protest against Western manipulation of the WTO. Instead we have the bizarre spectacle of at least one shrill radical environmentalist flying off to Seattle to join the street protests of Western NGOs and returning in self-satisfied triumph to proclaim victory through a press statement after the failure of the WTO conference. Small farmers in the

Philippines protested on the eve of the Seattle talks but there was, not surprisingly, a quiescent silence here. The will of our NGOs to protest has been diminished by constant flirtation with Western NGOs whose interests are often, though not always, in conflict with the livelihood of the poorest Indian labourers and farmers.

As for Government officials and ministers, their infatuation with the West has become obscene. While thousands of bloated, disfigured bodies of our countrymen and women were still being found in early November in the cyclone-ravaged fields of Orissa, the overwhelming concern of that state's Chief Secretary, S.B. Mishra, was to stick somehow to his plan to fly to the United States and he did manage to fly off to the promised land. A few thousand deaths and a few million fellow Indians on the verge of dehydration and starvation cannot come in the way of a glamorous trip abroad by our administrators and political leaders.

After all, Orissa's Chief Secretary was not exceptionally mindless. A few days later our President and Prime Minister also flew off abroad. On the eve of his departure for the Commonwealth summit in Durban and 12 days after the cyclone struck Orissa, the Prime Minister made the supreme effort of appointing a task force for Orissa headed by his man for all seasons, George Fernandes. The enormity of the disaster was apparent to the entire world within 48 hours but Mr Vajpayee, instead of mobilising succour from the entire nation and monitoring the relief and rescue effort on a daily basis, chose to treat it as a routine rehabilitation exercise. There was no attempt to set up a special cell within the Prime Minister's Office to oversee the Orissa situation and not even a radio and television appeal to the nation from the PM to come to the aid of millions of desperate Indian citizens. The President, who is said to be a sensitive man, carried on regardless with his state visit to an inconsequential country like Austria. On their flights back from Durban and Vienna, our two leaders addressed their accompanying press contingents and, by all accounts, were very pleased with themselves for having convinced various foreign leaders about the dangers of cross-border terrorism and military rule in Pakistan!

Having returned to Delhi, Atal Bihari Vajpayee and K.R. Narayanan will be spending an inordinate amount of time and official resources on laying out the red carpet for foreign visitors, now that the pleasant winter season has arrived in the capital. Such illustrious personages as the Vice-President of Uruguay have already been welcomed this winter. Flowery speeches at ritual banquets and renaming of roads after unknown foreign heroes will continue while banal decisions about such boring issues as universal primary education and rural health care will be kept in suspended animation for ever and ever.

Economic and Political Weekly, **December 25, 1999.**

Hindu-Muslim Hallucinations

WHILE middle America's insular ignorance about the world at large has been dented by the events of September 11, India's middle and upper classes have, since that day of infamy, gone into overdrive in their long-standing obsession with foreign affairs. Unwilling and unable to tackle our awesome economic and social crises at home, our dominant classes constantly turn outwards to an endless mental involvement with international issues which is reflected in the priorities of our pseudo-nationalist government. It is an age-old, self-deluding, psychological trick: avoid looking at the dung heaps at your doorstep by gazing at the stars in the distant firmament.

The pathological fallout here of September 11 has also brought into the open a hitherto hidden fracture which has long divided us. It is considered politically incorrect to examine the Hindu-Muslim societal fracture but it is about time we faced this gap squarely, without engaging in sanctimonious humbug. Far too many upper class and upper caste Hindus have psyched themselves into believing that they are the kissing cousins of 'Aryan' white Americans and far too many lower middle class Muslims see themselves as pan-Islamic brothers of sundry Arabs, Iranians and Uzbeks. (The poorer Hindus and Muslims have no time for such exotic diversions, involved as they are in seeking their daily starvation diets.) These pathetic pretensions are currently mirrored in the increasingly bitter feelings of betrayal by the 'other' community triggered by the generally conflicting – with some honourable exceptions – Hindu and Muslim reactions to America's war against terrorism/Afghanistan/Islam.

Muslims are embittered by Hindu indifference about the deaths of innocent Afghan children and women in the US bombing campaign while Hindus are angered by Muslim admiration for the defiant Taliban and Osama bin Laden. Hindus embrace the US as a saviour and ally in the global battle against Islamic terrorism while Muslims vilify the Americans as global oppressors who back such brutal regimes as that of Israel. The Hindu-Muslim crossfire is basically motivated by the obsequious cultural adoration by upper class Hindus for every vulgar American fad and the ridiculous search for spiritual solace by Sunni Muslims in the arid sands of Arabia and by Shia Muslims in the pomegranate groves of Iran. In the process, we end up deriding or ignoring the lustre and refinement of our own rich cultural and spiritual tapestry woven together through millennia with the purest silken strands of saffron, green and other brilliant colours. Not surprisingly, the BJP's young thugs who recently vandalised the Taj Mahal cannot comprehend that they are mocking at their own heritage.

There is much to appreciate in the wider Western and Islamic worlds but we have gone overboard in veneration for their least attractive segments, the United States and the Arabian-Persian Gulf. Though materially wealthy, in every indicator of human development the US and the Gulf region are relatively backward. Within the Western world, the United States lags behind in public health, social welfare and human rights and leads in criminal activity and police brutality. According to the *UN Human Development Report 2001*, the US ranks sixth in the world human development index (HDI) after Norway, Australia, Canada, Sweden and Belgium, though it has the second highest per capita income after the tiny banking haven of Luxembourg. In women's empowerment, it ranks tenth. In public expenditure on health as a percentage of total national income, the US falls behind 19 countries, including its former *bete noire*, Nicaragua. It has the highest number of people in prison in the entire world and its police forces have an international reputation for running riot. Along with its friend and ally, Saudi Arabia, it is one of the handful of countries which executes juvenile offenders.

Saudi Arabia, despite being one of the richest countries in the developing world, is medieval in the treatment of its populace. It is controlled by an avaricious, promiscuous and cruelly despotic royal family which publicly executes people for minor offences. In the past 20 years, Saudi Arabia's per capita income has dwindled by 40 per cent due to being squandered by the royal family on its thousands of opulent princelings, on wasteful defence purchases and by selling its oil wealth at depressed prices dictated by the US. Saudi Arabia ranks 42nd in per capita income but is much lower in the HDI at the 68th position. No wonder, the Saudi regime is currently feeling highly insecure that its populace could revolt against it. Iran is less medieval than Saudi Arabia, though it is hardly a paragon of virtue. Iran ranks 69th in per capita income and 90th in the HDI. The smaller Gulf countries are relatively better off but are in no hurry to become progressive societies.

Most Gulf Arabs, Iranians and Americans are deeply ignorant about the Indian sub-continent which is lumped together by them as an area of dismal darkness and degrading poverty. They have vague notions of a seething, monolithic mass of dark-skinned South Asians who cannot be differentiated between Indians, Pakistanis, Bangladeshis, Hindus, Muslims, Sikhs and pagans, all clamouring for immigration into their fair lands. These subliminal prejudices have surfaced forcefully in the US after September 11 in the form of hundreds of vengeful attacks and incidents of harassment against South Asians of all denominations. In the Gulf, South Asians are exploited and abused routinely by their Arab employers. In contrast, Muslim-majority Indonesia, Malaysia and Egypt are vibrant, liberal societies which have a genuine affection for Indians of all faiths. They are probably the only places left in the world where Indian visitors – not immigrants – are warmly welcomed.

Yet, so many Indian Muslims continue to be enchanted by Arabia and the Gulf region while upper class/caste Hindus remain entranced by the US. The schizophrenic Indian Muslim mind has been examined ad nauseam since September 11 by the Indian print media and by yuppie TV channels hosting verbose boxing bouts. It is seriously worrying that the same media have failed to investigate the paranoia of the upper caste Hindu psyche which feels insecure despite claiming to be the proud guardian of the cultural essence and historical memory of 850 million Hindus.

Outlook, **November 12, 2001.**

e-Patriots Online from California

E-MAIL, internet, worldwide websites are showing up the sad confusions of the great Indian middle class nationalist who goes ballistic about the power and glory of his motherland while sitting in front of his computer screen in California's Silicon Valley or in a gloomy apartment in New Jersey. Having satisfied his consumerist cravings and being overcome with syrupy nostalgia about a country which is at least 10,000 miles away, the Indian professional or businessman living in the

United States can afford to wax eloquent about Sanskritic civilisation and nuclear achievement. The problem is that very few of his white American neighbours or colleagues are impressed by Sanskrit or the Pokhran explosions and the nearest Indian friend is not easily available for a morale-boosting chat.

Solace is at hand and the patriotic US-Indian can broadcast to the world his paranoia and his yearning for India's greatness with a click of his computer-mouse. A typical example is an e-mail letter sent by an Indian living in Texas to *India Today* soon after the May 1998 nuclear tests: "….India made the right move by proving its nuclear capabilities. A weak India surrounded by powerful nuclear weapons states is a sure recipe for subjugation and the demise of the world's largest democracy. Now that India has shown the world the 'stick', it will have to work on the 'carrot' to maintain peace."

Ignoring the daily drudgery of hundreds of millions of labouring children, women and men in India, the US-Indian zips his e-mails to English-language dailies or weeklies in Delhi or Bombay, exhorting their readers to keep the faith and work for the abstract glory of the motherland. The Indian back home is routinely berated for his lack of patriotism by the Indian sitting in Los Angeles, Houston or New Haven. Indian periodicals are deluged with e-mail letters to the editor from Indians living in the West, particularly in the United States. These letters are usually hyper-nationalist in tone and aggressively defensive about the Bharatiya Janata Party (BJP). They often suggest that the lower castes and the religious minorities are to be despised or feared.

The recent rash of violent incidents in the Indian states of Gujarat, Maharashtra, Uttar Pradesh and Madhya Pradesh directed against Christian clerics and institutions by the BJP's sister organisations has not resulted in any significant condemnation by the US-Indian who half-believes that Christian "missionaries" have invited these attacks on themselves. The US-Indian has not yet realised that such attacks could lead to a backlash by white Christian fundamentalists against Indians living in the US, especially now that these assaults have been widely publicised by the US media.

Nor does the US-Indian notice the hypocrisy of vehemently promoting the grandeur of ancient Indian texts and traditions, of which he has no deep knowledge, as he has most likely been educated in India in schools and colleges run by Jesuits or other Christian orders while his children are now attending schools in the US which are as American as apple-pie.

For this breed of middle class, upper caste US-Indian, the debacle just suffered by the BJP in the November elections to the local legislatures of Rajasthan, Madhya Pradesh and Delhi could be most puzzling. It would be extremely difficult for the US-Indian to acknowledge that about 80 per cent of Indian voters belong to the labouring classes and to the so-called lower castes. The price of food and the quest for social and economic dignity are far more crucial for that 80 per cent than the jingoistic flag-waving and the abstract motherland-worship propagated by the BJP and its electronic warriors overseas.

Himal, The South Asian Magazine, **December 1998.**

Asses in Search of Lions

WHY are we always seeking a messiah? A Christ-like figure who will deliver us from evil and forgive us our trespasses? Why are we constantly looking for a great leader who will set the nation right and place it firmly on the path to greatness, prosperity and justice? Why do we always invest our hopes and wishes in one figure – a Gandhi, Nehru, Indira or Rajiv? And when the hopes die out and the wishes become a heap of ashes, we blame not ourselves but revile those same leaders who we once revered.

The current great white hope is Rajiv but the hysterical euphoria following his ascension to power after his acclamatory victory in last December's election, will soon wilt despite the success of his recent public relations exercises in France and the United States. Show-biz visits abroad are no substitute for hard-headed decisions at home. Rajiv had no business to be flaunting his charm and good looks abroad while his fellow citizens continue to be killed every day in the uncontrolled violence in Gujarat. His priorities seem to be disappointingly similar to those of his mother: glory on the world stage while chaos abounds at home.

But why blame Rajiv alone? Even with the best of intentions and the highest intelligence, Rajiv cannot possibly put right all that goes wrong in this country. Yet, even seemingly rational and educated people treat the Prime Minister as if he is a god with magical powers for good or evil. When the god fails – as he is bound to because he is held responsible for every happening and all disasters – he is resurrected as the supreme devil.

What are the reasons for the ruler being regarded as a god-devil by most of our countrymen? The age-old, kissing the feet of authority syndrome in an essentially feudal society is only part of the answer. The other part of the answer lies in the sloppy fecklessness of the Indian upper and middle classes who want endless favours and concessions from the Government despite being constantly pampered by it.

It is mainly these classes that Rajiv represents and he will have to continue pampering them. The businessmen and industrialists, who form a powerful segment of the upper and middle classes, will never be content with the deregulation and delicensing policies being carried out by Rajiv's Government. They will want continued Government incentives, subsidies and concessions together with deregulation and delicensing. Clearly an impossible combination. No Government can afford to opt for an open, competitive economy and at the same time subsidise inefficient sections of the private sector.

The plain fact is that Indian businessmen and industrialists are generally not a self-confident, independent, dynamic and go-getting entrepreneurial class. They are more of a *rentier* class who behave as if their customers are their tenants. Selling a shoddy, overpriced product is often regarded as doing a favour to the customer-tenant. Just queue up for a scooter or a moped and go through all the cumbersome harassment and botheration, and even the most ardent pro-capitalist will quickly lose his illusions about the Indian private sector. With such a parasitic *rentier* class pretending to be private enterprise, Rajiv's attempts to energise the economy are bound to fail.

The failure will of course be blamed on Rajiv as small minded nations always expect great leaders with magic wands. Great nations manage quite well without leaders of any great consequence. The United States has had only mediocre or dim-witted presidents, perhaps with the exception of Kennedy, ever since Franklin Roosevelt died in office in 1945. Truman, Eisenhower, Johnson, Nixon, Ford, Carter, Reagan, would not have qualified to be top executives of even a moderately successful company in their own country.

During the past decade or so, the Soviet Union has effortlessly retained its super power status with a succession of leaders in absentia who have been seriously ill during their tenures. Brezhnev was ailing for years before he died in office. His successors, Andropov and Chernenko, were sick throughout their tenures. Gorbachev, the present secretary-general, is an exception. He is healthy and does not function fitfully from a sick bed. China's great helmsman, Mao, was quite senile for several years before he died. But China, with the great legacy of an organised, grassroots Communist Party, continued its march to greatness.

Here, we rarely organise anything from the grassroots upwards, from small beginnings to the gradual and deliberate construction of strong and lasting foundations. Even our Communist Parties think they can take shortcuts to revolution through petty politicking during elections. The disease of gigantism is prevalent in the land. We want to take instant, giant steps into the 21st century. We want to be a nuclear, space-age power in one gigantic leap. India's elite likes to imagine that it can rocket India into being a major world power. Yet, this same elite is becoming increasingly captivated culturally, technologically and commercially by the West. Never since 1947 have the elite and the Government been as enraptured by the West as they are today. How such an imitative and derivative elite can ever think of converting India into a great power staggers the imagination.

In the elite's fevered quest for easy glory, the essentials are ignored. One of the most telling examples of this ignorance of essentials was our dismal performance in the Los Angeles Olympics. We, who make up one-sixth of all humanity, could not collect even one measly bronze. And this, after spending hundreds of crores on building fancy sports complexes for the New Delhi Asian Games. One of the major rationalisations for all that vast expenditure on the Asian Games had been that it would help to foster Indian sportsmen and women of world class. However, gigantic stadiums and swimming pools cannot conjure up Olympic stars when nutrition and education standards in the country are abysmally low. When the majority of India's youth remain malnourished and drop out of school at an early age for economic reasons, the choice of the sports talent which can only be selected from schools and colleges, is extremely narrow despite the country's huge population. As the expression goes, in sport you have to "catch 'em young" and train them from an early age. Unless we provide essentials like nutrition and education instead of fancy concrete buildings, which are now used as lecture halls for members of the Youth Congress, our performance in the Olympics will remain dismal.

With such weird priorities and such delusions of grandeur as are regularly exhibited by the upper and middle classes of this country, Rajiv or any other leader can hardly be expected to set this country on the path to true greatness. It was said of the British army during the bloodiest episodes of the First World War that it was an army of lions led by a bunch of asses. Would it be too much of an exaggeration to say that we of the Indian upper and middle classes are a bunch of asses looking in vain for lions to lead us?

The Telegraph, **July 10, 1985**

Pretending to be Americans of the Third World

FLOODLIT trumpeters silhouetted against the darkening sky. Black stallions galloping through hoops of fire. A magnificent spectacle in the forecourt of Rashtrapati Bhavan on the evening of October 6. The occasion: presentation of the presidential trumpet banner by Giani Zail Singh to the President's Bodyguard, proud descendants of Warren Hastings' 18th century "Troop of Mughals". Watching keenly, the Prime Minister, recently returned from London after inspecting the decor of the Indian High Commissioner's Kensington Palace Gardens mansion and from New York, after making a haphazard attempt at solving the world's problems. The decor is inspected and the spectacle is observed by the Prime Minister for one purpose: to declare them fit for the eyes of the British Queen who will dine next Tuesday with the High Commissioner in London and visit India next month.

The night before the spectacle: six bus passengers are picked out and shot dead by Sikh terrorists merely for being Hindus by birth. But no matter. The Prime Minister is a multi-faceted leader of "world class" who can take it all in her stride, from horse-shows to wanton killings in Punjab. As is her cool, chaotic style, President's Rule for Punjab is declared shortly before midnight, after the horse-show is over, and after the West Bengal Governor, B.D. Pande, has been instantly ordered to shift to Chandigarh, no doubt through a lightning trunk call as the STD phone service to Calcutta never works.

And no doubt, the upper crust which still dominates this country, despite all the learned treatises on sociological change and social mobility, will appreciate and applaud the Prime Minister's style and aplomb. The lack of substance, the lack of concentration, planning and priorities are all part of our Indian style epitomised by the upper crust and by Indira Gandhi.

Perhaps, Mrs. Gandhi's scattiness and lack of concentration is a global phenomenon now that US President Ronald Reagan has been noted to cast aside any memo which is more than a page long and to tire of reading anything more complex than *Reader's Digest*. Politically, Mr Reagan and Mrs Gandhi seem to be at loggerheads but personally they get on famously as was noticed during Mrs Gandhi's official visit to the United States last year.

Their rapport is reinforced by their common bond of personal and strategic aggressiveness. This is especially clear in their foreign policy postures. If Mr Reagan wishes to exhibit American muscle from EI Salvador to Lebanon to the Sea of Japan, Mrs Gandhi must at least show off Indian power and glory from the Khyber Pass to Kandy. Unfortunately, we have only one aircraft carrier and no nuclear missiles and therefore cannot send our gunboats much beyond the Bay of Bengal or noisily rattle any missiles, even though many of Mrs Gandhi's pocket strategists at Delhi's Sapru House or at Bombay's Bori Bunder newspaper would dearly love to do so.

Massive defence spending is a logical corollary to a macho foreign policy. The United States and India have hiked their armaments expenditure greatly since the Reagan and Indira administrations took over in the two countries, though the Soviet threat to the United States or the Sino-Pak threat to India have not increased substantially since Carter and Morarji were in power in Washington and New Delhi. Mr Reagan's Soviet blackmail cacophony and Mrs Gandhi's foreign hand refrain are smoothly swallowed by the flag-waving middle classes of the world's two largest hypocrisies.

The social and political consequences for India of an increasing defence burden are likely to be explosive. A powerful economy like that of the United States can better afford the burdens of a gung-ho foreign and defence policy than we can. Here, we are already witnessing the disastrous internal insecurities created by concentrating on external security and by pouring our scarce resources into defence and show-biz projects like satellites, fast-breeder reactors and expeditions to Antarctica instead of investing more in the training and employment of the young in Assam, Punjab and all the other territories of India. The Assam agitators and the Punjab extremists have their common grievance of economic neglect by the Centre. But where is the money to come from? The Centre is far too busy with show-biz attempts to catch up with the outer world while Assam, Punjab or Bihar go to pot.

This craving to cut a dashing figure on the world stage is part of the 'America syndrome', a disease currently raging even more feverishly than the dengue virus in the upper-middle crust of Indian society. We, which includes many of those who read this page, like to think we are the Americans of the Third World. We are superior to all those pesky Orientals, Africans and Latin Americans. Culturally, we are part of the American and Western world. Our upper crust women spout Western feminist slogans, our executives mouth the latest Harvard Business School slang and our I.G. Patel is appointed Director of the prestigious London School of Economics. See, the Westerners recognise that we are almost as white as they are. The bride being burned to death next door or the leper withering to death on the pavement downstairs are distant phenomena. It's an old psychological trick: look at the stars on the Western horizon, so that we can avoid looking at the rubbish on the doorstep. The mental comfort is ephemeral as the rubbish on the doorstep is likely to pile up.

But we will not help clear our accumulated rubbish. It is too menial a task for the gentry. Instead, we will bicker increasingly about who is responsible for piling up our heap of social and economic depravity. The lower strata will be held solely responsible and 'popular' political movements will be launched against them in each 'ward' – not to clear the pile but to fix the blame.

Precursors of such movements have already made their appearance in the form of the anti-reservation agitators in Gujarat, Sharad Joshi's fattened farmers in Maharashtra, NTR's Telegu drum-beaters, the Assamese fanatics and the Sikh terrorists. Each of these 'popular' movements has identified and attacked its lower strata victim – the aspiring Harijan student, the landless rural labourer of Maharashtra and Andhra Pradesh, the toiling agriculturist from East Bengal, the Hindu petty trader in Punjab's towns. And all these 'popular' movements, especially the All-Assam Students' Union and the Khalistanis, look for inspiration and aid to the great Western 'democracies', just like the rest of us in the upper-middle crust do.

Culturally captivated by the Anglo-Saxons, we cannot be enthralled by any Japanese, Korean, Chinese or Russian success story. New Delhi's cosiness with the Russians or Mrs Gandhi's socialist slogans (at a lesser pitch for the moment) have long been recognised for what they are: tactical manoeuvres to keep the Pakistanis and Chinese at bay and to placate the aspirations of the domestic serfs.

These tactics have a short life-span. Nasser's Egypt, Nkrumah's Ghana, Sukarno's Indonesia, all went through the drama of fake socialism and false national glory. Finally, the dominant crusts of those countries came out in their true colours and opted openly for their cultural and economic masters – the Americans.

We may delude ourselves that we are unique but we are not too different from the dominant crusts of other Third World countries except in size. There is no need for any foreign plot here. The CIA and the foreign hand are within our hearts. We are Orientals trying, oh so hard, to be second-rate occidentals.

The Sunday Observer, **October 23, 1983.**

Is Rajiv Catching the Indira Virus?

ON Sunday, Prime Minister Rajiv Gandhi arrived in Oman. Next week, he will be in Vietnam and then in Japan. Next month, he will be in Bangladesh and next February, he is expected in Australia.

Last month he visited the Bahamas, Britain, Cuba, the Netherlands, the Soviet Union and the United States. Last June he toured Algeria, Egypt, France and the United States. Last May he toured the Soviet Union which he had also visited last March for Chernenko's funeral.

Isn't he overdoing his foreign role a bit? Of course, there are rationalisations for his trips: summits of world leaders in Nassau and New York and regional leaders in Dhaka, strategic imperatives in Moscow, building bridges (which are collapsing again) in Washington, economic cooperation in London, Paris and Tokyo. His personal charm and direct manner have created some extra goodwill for India but no foreign country has succumbed to Mr Gandhi's charms by dramatically shifting its stance towards India. Nor was any such dramatic shift expected in the tough terrain of international diplomacy.

Then what is the pressing need for this flurry of foreign trips? Could it be that Mr Gandhi is catching the same virus that his mother suffered from? Of playing the prima donna on the world stage. Of getting diverted by the glitter of international jamborees. Of hosting Non-aligned and Commonwealth summits while Assam and Punjab went to pot.

It is apparent that Mr Gandhi has devoted his considerable energies to solving the domestic problems left behind by his mother. The Punjab accord has not only been a striking domestic achievement but it has also raised India's and Mr Gandhi's image in the world to a much greater extent than all of Mr Gandhi's foreign trips put together.

Political consolidation and economic development at home bring a nation much greater rewards in terms of power and prestige on the international scene than any amount of diplomatic razzle-dazzle. This rather obvious axiom is usually forgotten by our external affairs bureaucracy, our professors of international relations and our rising middle classes, all of whom want instant, international star status for India through quick fixes in diplomacy or through cultural circuses like the Festivals of India. (Have you ever heard of the Governments of great powers like the Soviet Union and the United States focussing on festivals?)

The desire for international social climbing, so evident among the Indian middle classes, must be firmly resisted by the Prime Minister if he wishes to avoid the virus his mother was afflicted by. The honeymoon period of domestic bliss for the Prime Minister is coming to an end and the long-standing political problems arising from mass economic and social deprivation are bound to surface again. While the per capita income and living standard of our people remain among the eleven most wretched in the world, comparable only with those of the peoples of countries like Burundi and Mali, the Prime Minister of India must concentrate his mind and his administration on efforts to reduce deprivation.

No amount of myth-making by the middle classes will make this country a great nation till the vast majority of the people suffer from servitude within India's boundaries. In our present circumstances, delusions of national grandeur are anti-national.

The Telegraph, **November 19, 1985.**

Bumblebees that Produce no Honey

THE British just cannot manage to get anything right these days. Northern Engineering Industries (NEI), the British company building the giant 1,000 MW Rihand thermal power station in Uttar Pradesh, has made such a hash of it that the completion of the first phase of the British-aided project has already been delayed by a year. Further delays are expected due to the British company's "slippage in design and manufacturing activities", as pointed out in a confidential document prepared by British Electricity International, consultants to India's National Thermal Power Corporation. The consultants further state that there is not much "confidence that a significant improvement in NEI engineering will occur".

The Westland helicopter deal with Britain is again in the news. Last May in parliament, Prime Minister Rajiv Gandhi had rejected the British offer of 21 Westland helicopters for the offshore operations of the Oil and Natural Gas Commission, despite their entire purchase price of 65 million pounds being financed by a British Government grant. One of the major grounds on which he had rejected the British helicopters was that their Rolls-Royce engines were extremely fuel-inefficient. He had said that the fuel-guzzling Westland helicopters would prove more expensive too operate over a period of several years than other available (non-British) helicopters, even if their purchase was covered by a British grant. Now the British are reportedly also offering to pay for part of the operational costs, Prime Minister Gandhi has said that India may re-consider buying the helicopters if certain India specifications are fulfilled.

It seems that British industry just cannot compete in the international market without British Government subsidies or special appeals. That great advocate of free market forces, Prime Minister Margaret Thatcher, has been virtually reduced to begging for foreign contracts. *The Sunday Times* of London reported on September 8 that she had written to US President Ronald Reagan, imploring him to award the 4.5 billion dollar contract for a sophisticated combat telephone system to the British firm, Plessey Electronics, rather than to the French competitor, Thomson CSF. Mrs Thatcher claimed that Britain deserved preferential treatment because it was a more dependable ally than France. A US official is quoted as having responded to the appeal by saying, "Mrs. Thatcher feels the United States owes her one."

That is the British hang-up, the British delusion. That the world owes them a living for their past greatness, no matter how second-rate they may be now. The British continue to bluster where they can get away with it, though it all sounds rather pathetic when their only unmatched products are football hooligans.

One of the few countries where the British can get away with their bragging and bluster is India where the white sahib is still looked up to in the caste hierarchy of social and cultural status, though he is no longer regarded as superior in political terms. The obverse side of fawning on the white sahib is the common Indian middle class delusion that we are a cut above other Asians, Africans and Latin Americans, that we are somehow 'whiter' than other coloured peoples. No wonder the blacks in Britain and South Africa have been attacking Indian enclaves in Birmingham and Durban.

An economically bankrupt and socially archaic Britain likes to believe that it is still a leading power in the world. India, with one of the lowest per capita incomes in the world and a primitive social structure, keeps harping about being a major power. Both India and Britain live in a thick fog of a chauvinistic self-delusion.

The fog is made denser in both countries by highly articulate and voluble politicians, journalists and academics. If Britain excels in anything, it does so in BBC broadcasts, book publishing and theatre. We Indians are also masters in the art of self-expression.

There is the recurring story of Indian experts at international economic conferences ceaselessly holding forth on how the Sixth or Seventh Five-Year Plan will change the face of India and how India has succeeded in becoming a major industrial power while the tongue-tied Japanese delegates can only manage to say, "But.... but...."

Watch a Doordarshan interview and see the foreign guest

left gaping while the Indian interviewer does all the talking, including answering his own questions.

Perhaps, a common feature of decadent nations is that they are great talkers but not great doers. They are like the bumblebee which is described as a large, loud-humming bee that flits from blossom to blossom but produces no honey.

The Telegraph, **September 18, 1985.**

Chapter-11

Nuclear Follies

TWO of the most powerful, rational arguments for going overtly nuclear in May 1998 were: Pakistan would be deterred from launching adventurist military actions against us and our defence expenditure on conventional forces would go down as a result of our nuclear capability. In the light of our experience since May 1998, both arguments have been proved to be wrong-headed. Pakistan launched its Kargil adventure in May 1999 and has stepped up its support for armed forays into Kashmir. Defence expenditure has continued to rise since the Pokhran blasts. In the 2000-01 budget it went up by 18 per cent over the 1999-2000 budget. In the 2001-02 budget defence spending increased by another 13 per cent. These increases are overwhelmingly for our conventional defence forces. Most of the expenditure for the nuclear deterrent remains shrouded under the cloak of substantial financial outlays for the Departments of Atomic Energy and Space. Details of how the funds for the two Departments are utilised remain confidential.

Diverting scarce funds to such essentially non-productive sectors as space and atomic energy means that there is little left to spend on nurturing our most valuable resource – human potential. It has been repeatedly demonstrated in Japan, China, South Korea and Southeast Asia that state investment in education, health and social welfare, benefits national economies exponentially and leads to immense gains in the national power and prestige of individual countries.

Rational debate on the nuclear issue was submerged in May 1998 under a flood of rhetoric pandering to wild emotions and to domestic political interests. The BJP-led Government encouraged the absurd euphoric sentiment that the Pokhran explosions would overnight convert the world into regarding India as a great power. As for the BJP's expectation that Pokhran would pay off in terms of votes, the November 1998 assembly elections in Delhi, Himachal Pradesh, Madhya Pradesh and Rajasthan proved to be a major setback for the party. The BJP lost the elections in all the states except Himachal Pradesh. The sophisticated Indian voter demonstrated once again that basic economic issues like employment and inflation are much more important for him than delusions of grandeur.

Disarmament Diary

'Kalamity'

FOR a cynical city like Delhi to disgorge over 5,000 of its residents onto its streets on the hot and humid morning of August 6 for a fundamentally moral cause like global nuclear disarmament was a heartening sight for a handful of us who had set out to organise the citizens' march to mark that horrific event when the United States had devastated Hiroshima as the world's first nuclear target even as the Second World War was already reaching its inevitable end. The target of the citizens' rally was not just the United States but also our own Government and nuclear-security establishment which have callously invited the distinct possibility of turning some of our own cities, including Delhi, into smouldering and radioactive Hiroshimas. It will not be much of a recompense for any survivors of a nuclear weapons exchange to see that Islamabad or Karachi have also been turned into Hiroshimas along with Delhi or Bombay. The security-mongers have only succeeded in making every Indian citizen more insecure!

Our top security guru, A.P.J. Abdul Kalam, and his brethren were predictably agitated at the very thought of some thousands of their fellow-citizens challenging their smug strategic scenarios. In a *Times of India* interview on August 8, Kalam said that we should have held demonstrations in Washington and Moscow to put pressure on those Governments to get rid of their huge stockpiles of 10,000 nuclear weapons each. Unfortunately, most of us who participated in the Delhi rally do not have the money or the time to fly to foreign capitals. More pertinently, we do not believe that India's and Pakistan's additional contributions (however small) to the world's huge stock of nuclear bombs and missiles enhance South Asian or global security. Indians, Pakistanis, Americans, Russians, British, French and Chinese must necessarily demonstrate against the nuclear follies of each of their own Governments. That is the only way to work towards a safe world without nuclear weapons.

Bombnik

ANOTHER veteran security strategist, K. Subrahmanyam, who has been shrilly advocating for decades that India must overtly demonstrate its nuclear weapons capability, attempted to rubbish peace movements in general in an article on August 10 (also in *The Times of India*). He declared that while peace movements in the West had not succeeded in eliminating a single nuclear warhead, the understanding about the impossibility of fighting and winning a nuclear war had led to some reductions in the number of nuclear warheads under the START I and II international treaties. It is not all surprising that Subrahmanyam has chosen to whitewash the fact that this understanding about the impossibility of winning a nuclear war has been a defining argument of peace movements for the past 45 years, an argument which has directly led to the reductions in nuclear warheads.

In the same article, Subrahmanyam has also been hilariously bizarre in suggesting that India could move towards a non-violent, anti-nuclear resistance policy after having defied the five hegemonic nuclear powers through its nuclear blasts.

According to Subrahmanyam, this non-violent policy would be complete with India's declaration that it would not be the first to use nuclear weapons. This is as weird as suggesting that Gandhi should have led our country's non-violent struggle for independence with a fully-loaded revolver strapped to his dhoti while declaring that he would never be the first to use his holstered firearm!

Sleuths and Schoolgirls

ABOUT half the participants in the anti-nuke rally were enthusiastic children from a wide variety of schools, numbering more than 20. The rally also attracted the zealous participation of plainclothes police sub-inspectors from our intelligence agencies. I saw and heard at least two of them asking some schoolgirls about which school they came from even as they were carrying a big banner proclaiming the name of their school. One of the sleuths readily admitted to me that he was from the Intelligence Bureau while writing some names in his note-book. I naively asked another sleuth that were we not citizens of an Azad Hind? He smiled generously and continued his jottings.

Clinton's Spheres

I WAS the recipient of boisterous cheers from many teenage schoolgirls and schoolboys during the march as I had made my own placard which read – CLINTON, PULL UP YOUR PANTS! DROP YOUR BOMBS! I was sorely disappointed that my adult comrades, especially those of the pink variety, failed to see the point and kept asking me what I was getting at? Obviously, the old comrades could not make the connection to Clinton's affair with Monica. The teenagers were obviously brighter!

Frightened Foreigners

IN an attempt to give the rally for global nuclear disarmament an international dimension, we had asked some foreigners working and living here to join the march. Most of them declined, saying that while they supported the cause, it was a sensitive issue and their participation could possibly lead to their Indian residence visas being withdrawn. The Americans seemed to be the most wary of participating in the march. The British were quite willing to consider our request. The Tibetans declined and the French ignored us. In the event, only 10 or 12 foreigners participated in the march. However, the foreign media were far from shy about covering the march.

Routed

SOME friends have asked why the marchers did not protest at the gates of the embassies and high commissions of the six other countries which are overt nuclear powers. The original idea was to protest in front of their very gates in Chanakyapuri, to be followed by a protest near the Prime Minister's residence. This would also have been most convenient as all the relevant legations are bunched together and the PM's house is also quite close by. However, strict police regulations absolutely forbid any large demonstration in the Diplomatic Enclave or near the PM's bungalow. We had to make the best of marching from Shanti Van to Ferozeshah Kotla grounds.

Friday Vigils

THE big march was preceded from May to July by small gatherings of enthusiasts handing out leaflets about the dangers of nuclearisation on Friday evening rush-hours to commuters at crowded road junctions. The usual reaction, as I saw it, was the tired and exhausted indifference of most commuters returning home after another day of relentless heat and hassle. The pedestrians walking past us at Chandni Chowk and the bus passengers at the Medical Institute-Ring Road intersection seemed to be the most exhausted. There were some angry remarks and crumpling of leaflets by a few young, educated, male punks at Laxminagar and Nehru Place. Immediately after the Pakistani nuclear blasts, several Maruti-borne commuters gave us the thumbs-up sign at Parliament Street as our placards showed our opposition to both Indian and Pakistani tests.

Outlook, **August 24, 1998.**

Drop the Bomb!

THE Government and its critics, in parliament and outside, have debated the vital issue of whether we should build an independent nuclear weapons system or not, at a frighteningly simplistic and absurdly uninformed level. Attempts at gaining political capital have not stopped even here.

This political frivolity raises the question of whether our political system and its operators are capable of providing the firm, long-term political backing and continuous financial support that a nuclear defence programme will demand. Political pressures resulting in stop-go methods and financial jugglery will not do. Clear directives will be required from the Government. Flexibility and initiative at every level of decision-making will be demanded of administrators and scientists. The argument that building the Bomb will provide the incentive to clear up well-established political and administrative cobwebs is wishful thinking. With the political system in a state of flux, the continuance of parliamentary democracy itself cannot be taken for granted. The discipline and firm leadership required for such a project along with the ultra-nationalism it might generate could precipitate a change in the political system towards right-wing authoritarianism, an eventuality which parties like the Jan Sangh would no doubt welcome.

Building a nuclear weapons system presupposes the capacity to deter not only China but also the other nuclear powers – the United States, the Soviet Union, Britain and France – as the presence of a nuclear force on our soil will arouse the suspicion of those who have a monopoly of nuclear armaments, in spite of our present cordial relations with them. We shall, once we have exploded our first nuclear device, be entering a nuclear weapons race of unfathomable proportions. The entire concept of nuclear deterrence is based on the psychological premise of maintaining a parity of fear.

There is a plausible argument for manufacturing nuclear weapons in order to play a more forceful part in the anti-imperialist struggle on the continents of Africa, Asia and Latin America against US and Soviet economic and political interference. By the end of this century the rich world will feel increasingly threatened by the poor world seeking a greater and fairer share in the exploitation of world resources. Nuclear blackmail by the rich against the poor is a scenario which could become a reality a couple of decades from now, if the poor world forges its own path towards economic fulfilment. Building the bomb for this reason is, however, a non-starter, since our political leadership and public opinion are hardly aware of or willing to concern themselves with these matters at the moment.

Much of the recent outcry for the development of nuclear weapons is based on an incorrect analysis of Chinese political and strategic goals. As was demonstrated in 1962, in NEFA, the Chinese are not interested in territorial conquest for its own sake even if they have the military potential for it. Mao's philosophy is explicit on this point. The decisive factor both in war and economic development is people, not material resources or military systems based on the advances of modern science. The support of revolutionary movements is a much more likely Chinese line. Such movements cannot be countered by military means; nuclear armaments are totally irrelevant in these situations.

The imposition of a top-heavy and extremely costly defence system on an insecure social and political structure and weak economic base might indeed prove to be a good way of promoting violent liberation movements within this country. National security is bound to be illusory if it diverts limited resources away from the primary goal of wiping out economic and social deprivation. The diversion of economic resources to unproductive sectors like nuclear defence will result in a significant drop in the rate of growth of the economy. The idea that the technological fall-out from the development of nuclear arms and auxiliary equipment will be an economic asset does not hold water either, as is proved by the consequences for the economy of the sharp increase in defence expenditure after the India-China conflict in 1962.

The Bomb must not be built. It is politically dangerous, is likely to endanger our security and will be economically a criminal waste. Those who fervently advocate nuclear weapons for India have not analysed the issue thoroughly or have got carried away in a burst of emotional nationalism. If our main concern is to seek a better and more secure life for our people, then it is callous to demand the Bomb. But the worst of all alternatives would be to drift into making nuclear weapons without serious thought, as the Government seems in danger of doing.

Economic and Political Weekly, **May 23, 1970.**

Internal Political Cost of the Bomb

THE diplomatic, strategic, military and economic aspects of this sub-continent's steady drift towards nuclear weapons and nuclear confrontation have been widely discussed. But the most important aspect – the internal political consequences for both India and Pakistan of going nuclear – has hardly been touched in the nuclear debate. Perhaps the silence on this aspect is deliberate as the domestic political consequences may be too appalling to contemplate in a clear-headed fashion. However, an attempt must be made.

For India, the most obvious consequence of creating and maintaining a credible nuclear deterrent force would be the increasing usurpation of political power by administrative, scientific and military officers, that is, by the bureaucracy. Politicians, which includes ministers and members of parliament, would find themselves handing over their power to make complex policy decisions to the bureaucrats with nuclear and allied expertise, as is already happening in the GOI's Departments of Atomic Energy and Space.

The need for secrecy and efficiency would become an excuse for no public accountability. Budgetary control and allocation by parliament of the annual outlays on the defence, atomic energy and space sectors is already woefully lax due to a misplaced sense of patriotism and due to a lack of expertise in these fields among MPs. The situation will get much worse as the nuclear deterrent force becomes a god in its own right.

Another major political consequence of maintaining an effective nuclear force would be greater centralisation of power with the Central Government in New Delhi at the cost of the states. All Central directives to the states regarding the allocation of power, labour, water, land and other resources for the expansion of the nuclear estate would have to be promptly carried out. In fact, the Centre may gradually eat into the state and concurrent lists of the Constitution, endangering the federal nature of our polity in the name of the growing nuclear estate.

For Pakistan, a serious commitment to a nuclear strike force would have far more immediate and far more disastrous domestic political consequences than such a commitment would have for India. For a start, Pakistan is a much weaker and smaller state than India and it is, therefore, much less capable of carrying the economic burden of nuclear weapons and delivery systems than India.

More important is the fact that the political structure of Pakistan is already highly bureaucratised, centralised and anti-democratic. Clearly, Pakistan has no political shock-absorbers to cushion the Government against popular and regional movements set off by any slight spark. Any further repression by the Government in the name of national defence or a national nuclear armoury and in the absence of any broad based national political party, could well cause the break-up of Pakistan.

The main proponent of a nuclear armoury in Pakistan is the Punjabi military and science establishment. The Baluchis, Pathans and Sindhis have no love lost for this Punjabi clique. In these circumstances, if the Punjabi clique persists in its plans to complete its nuclear armoury at any cost, the consequences would be shattering for Pakistan and extremely dangerous for India.

In effect, Pakistan or what was left of it, would have succeeded in producing something much nastier than an Islamic bomb, which would be a Punjabi *Mussalman* bomb. To counter it, we would be producing a bomb controlled by an irresponsible bureaucracy, a Brahmin *babu* bomb. The scenario for the sub-continent cannot possibly be more explosive. The Pakistan-India nuclear nightmare must be stopped in its tracks by the political elites of the two countries for they will be the first to be swallowed up by it if it is allowed to proceed along its terrible path.

There is a limited and simple way to begin the process of stopping the nuclear nightmare in its tracks. The psychological knot of distrust between the two countries can be cut by a solemn joint agreement signed by Prime Minister Rajiv Gandhi and President Zia-ul-Haq at the forthcoming first South Asian summit at Dhaka in December, declaring that both countries will abstain from nuclear test explosions of any kind, overground or underground.

Such an agreement would at least for some time prevent the sub-continent from going over the threshold into an open nuclear arms race. This kind of mad race would become inevitable if Pakistan or India were to explode a nuclear test device in the present climate of suspicion.

The Telegraph, **August 21, 1985.**

Chapter-12

Despots in the Making

IS there any outstanding trait, any winning formula which propels some individuals to the top as national leaders? Or is it all a question of a random series of events and a good deal of luck which gets them to the pinnacle? The family backgrounds of some leaders provide them with an easy ride on the elevator but with others it is a matter of grabbing an opportunity when it presents itself. The childhood and adolescence of a national leader are always intriguing as some nuggets from the past can always be dug up and accepted or rejected as possible pointers to political destiny.

In the case of Zia-ul-Haq and Zulfikar Bhutto, the country they would head was not a reality when Zia was at St. Stephen's College (1940-44), Delhi, and Bhutto was at Cathedral School (1939-46), Bombay. Both institutions were set up by British Christians to nurture a colonial elite resembling the upper crust of those grey isles in the North Sea. St. Stephen's produced brown caricatures who populated the IAS and IFS from the late 1940s well into the 1980s while Cathedral continues to provide rotund boys and girls to worship Mammon in the business, banking and industrial houses of Bombay. Most students at both institutions were, and continue to be, from prosperous or comfortably placed families.

Bhutto was from one of the richest landed families of Sindh. Zia was an exception at St. Stephen's. He was the son of an army clerk. Bhutto was a loner while Zia was a team player.

Little did they know that their destinies would meet three decades later. There were no obvious signs in school or college that they would rise to the top. The creation of Pakistan helped to get them to the top, though both would probably have done quite well for themselves in politics and the army in an undivided India. In Pakistan, their careers peaked because of the feudal-military alliance which dominates that state. With the exceptions of Jinnah and Nawaz Sharif, both from business families, all the other Pakistani heads of state and of government have been from the feudal gentry, senior bureaucracy or the army's officer corps. The army has been relatively egalitarian as it has allowed senior officers to emerge from humble backgrounds while big landlords have continued to dominate the political breed.

Leading political figures from East Pakistan were also from propertied families except the one challenger who was denied the prime ministership of Pakistan in 1971 despite having won a clear parliamentary majority, Mujibur Rehman. The man who foiled Mujib's challenge and divided Pakistan in the process was Bhutto. India's military assistance was the major factor in liberating Bangladesh from Pakistani military rule, in bringing Mujib to power in Dhaka and also, ironically, in bringing Bhutto to power in Islamabad. The events of 1971 demonstrated yet again that India and Pakistan are Siamese twins organically connected at birth. The past and future of the two states are linked, though this would be disputed by Pakistani ideologues bent on advancing a separatist identity.

The rhetoric of helping the poor has pervaded the populist politics of both countries. Two dynastic and aristocratic families, the Nehru-Gandhis and the Bhuttos, have been the foremost proponents of 'socialist patterns of society'. Indira Gandhi sought votes on the basis of "*Garibi Hatao!*" and Zulfikar Bhutto stirred voters with calls for "*Roti, Kapda aur Makan!*". No persistent and sincere attempts were made to implement the slogans. The rhetoric of India-Pakistan hate campaigns was another populist speciality of the two leaders. It soon became apparent that personal power and dynastic succession were the only real goals of the two leaders. Their popularity waned but the charisma of the ruling families remained. Rajiv Gandhi and Benazir Bhutto succeeded to power with a vengeance after the 'martyrdom' of Indira and Zulfikar. Sonia has slipped effortlessly into being the leading light of the Congress Party after Rajiv's assassination and Benazir still heads the Pakistan People's Party despite being in exile abroad.

'Zulfi' at Cathedral School

IF there were to be an epitaph for Zulfikar Bhutto, it would read: "A man who inspired love and hate in equal measure." The capacity to incite extreme emotion was evident in Bhutto from childhood. Even while he was a schoolboy, he was loved as "the most gentle and sensitive" of souls and hated as the "arrogant, heighty-mighty son of a rich landlord." Which was he? Evil or gentle? Or perhaps, he epitomised a mixed-up, upper class, sub-continental generation which grew up in the 1940s and 1950s and gained the fruits of power far too easily, almost as of birthright? A generation which with its sense of ease turned easily from sensitivity, to self-righteousness, to abounding self-indulgence?

"There he stood whilst bad wolf fed.
And soon his flock of sheep lay dead.
Oh! foolish boy, you deserve your fate
Repentance now has come too late."

This poignant verse was written at the age of 11 by Z. Bhutto and R. Sopher in their school magazine of December 1939. Forty years later, the verse sounds sadly ironic as one of the young men who wrote that poem has been hanged after a tempestuous and emotive political career.

Zulfikar was emotional from boyhood. His masters at the Cathedral School, Bombay, remember him as "very, very emotional". Mr C.B. Nix James, 78, now blind but crystal clear in mind, knew "the boy" well. Zulfikar often used to come and talk to him. It was the need of a lonely boy. Mr Nix-James explains: "I have the impression that he did not receive the attention from his father that a boy should have. I wonder whether he found in me a sublimation for fatherly affection or the need for a father."

The father was usually away on some business or other and Zulfikar saw him only during the holidays. Mr. Nix-James says that "the boy used to live all by himself in one wing of a big, sprawling house. He looked introvert and almost solemn at times. He was serious-minded and I would give him credit for intellect. He was thoughtful rather than studious."

Another school-master, Mr C.J. Olliver, also found that Zulfikar was a "a rather emotional youngster who was more politically conscious than most schoolboys generally are." This emotionalism was often expressed in the form of anti-Indian politics even before partition and his basic loneliness was sought to be forgotten through the formation of extremely close friendships.

Among his close friends was Piloo Mody, who is now an eminent Janata Party MP. Piloo's cousins, Jehangir and Silloo Mugaseth, were Zulfikar's closest friends during his childhood and adolescence. To Silloo, Zulfi was the "most gentle" of young men. To Rati Guzder (now Mrs Sethna), he was "timid". Silloo can never think of him as anything but the most quiet and sensitive of persons. Even when she met him for the last time in 1974 at his country home at Larkana in Sindh, she found that his solitary concern was his old Bombay friends. He constantly enquired about how they were and where they were. Silloo says: "To me Zulfi was Zulfi and will always stay Zulfi". His politics, his prime ministership, his eminence, matter little to Silloo whom Zulfi always called "Sis".

The fire and fury were reserved for school debates. What stands out in Silloo's mind is that "he was awfully well-mannered and never scruffy in dress". But behind the conditioned exterior, there was impulsiveness. This came out in his speeches and his sport. In the school magazine of December 1942 he is mentioned as one of the personalities of the junior debating society. His character is described pithily: "Z. Bhutto seconded O. Kureishi in the challenge contest. Has often spoken well, clearly and cleverly but ruined many a good speech by its unnecessary length."

A certain impatience and disdain for the lower middle class was evident to other school boys who new him. To Hiro Shroff, "He was heighty-mighty, a rich man's son". But this was in a school which had quite a different ethos from Cathedral where the upper classes sent their sons and daughters. For one school term in 1940, Zulfikar went to a more rough-and-tumble, less affluent, school in Karachi. There at St. Patrick's, the feudal arrogance of a rich landlord's son came out in Zulfikar. A young, not-so-rich boy like Hiro was angered that Zulfikar "always came by car, while we came by cycle. He ate from his tiffin box while we ate from the street vendor. He acted rich from the beginning."

The smouldering resentment burst out one day and Hiro Shroff gave Zulfikar Bhutto a hammering and pushed him against a wall. Hiro and his friends then ate from Zulfikar's tiffin box while he watched. But no grudge was held by Bhutto who invited Shroff to a duck-shoot near Larkana when Shroff went back to Karachi in the 1950s as a PTI correspondent. Even there, Bhutto's feudal expansiveness displayed itself. The duck-shoot was a big affair with dozens of beaters and retainers hanging around. When a duck soared by, Bhutto would take a pot shot. His retainers would also fire at the bird. With such a fusillade, the hapless duck would always fall. But the credit for having bagged the bird would always be given to Bhutto and he would never refuse such credit. The duck-shoot only confirmed Hiro Shroff's intense feeling that in such a landlord family, "ordinary people are treated as a commodity".

Even today, Shroff has little doubt that Bhutto was guilty of murder and his hands were not clean in getting rid of his opponents.

To Nix-James, Bhutto's guilt or innocence is unknown. What Nix-James sees is "his great bravery in not pleading for mercy" right to the end. The aristocratic dignity of the man when he was a boy was evident to C.J. Olliver even in school. To Nargis, the film actress, the only striking features about Zulfikar as a young man were that "he was very elegant . . . like an aristocrat . . . fond of dressing . . . perfumed. The image of an angry young man was put on. He was actually very soft spoken. He was like any normal student in his reaction to the film world. He used to come and watch the shooting of the first Mughal-e-Azam in which I was acting around 1944. Of course, this film was never completed."

Nargis dismisses the suggestion that Zulfikar was in love with her. It was his half brother, Sikander, who jokingly used to tell her, "I will take poison if you don't marry me". Those were the days of picnics and parties at Juhu beach in Bombay. Zulfikar was always very quiet at these parties and not in the least arrogant. The flamboyant one those days was Sikander who used to drink and playfully tease the girls.

In Cathedral School, however, Zulfikar came to be known as a ladies' man. On a school holiday to Mussoorie, Zulfikar "was quite the rage" among the girls. At school socials, he was a good dancer. Jitterbugging was the dance of those days.

Despite the dancing, the elegance, the perfume and the beach parties, Bhutto's ambitions were far more serious. He was a great admirer of Napoleon Bonaparte and used to read everything about him. One of his legacies is probably the finest library on Napoleon at his home in Clifton, Karachi. The serious intent became clear to Rati Guzder when she met him again at Oxford in the early 1950s: "He knew where he was going and what he wanted to do." He always wanted to be a diplomat or a politician.

While talking of politics to Silloo, he always spoke of the poor and felt that something should be done for them. Even at Larkana at his big country home, he expressed his concern for the poor. The concern was distant and abstract as it usually is with the upper classes. His contempt was reserved for the lower middle class. He was to display this contempt in his disruption of Pakistan's lower middle class civil service and, to some extent, the army's officer corps. He treated Zia, the man he promoted to chief of the army over six senior generals, with ill-conceived contempt. Even when Zia had just overthrown Bhutto in July 1977, Bhutto's contempt for the lower middle class general was withering. Bhutto told Zia that with his brains and Zia's military muscle, the two could rule the country for ever. Such a snide slap in the face was probably never forgotten by Zia, the son of an army clerk, who took his class revenge on 4 April 1979 when Bhutto dropped from the gallows.

Bhutto the man may have gone but the love and the hate that he inspired will live on in Pakistan. As he said in a school essay written by him in December 1946 on the 'World of Tomorrow': "I know, for it is no prophecy, that the world of tomorrow will be modelled on the events of today."

New Delhi magazine, **April 30, 1979.**

Zia at St. Stephen's College

ST. STEPHEN'S, that distinguished college which has produced so many square pegs to fit into Delhi's semi-smart elite, has also contributed to the ruling elite of Islamabad.

At the top of the pyramid in Pakistan is an old Stephanian, General Zia-ul-Haq. In 1941, Zia was a cadet in the University Training Corps (the predecessor of the NCC) of the college. Platoon Sergeant D.P. Basu mentioned him in a report in the college magazine, *The Stephanian*, of November 1941, which indicates that Zia even at the age of 17 had a punctilious regard for outward form and, perhaps, also a whimsical streak.

Sergeant Basu wrote: "Caleb, Paul and Zia. This trio set up such a high standard in very smart turn-outs that even sergeants were ashamed to stand beside them. It became a mania for them to polish their boots and equipment."

A fanatic tendency was noticed by a condescending colleague, K.K Mehra, who is now a Vice-President in the management hierarchy of the Oberoi hotel chain. Mr Mehra recalls that Zia usually wore an achkan while most of the other students wore western clothes. Zia also came from "a different educational background". This gave Mehra the impression that Zia was a "kattar (fanatic) Muslim."

Zia was "different" from many of the students at St. Stephen's in that he was from a humble, lower middle class, Jullundur background while some others believed they were koi hais because they came from half-westernised families. Mehra is convinced that the young Zia was "different". "We used to avoid him", Mehra snorts. "Zia was one of the outsiders trying to be in. I will tell you what was most distinguished about him.... nothing."

Wing-Commander K.K. Ganguly (retd.), now Director Corporate Planning of Hindustan Milk Foods which produces the nutritious nightcap, Horlicks, does not recall any fanatic streak in Zia. Ganguly did not notice any signs of Zia being ultra-Islamic or particularly religious. He was an open, friendly sort who did not offend anyone, Ganguly says. He had no inhibitions and was a good mixer.

Ganguly remembers that Zia "would not do anything that would violate the norms, the rules. Yet he was not one of those goody, goody types." But there was nothing outstanding about him. He did not stand out physically, mentally or otherwise in any sphere of college life, Ganguly feels.

C.S. Pandit, now an eminent journalist, confirms Mehra's and Ganguly's image of Zia as a nonentity. Mr Pandit says: "Here was a man who did not leave an impression on you. He was innocuous. There was nothing special about him except his huge, expressionless eyes." Pandit "can't think of anybody who was Zia's great friend. He was a loner."

Sookhia, the wizened old man who has been selling samosas

and pedhas to Stephanians since 1930 when the college was at Kashmere Gate, remembers droves of old boys since most of them kept credit accounts with him. But of Zia he has no recollection.

There were a number of other Stephanians of that time, "far brighter" than Zia, who later went off to Pakistan. Among them was Iqbal Butt, who is now working under Zia as Director of External Publicity. Zahur Azhar, another Stephanian of the same vintage, was Secretary of the Pakistani Ministry of Information and Broadcasting until recently when he was thrown out in a political purge. The Bokhari brothers and Ahmed Shah Nawaz are also remembered by their contemporaries, but mention Zia and many of the old boys of that time do not even know that he was a student with them.

On one point concerning those times, there is unanimity among the old boys of St. Stephen's. There was no communalism in the college. There were cliques and sets and groups but they had nothing to do with religion. Ganguly says that, unlike at Hindu college, there was very little interest in politics at St. Stephen's. So the question of Pakistan which had just been raised was hardly an issue for the students of the college.

For some like Dharambir Mohindra, the concept of Pakistan was a hilarious fantasy. In the March 1941 issue of *The Stephanian*, Mohindra wrote a parody, 'If Delhi Were Pakistan'. The second paragraph of the parody displays a sweeping imagination: "The Muslim idealisation of gardens will find scope for expression. Imagine a lovely garden running from Fort to Delhi Gate and another in place of Qarol Bagh and a third instead of Connaught Place. Imagine the picnics on moonlit nights. There will be water (not wine), dancing girls and boys, fan-tailed pigeons, beautiful ghazals and poetry, appetising feasts, scented 'paans', gorgeous hookahs, magnificent carpets and a general community of Lotus-Eaters drunk with the pleasantness of everything. Only the call of the Muezzins will take the men to duty and the coming day."

02610709017
Rs – 295-

The last paragraph of Mohindra's parody is skeptical: "A sweet dream is the best of all temporary pleasures; and Pakistan, especially in Delhi, is at best a very sweet dream indeed." Mohindra could not have dreamed that one of his co-students would become President of Pakistan. Nor did Zia have any such dreams.

Zia's only interests at that time were football and the University Training Corps. On the football field, Pandit was a forward while Zia was a back. Zia played a clean game "but opposing players were afraid of him as he was a tough tackler".

The musty yellow admission register in the office of the veteran college head-clerk, Mr Roberts, contains all the cryptic biographical details of Zia's early years under the usual section headings. Date of birth: 12-8-24. Father's address: Medical Directorate, Army Hqrs., Simla. Last exam passed: Matric from Punjab. Division obtained: II. Date of entry into college: 27-5-40. Subjects offered: Hist. Eco. P. (The P probably stands for Politics.)

Others who figure in the admission register on the same page as Zia are: Suresh Narain, Swami Nath Segal, Syed Iqbal Imam, Virendra Mohan Saksena, Ajit Kumar Ghose and Mary Ware, an English girl whose father's details are listed as Animal Husbandry Commissioner, 12, Tughlak Road, New Delhi. There were a handful of girls at St. Stephen's during those days. Then for many years, St. Stephen's became a bastion of male privilege. The girls are back now and in much larger numbers.

As the register indicates, Zia took a pass course and not an honours course. He did not finish his course as he joined the army's Officers Training School at Mhow in 1944. Unlike at St. Stephen's, he made a mark in the army right from the beginning.

New Delhi magazine, **April 2, 1979.**